IN THEIR PARENTS' VOICES

Reflections on Raising Transracial Adoptees

Rita J. Simon and Rhonda M. Roorda

D0950259

COLUMBIA UNIVERSITY PRESS
NEW YORK

COLUMBIA UNIVERSITY PRESS
Publishers Since 1893
New York   Chichester, West Sussex

Library of Congress Cataloging-in-Publication Data
Simon, Rita James.
 In their parents' voices / Rita J. Simon and Rhonda M. Roorda.
   p.   cm.
 ISBN 978-0-231-14136-9 (cloth : alk. paper) — ISBN 978-0-231-14137-6
(pbk. : alk. paper — ISBN 978-0-231-51235-0 (ebook)
  I. Interracial adoption—United States. 2. Adoptive parents—United States.
  I. Roorda, Rhonda M. 1969– II. Title.

 HV875.64.85577 2007
 649'.14508900973—dc22

                                    2007005678

Columbia University Press books are printed on permanent
  and durable acid-free paper.
This book is printed on paper with recycled content.

Printed in the United States of America
c 10 9 8 7 6 5 4 3 2 1
p 10 9 8 7 6 5 4 3 2 1

In Their Parents' Voices is dedicated to the parents who share their experiences here and to parents throughout the United States who have adopted children and who are striving to uphold their commitment to nurture them.

This book is also dedicated to the many children who are languishing in this country's foster care system, desperately hoping for a loving and stable family. We hope that heightened awareness of the vitality of adoption and the urgent need of these children to have a solid foundation will encourage more people to step forward to provide them with good homes.

CONTENTS

Introduction   ix

PART 1: THE CHILDREN FROM *IN THEIR OWN VOICE*S   1

Author's Note   11

PART 2: THE PARENTS   15

John and Marian Pelton   17
Jim and Alice Bandstra   26
Jim and Kathy Stapert   34
Ron and Dorothy   51
Paul Goff   65
Barbara Tremitiere   73
Nora Anker   86
Marjorie Gray   96
Edson and Judith Bigelow   105
Aaldert and Elisabeth Mennega   114
Rikk Larsen   122
Charles and Pam Adams   136
David and Lola Himrod   145
Ken and Jean   158
Winnie   172
Rodney and Joyce Perry   183

PART 3: CONCLUSION   201

Afterword   209

Postscript   215
Acknowledgments   217

INTRODUCTION

IN THEIR PARENTS' VOICES: *Reflections on Raising Transracial Adoptees* is the second of two volumes on black and biracial men and women who were adopted primarily in the 1970s by white parents when most of the children were younger than 2 years old. *In Their Own Voices: Transracial Adoptees Tell Their Stories* (2000) reports the experiences of twelve women and twelve men then aged 22 to 31 (with one male outlier who was 57) and who were transracially adopted. The stories of these transracial adoptees were obtained mostly through telephone interviews, with a few done in person. We found participants through referrals from individuals and organizations, responses to an ad in *Interrace* magazine, and through the Internet. Some initiated contact with us. Some were well-known personalities whom we sought out for interviews. The interviews lasted at least two hours.

The stories told by the adoptees in *In Their Own Voices* reveal their thoughts about family, adoption, and self-identity issues from their adult perspective. This book substantiates the claims empirically demonstrated by traditional researchers (from the mid-1970s to the early 1990s), primarily in the fields of social work and child development, that love and stability are essential in establishing healthy families, including those families made through transracial adoption. But *In Their Own Voices* further stretches the reader to ask the critical question: Is love (and stability) enough? Do parents of transracial adoptees have to make changes in their lives, such as the neighborhoods they live in, the churches they attend, and the friends they have?

In Their Parents' Voices picks up where *In Their Own Voices* leaves off, this time drawing from the personal accounts of the adoptive parents, many of whom had the opportunity to read their sons' and daughters' intimate discussions of their adoptive experience. The parents reflect upon their journeys, which entailed adopting and raising black and biracial children against the backdrop of the civil rights movement and amid the controversy about transracial adoption. In this second volume parents representing sixteen families from the first volume talk candidly about their reasons for adopting, the adoption process, the challenges and triumphs they encountered in raising their children, and the relationships they have with their adult children and, in many cases, with their children's spouses and children. The parents express their opinions about transracial adoption and the stance taken in the early 1970s in opposition to transracial adoption, and they offer recommendations to other adoptive families who are in the process of raising children of color.

Our research design for this book was similar to the one we used for *In Their Own Voices*; we primarily interviewed participants by telephone (with the exception of two couples and one parent). The interviews lasted on average 1.5 hours and were then transcribed and mailed to each participant for her or his review and consent before publication.

Although the parents in this volume reflect on the often bitter debates carried on for more than thirty years about the consequences of transracial adoption, it is no longer a factor for families seeking to adopt today. The debate formally ended in 1996 with the passage of the Adoption and Safe Families Act, which in essence stated that race shall not be a factor in adoption.

Unfortunately, statistics about transracial adoption remain difficult to pinpoint. Most would agree that the actual numbers of transracial adoptions of U.S. citizens by U.S. citizens are still very small. Some scholars continue to use data from a 1987 study because of the scarcity of statistical information on transracial adoption; it found that "92 percent of all adoptions involve an adoptive mother and child of the same race.... In only 8 percent of all adoptions are the parents and children of different races."[1] But as noted in *In Their Own Voices* (2000) the 8 percent figure also included thousands of international adoptions, and in actuality, in those cases where a black American child had been adopted by a white family domestically, the figure could be as low as 1.2 percent of all adoptions.[2]

TRANSRACIAL ADOPTION

The institutionalized beginnings of transracial adoption of black children in North America trace to the activities of the Children's Service Center and a group of parents in Montreal, Canada, who in 1960 founded an organization called the Open Door Society.

In the United States 1961 marked the founding of an organization whose original purpose was to provide placements for black children in black adoptive homes. Parents to Adopt Minority Youngsters (PAMY) was founded in

Minnesota and worked with the Minnesota Department of Public Welfare. PAMY was one of the first groups formed in the United States along the lines of the Open Door Society and provided similar referral and recruitment services and handled public relations. But PAMY's involvement with transracial adoption, unlike that of the Open Door Society, came as an unexpected by-product of PAMY's original intent, which was to secure black adoptive homes for black children. From 1962 through 1965 approximately twenty black children in Minnesota were adopted by white families through the efforts of PAMY. These adoptive parents seemed not to fit the stereotype of the adoptive family, an infertile couple. For the most part they were not infertile, and they did not regard their act as a substitute for biological parenthood.[3]

By 1969 the United States had forty-seven organizations similar to the Open Door Society. Among the major ones were Families for Interracial Adoption, the Council on Adoptable Children, Opportunity, the National Council of Adoptive Parents, and Adopt-A-Child-Today.[4] Their primary function was to help secure adoptive homes for all parentless children, with particular emphasis on children with "special needs," a category that included children of color.

Historically, both private and public adoption agencies have had a bank of white adoptive families larger than the number of available white children. For example, a 1957 study found that at any given time two to eight approved white adoptive homes were available for every white child, whereas only one approved black family was available for every ten to twenty black children.[5]

By 1970 the number of available nonwhite children still far exceeded the number of approved nonwhite homes. That year, 21,416 approved white homes were available for 18,392 white children, and 1,584 approved nonwhite homes were available for 4,045 nonwhite children. This meant that 2,461 nonwhite children had little hope of being adopted into nonwhite homes.[6]

The 1970 study provided combined figures for public and private agencies that showed that 116 approved white homes were available for every 100 white children and only 39 approved nonwhite homes were available for every 100 nonwhite children.[7] The following statement, from the Child Welfare League of America (CWLA), demonstrates that the agencies in the 1970 survey did not even consider transracial adoption as a way of finding homes for the nonwhite children for whom nonwhite homes could not be found: "Again, the reader must be cautioned that the data do not take account of the white adoptive homes that are in fact available for the placement of nonwhite children. If it were possible to place a nonwhite child in about one out of every nine approved white homes, there would be an available adoption resource for all children reported by the 240 agencies."[8] Clearly, the assumption in 1970 was that it was impossible to consider placing nonwhite children with white families.

Adoption agencies that serve black children predominately tend to have a higher proportion of black social workers on their staff than agencies with small populations of black children. Studies have shown that a social worker's race is one of the strongest factors affecting attitudes toward transracial adoption, with black social workers disapproving more often than white social workers.[9]

At its 1972 national conference the National Association of Black Social Workers (NABSW) presented a position paper that attacked and repudiated transracial adoption. The following excerpt establishes the flavor of the attack:

> Black children should be placed only with black families, whether in foster care or adoption. Black children belong physically, psychologically and culturally in black families in order that they receive the total sense of themselves and develop a sound projection of their future.... Black children in white homes are cut off from the healthy development of themselves as black people.
>
> The socialization process for every child begins at birth. Included in the socialization process is the child's cultural heritage, which is an important segment of the total process. This must begin at the earliest moment; otherwise our children will not have the background and knowledge which is necessary to survive in a racist society. This is impossible if the child is placed with white parents in a white environment....
>
> We [the members of the NABSW] have committed ourselves to go back to our communities and work to end this particular form of genocide [transracial adoption].[10]

The popular black press, especially *Ebony*, continued to feature articles in which adoption and transracial adoption were the central themes.[11] These were wide-ranging reports that attempted to present the gamut of positions and ramifications involved in black adoption. In August 1974 *Ebony* devoted an entire issue to the black child, with the adoption controversy woven throughout several reports.

Many of the readers' letters that *Ebony* published after that issue appeared contained the following sentiments: Whites are responsible for having produced a white racist society. Their act of adopting blacks is insulting and psychologically damaging and dangerous. It's ironic; once whites enslaved us because they considered themselves superior, and still do. Yet now they want to "rear and love us." Why?[12]

In 1974 the Black Caucus of the North American Conference on Adoptable Children recommended "support [for] the consciousness development movement of all groups" and "that every possible attempt should be made to place black and other minority children in a cultural and racial setting similar to their original group." In May 1975 the dean of the Howard University School of Social Work, who was also president of the NABSW, stated that "black children who grow up in white homes end up with white psyches."[13]

Most black writers opposed to transracial adoption challenged two main hypotheses: The number of black couples willing to adopt black children is insufficient; and the benefits that a black child will receive in a white family surpass those received in an institution.[14]

They observed that many potential nonwhite adoptive parents are disqualified because adoption agencies widely use criteria adopted for screening white middle-class parents for selection. The writers also observed that blacks historically have adopted informally, preferring not to rely on agencies and courts for sanction. Therefore the figures cited by agencies were an inaccurate reflection of the actual number of black adoptions. Critics also claimed that no longitudinal outcome data were available to show that transracial adoption of black children outweighed the known disadvantages of institutional or foster care and predicted that black children adopted into white families would suffer family and personal problems as the children grew into preadolescence and adolescence. A leading black organization pointed to transracially adopted black children who were being returned to foster care because the adoption was not "working out" or were being placed in residential treatment by their white adoptive parents because they could not manage them.[15]

Black professionals and organizations cited two National Urban League studies as further evidence that institutional racism is one of the primary reasons that more black children are not given to prospective black adoptive families.[16] These studies reported that of eight hundred black families applying to become adoptive parents, only two families were approved (0.25 percent), compared with a national average of 10 percent.[17] Another study concluded that 40 to 50 percent of black families sampled would consider adoption.[18]

What is the explanation for the discrepancy between the apparently widespread desire to adopt among blacks and a dearth of approved black homes for adoption? First, blacks have not adopted in the expected numbers because child welfare agencies have not actively recruited in black communities using community resources, the black media, and churches. Second, many blacks have a historic suspicion of public agencies and therefore restrict their involvement with them to whatever extent possible. Third, many blacks feel that no matter how close they come to fulfilling the criteria established for adoption, the chances of winning approval are slight because many reside in less affluent areas.[19]

On August 20, 1996, President Bill Clinton signed into law the Adoption and Safe Families Act, which prohibits "a state or other entity that receives federal assistance from denying a person the opportunity to become an adoptive or a foster parent solely on the basis of the race, color, or national origin of the person or of the child involved." The provision also prohibits a state from denying or delaying the placement of a child for adoption or foster care solely on the basis of the race, color, or national origin of the adoptive or foster parent of the child involved. The federal statute went into effect on January 1, 1997.

RESEARCH FINDINGS

Beginning in 1971–72 Rita Simon and Howard Altstein conducted a twenty-year study of families who adopted across racial lines. They interviewed the parents, the birth children, and the adopted children in 104 families living in the Midwest. The major findings showed that the transracial adoptees clearly were aware of and comfortable with their racial identity. They both laughed at and were somewhat scornful of the NABSW's characterization of them as "Oreos: black on the outside, white on the inside." As young adults the black adoptees stressed their comfort with their black identity and their awareness that they may speak, dress, and have different tastes in music than inner-city blacks—but that the black experience is a varied one in this society, and they are no less black than are children of the ghetto.[20]

Throughout the study Simon and Altstein also described how the birth children were reacting to the transracial adoption experience. In the early years Simon and Altstein reported siblings' occasional expressions of annoyance and anger at how much time and energy the parents were devoting to their adopted child: "Our family life has been turned upside down since 'D' came home," or "'M' gets all the attention." But these remarks were few and far between. In the large majority of the families, the black adoptee was "my brother" or "my sister"—to be cared about, played with, and, if necessary, protected. Race had receded into the background.[21]

Other studies conducted of families who adopted across racial lines have reported similar findings. Elizabeth Bartholet, who teaches civil rights and family law at Harvard, surveyed the literature and reported:

The evidence from empirical studies indicates uniformly that transracial adoptees do as well on measures of psychological and social adjustment as black children raised inracially in relatively similar socio-economic circumstances. The evidence also indicates that transracial adoptees develop comparably strong senses of black identity. They see themselves as black and they think well of blackness. The difference is that they feel more comfortable with the white community than blacks raised inracially. This evidence provides no basis for concluding that, for the children involved, there are any problems inherent in transracial placement.[22]

After more than thirty years transracial adoption, particularly the adopting of black and biracial children into white homes, continues to be an intriguing subject. Many questions about the identity and racial identity development of these children remain unanswered, and the lessons learned from parents who first ventured on this path and have raised their children to adulthood have not been completely explored or openly discussed. We hope that the experiences described here by these courageous and generous parents will provide insights into the complexities of the transracial adoption phenomenon.

NOTES

1. Center for the Future of Children, "Adoption," *Future of Children* 3, no. 1 (spring 1993): 29.

2. Rita J. Simon and Rhonda M. Roorda, *In Their Own Voices: Transracial Adoptees Tell Their Stories* (New York: Columbia University Press, 2000), 6.

3. Elizabeth Shepherd, "Adopting Negro Children: White Families Find It Can Be Done," *New Republic*, June 20, 1964, 10–12; Harriet Fricke, "Interracial Adoption: The Little Revolution," *Social Work* 10, no. 3 (July 1965): 92–97.

4. Bernice Madison and Michael Shapiro, "Black Adoption—Issues and Policies," *Social Service Review* 47, no. 4 (December 1973): 531–54.

5. Michael Shapiro, *Adoption of Children with Special Needs* (New York: Child Welfare League of America, 1957), 86.

6. Lucille J. Grow, *A New Look at Supply and Demand in Adoption* (New York: Child Welfare League of America, 1970), 8, table 4.

7. Ibid.

8. Grow, *A New Look at Supply and Demand*, 9.

9. Anne Stern Farber, "Attitudes of Social Workers toward Requests for Transracial Adoption," research project, University of Maryland School of Social Work, 1972; Dawn Day Wachtel, "White Social Workers and the Adoption of Black Children," paper presented at the August 1973 meeting of the American Sociological Association, New York.

10. William T. Merritt, chair of the committee on transracial adoption, speech to the National Association of Black Social Workers National Conference, Washington, D.C., 1972, quoted in Rita J. Simon, Howard Altstein, and Mary Gold S. Melli, *The Case for Transracial Adoption* (Washington, D.C.: American University Press, 1994), 40.

11. Helen H. King, "It's Easier to Adopt Today," *Ebony*, December 1970, 120.

12. Letter to the editor, *Ebony*, August 1974.

13. Sandy Banisky, "The Question: Is It Bad for Black Children to Be Adopted by Whites?" *Baltimore Sun*, May 28, 1975, B1.

14. Rita J. Simon and Howard Altstein, *Adoption, Race and Identity*, 2nd ed. (New Brunswick, N.J.: Transaction, 2002), 16.

15. New York Chapter, National Association of Black Social Workers, "Transracial Adoption Update: 1978," mimeograph, 4–5.

16. Simon and Altstein, *Adoption, Race and Identity*, 17.

17. "Black Children Facing Adoption Barriers," *NASW News*, April 1984, 9.

18. Ibid.

19. Simon and Altstein, *Adoption, Race and Identity*, 18.

20. Ibid., 222.

21. Ibid., 222–23.

22. Elizabeth Bartholet, "Where Do Black Children Belong? Politics of Race Matching in Adoption," *University of Pennsylvania Law Review* 139 (1991): 1163.

IN THEIR PARENTS' VOICES

PART 1

THE CHILDREN FROM
IN THEIR OWN VOICES

TWENTY-FOUR MEN and women participated in *In Their Own Voices*. The twelve women ranged in age from 22 to 28. Eight were adopted when they were 3 months old or younger. The other four were 1 year; 18 months; 2 years; and 6 years old. But the 6-year-old had been living with the family as a foster child since her birth. The respondent who was adopted when she was 2, Rhonda, had been in foster care with an African American couple who may have wanted to adopt her but were not allowed to because of their age. Rhonda had been abandoned by her birth mother and was taken directly from the hospital to the black family. Five of the twelve describe themselves as "mixed," the others as black. Kimberly, who described herself as mixed, was married to a white man and was the mother of two sons. Two mixed respondents were married to black men; another was unmarried and had a son who was two and half. The fifth was unmarried and recently had moved back to her parents' home. Eight women had at least a bachelor's degree, one was working toward her Ph.D., one had a master's in speech communications, and one was working toward a master's degree in social work. Three were completing their bachelor's degrees, and one was a high school graduate who had taken college courses but was not working toward a degree.

Of the twelve male participants, eight were adopted before they were 6 months old, one was adopted when he was 2, two were adopted when they were 5, and one was a teenager (13 to 18) when he lived with a white family in a southern, rural Virginia community from 1954 to 1959. Four were born and raised in Iowa, Michigan, Illinois, and Oregon. The other eight were born and reared on the East Coast in Connecticut, Vermont, Massachusetts, New York, Maryland, and Virginia. Eleven ranged in age from 23 to 31, and one was 57. Six were married, three to white women, one to a Haitian woman, and two to American black women. Four had children; one adopted a black child when the child was 6 months old. One was a single father. Eight men had at least a bachelor's degree.

The work lives of our respondents showed a good deal of variety. They included a professional athlete and Olympic gold medal winner, minister, property manager, ninth-grade teacher, aspiring screenwriter, student, stockbroker, actor, police officer, technical writer, and a retiree from the Department of the Army. At the time the interviews were conducted most respondents lived in small or medium-sized cities.

Just before this book went to press, we caught up with the children (nine women and eight men) from *In Their Own Voices* whose parents participated in this new book.

Shecara (pseudonym) was interviewed in 1998. Today, she says, she still feels that her role in society is to be the "go-between for the black and white sides." She believes that being a biracial woman and a transracial adoptee gives her an edge in narrowing the racial divide. Shecara and her husband, Arsale, moved from the college community of West Lafayette, Indiana, to a predominately black community in St. Louis, Missouri. Shecara had worked as a nurse in Indiana for six years; now she stays at home to care for their children. Arsale, who is African American, is a high school teacher and a football coach who is highly regarded in the community. Shecara and Arsale now have four children: India, 16; Asante, 9; Kiya, 5; and Alexis, 3. India maintains a 4.0 grade-point average. When asked about any differences in how she and Arsale view issues, Shecara paused and then laughed. She said that while she and Arsale have a good marriage and family life and agree on most things, the bone of contention remains (it was evident in her interview in 1998) how to discipline their children, particularly India. Shecara attributes the difference to their cultural backgrounds. Arsale was raised according to the old rule that "children are seen and not heard," whereas she was encouraged to express herself within specific parameters. Recently, Shecara and her family visited her adoptive parents in West Lafayette to celebrate her dad's seventy-fourth birthday.

Ned and his wife, Sharon, are making their dreams come true. They have built their family through the gifts of adoption and birth: Gabriel, 10; Michael, 8; and Joy, 3. Ned is a middle-school history teacher who enjoys making a difference in the lives of his students. Ned still believes, as he did in his 1997 interview, that family is the defining factor in life, but he continues to be amazed at how important race is to other people. Ned and his family remain in Grand Rapids, Michigan, and have a good relationship with his adoptive family.

Since her interview in 1997 Laurie has worked in supervisory positions within the social service arena in the Los Angeles area. Among the organizations with which she has worked are Mothers Against Drunk Drivers, AIDS Project Los Angeles, and Planned Parenthood. She has also worked for Kaiser

Permanente. Laurie remains very supportive of transracial adoption. She says that if she had not been adopted, she would not have been able to do anything that she has accomplished in life to this point. In *In Their Own Voices* Laurie described her reluctance to meet her biological father after witnessing how he behaved toward his family; today, she says, she has nothing to do with him. She says that maintaining her biological connection is not a priority for her. Laurie recently moved to the State of Washington to be closer to her adoptive family and close friends. She hopes to land a job soon in the social service field, specifically, in health and education.

Interracially married, Pete and his wife, Brenda, now have two boys aged 5 and 7. They continue to live outside Ithaca, New York. Pete now is sergeant of the Ithaca Police Department, the first black officer to serve in that position. The local black community has recognized Pete for this achievement, an honor of which he is especially proud. He still volunteers with the local fire department when time permits. In 1997 Pete had recently located both his birth parents, connecting his Nigerian and Caucasian roots. Today he remains in contact with both of his biological parents as important links to his identity. But paramount in his life is his role as father and husband. Adding to the happiness of Pete and his family is their recent move to a beautiful, custom-built home.

Rachel Anker's life has been on the upswing since we talked with her in 1997. She was married in 2005 to a young African American man who complements Rachel well. After a long journey in pursuit of her degree, she was expecting to graduate in the spring of 2007 with a B.A. in elementary education and music. She recently located her birth mother through a postadoption agency. Rachel and her husband, Robert, who works as an independent sales distributor for a major food company, have attended gatherings with her birth mother and other birth family members. All in all, Rachel says, since her interview she has become stronger both physically and spiritually, and she has a healthier sense of racial identity and self-esteem yet still struggles with both at times. In addition to her studies, Rachel is director of a day care center. She and her husband spend quality time with her adoptive family and live only twenty minutes from South Holland, Illinois, where her parents still live and where she grew up.

The title of an old Negro spiritual is "Ain't Gonna Let Nobody Turn Me Around." If you were to ask Rev. Keith J. Bigelow if its words remain meaningful to him ten years after his 1996 interview, he would say amen. He clearly is moving forward in his journey. In recent years he has formed Antioch Full Gospel Ministries of Lansing, Michigan, which he now serves as senior pastor; he also has been promoted to master sergeant in the Air National Guard.

The Antioch church is a multicultural ministry, the majority of whose members are participating in or planning to participate in foster care and/or adoption. Keith says his vision for the ministry is to expand and ultimately create a full-fledged foster care and adoption program that is spiritually based. He and his wife, Francoise (Magda), who is Haitian American, are raising their two children, Taryn, 12, and Keith II, who is 5. Keith continues to believe that adoption means that the good Lord is looking out for you—whether you look like or appear to be different from the rest of your family members.

Andrea Bandstra was married in 1998, a year after her interview, and moved from Portage, Michigan, to a suburb of Detroit. Her family has grown from one child to three: Antonio Jr., 16; Latrelle, 12; and Arya, 5. Andrea is an aquatic director and expects to soon complete her bachelor's degree in general studies with a minor in exercise science. She has plans to earn a master's degree (her husband, Antonio, already has one). Andrea says she continues to support transracial adoption, that love within a family is the most important factor in a child's growth and development, and that one's identity should be based on one's character, achievements, and purpose. However, she now recognizes the benefits of having an African American father and role model for her children, because he provides them, especially the boys, with guidance based on his experiences as a successful black man in American society. Andrea says she is very appreciative of the upbringing her adoptive parents gave her.

Daniel Mennega reports that not much has changed since his interview in 1998. He still lives in Austin, Texas, and is enjoying the uniqueness and ethnic diversity of that community. He is supportive of transracial adoption and still believes his identity is strongly guided by his interests and individuality, although he understands that he is part of both black and white worlds. Daniel is employed as an advertising copywriter and enjoys mountain biking, bird watching, cooking, and reading. He stays in contact with his adoptive family.

Shortly after his interview in 1998, Seth D. Himrod married DarLisa, whom he has known since high school. They have four daughters and a son: Nadia, 1; Nia, 5; Nykel, 6; Destini, 8; and Tim, 17. Seth, who was working as a stockbroker in 1998, now is employed in the sanitation department of the City of Evanston, Illinois. When he can find the time, he continues to speak to groups on transracial adoption. Seth's adoptive parents are very much a part of his family's life today as active and caring grandparents.

Nicolle Tremitiere has divorced since her 1997 interview and is living back in York, Pennsylvania, with her daughter, Azariah, 14, after a stint in Colorado. Nicolle is working toward her master's in social work at Temple University, where she has a 4.0 average. This is an especially significant accomplishment for Nicolle, because she experienced serious academic difficulties throughout her K-12 and college years. In 1997 Nicolle was finally diagnosed with dyslexia and spent two years "relearning how to read" with a reading specialist. Her experience with dyslexia is one focus of her graduate studies as she prepares herself for developing an intensive adult training program for adults with unremediated dyslexia who want to complete postsecondary education or vocational training. Grounding Nicolle through all of this is her faith in God, which she sees as central to her core identity. Transracial adoption is a part of Nicolle's history and familial reality, but it no longer defines her. Her focus is on being a good parent, as well as her professional preparation and growth. Nicolle maintains a close connection to her adoptive family and continues to be supportive of transracial adoptions that are well thought out for children who do not have access to an appropriate parent who shares their cultural identity.

Every entrepreneur experiences the highs and the lows of a business. David T. Adams is no exception. In 1998, a year after his interview, he launched his own film company, the Indie Film Group (IFG), in conjunction with the premiere of the film of his first screenplay, *Connection*. David is the educational coordinator and instructor for IFG, which provides an opportunity for young filmmakers to network while learning more about their craft from experienced and well-known professionals in the field. IFG also offers a hands-on component, Screenwriters' Boot Camp, which requires both novice and experienced screenwriters to complete a screenplay in sixteen weeks. David also speaks to schoolchildren about his experiences as an educator, writer, filmmaker. David and his wife, Shari, live in northwestern Washington State with their sons, who now number four: Luke, 16; Josh, 13; Andrew, 7; and Jordan, 5. David continues to believe that race is not an issue for him, either as a black man or as someone who is interracially married. He says that in his profession people see his work and his personality—which are all that count. David and his family remain in contact with his adoptive family.

Rhonda M. Roorda was married in 2000 to an African American man who is her number one supporter and her better half. She has dedicated her life to helping to bring about a better understanding of transracial adoption and its impact on families over time through writing and speaking engagements and by collaborating with others on adoption projects. She stays in contact with her adoptive family, although her relationship with her father is not strong. Rhonda's godfather remains as active in her life as he was in 1997, as are her mentors, who are from different racial and ethnic backgrounds. Rhonda continues to serve professionally with a nonprofit educational advocacy organization in Lansing, Michigan.

Tage Larsen's classical music career has spanned more than ten years. In 1997 he was performing with the prestigious U.S. Marine Band, which is based in Washington, D.C. Today Tage is in his fifth season as a trumpet player with the Chicago Symphony Orchestra, its first full-time African American member. His career so far has taken him to Australia, England, Germany, Hungary, Switzerland, and Japan. When he is not performing on stage or in rehearsal, he teaches at Chicago's Roosevelt University and gives private trumpet lessons. He also reaches out to children and young people who have had little exposure to classical music and introduces them to it. Although he says that his goal is to play music as well as possible and that he does not focus on race, Chicago's large and influential African American community has a different perspective. Although the community is proud of Tage's accomplishments as a musician, it is even more proud that an African American was instrumental in helping to bring down racial barriers within the symphony. Tage is married and has two children, Zachary, 5, and Ethan, 4. He maintains a close relationship with his adoptive family and is an advocate for transracial adoption.

In 1997 Jessica Pelton described her identity this way: "I always felt 'half-baked.' I mean I didn't feel completely done." Much has changed in her life since then. After spending years outside her home state of Vermont, Jessica returned and worked for three years with a small, private adoption agency as a caseworker, with much of her work focused on building a more comprehensive educational component for families pursuing transracial adoption. She also worked with pregnant women and couples who were considering putting their child up for adoption and with birth parents involved in open adoptions. She says that experience did more good for her personally than she could have imagined and helped move her forward with her own issues of grief and loss.

After she returned to Vermont, she also decided to search for both sides of her birth family; through her birth mother's family she was able to contact her birth father. In this bittersweet reunion (which her adoptive parents touch on in their interview here), Jessica learned that both her birth parents have other children by people of a different race. Her African American birth father had six children (including Jessica), all with white women. And her white birth mother has three sons, all with African American men. Jessica says, "It is incredible—all of us kids look so much alike!" What is even more incredible is her realization that, as she says, "You belong to who you belong to." She remained in close contact with her adoptive parents and her friends throughout her search and reunification process. Feeling their unconditional love and support helped her to realize that she belongs where she is.

Jessica recently married Steven, whom she describes as an "old school" black man. Their daughter, Olivia, is 18 months old, and their family includes Steven's children, Steven Jr., who is 8, and Akira, who is 21. Jessica is the coordinator of multicultural affairs at a nearby community college and is working on her master's in counseling. Steven is employed as a project manager and supervisor with a company called New Visions that offers a wide variety of programs and services for individuals with developmental disabilities in the greater Albany, New York, area. He oversees one of the company's ten consumer services departments. Jessica and her family live in Niskayuna, New York, about ninety minutes from West Rupert, Vermont, where her parents still live. Jessica reports that they have embraced Steven and all their children. Steven, who lost both his parents as a young man, has developed a close relationship with Jessica's adoptive parents too.

In the decade since her 1997 interview, Kim Stapert's journey as been marked by great success but also new challenges, pain, and loss. Kim's transformation as a woman of faith, transracial adoptee, birth daughter, and mother has been marked by the challenges that she has confronted in her own life. Divorced only a few months after her interview, Kim and her two children moved back to Grand Rapids, Michigan, so they could be closer to her adoptive parents. She worked as social worker for a Christian adoption agency, in charge of postadoption services for families who had adopted older, special needs children and children of color. Kim then took a position with a community mental health agency and has worked as a social worker in the emergency room of a local hospital.

While still reeling from the loss and pain of her first marriage and still exploring her racial identity, she met and married an African American man with whom she had two children. Then, in 2002, one of her younger adoptive brothers, who suffered from an addiction, committed suicide. Three years later one of her biggest advocates, her adoptive father, died of a massive heart attack. Kim recently divorced her second husband, citing spousal abuse.

Kim believes that these losses have made her a more "authentic, humble person" who "pulls from her faith in God and the loving comfort" of her adoptive mother and family. She has since launched a nonprofit organization called Living Water, Inc. Living Water, a faith-based initiative, runs an outpatient center for women and children. Services focus on crisis intervention, computer education, and counseling to keep families together. Living Water also maintains two recovery houses, both with the capacity to offer long-term housing to traumatized women and children who have fallen through cracks in the government safety net.

Now a single mother of four—Alex, 15; Zach, 12; Miles, 7; and Nia, 4—she is a deacon of her church. She is in contact with her birth mother and is thankful for this connection as it is gives her a better understanding of her birth history, and she and her birth mother have found they have much in common: losses, choices, and patterns of relating. Kim believes that her relationship with her birth mother has helped her to resolve issues involving abandonment, attachment, and loss resulting from her being put up for adoption. Kim continues to enjoy a wonderful relationship with her adoptive mother and family. She says her mother "is an inspiration of faith in God," a "prayer warrior" for her children and grandchildren, and an "amazing person who has a great Christian perspective."

Now retired from the WNBA, Chantel Tremitiere continues her commitment to community and to children, especially those in need of homes. In 2005 Chantel was the guest speaker at the annual conference of the North American Council on Adoptable Children. She has also done charity events and participated in other activities designed to support children domestically. Since her 1998 interview Chantel appeared in a Disney movie called *Double Teamed* (2002) and is in negotiations to have her life story made into a movie.

But a main focus of her time today is her young company, called BLANK Entertainment, in Louisiana. As CEO of BLANK Entertainment, Chantel Tremitiere oversees the development of commercials and music videos. BLANK Entertainment also houses a recording studio. Her business influence has been recognized by the Association of Business, Engineering and Science Entrepreneurs, which hosts a Louisiana Tech "Top Dawgs" Business Plan Competition designed to give students experience as entrepreneurs. One message about adoption that Chantel Tremitiere would like to get out is that thousands of children in the United States are waiting desperately to be adopted. If more funding and attention were devoted to these children, they would, she believes, have homes. Instead she fears that adoption is becoming a fad because of the current media frenzy about celebrities adopting children abroad. She says that stories about adoption should be focused on everyday people and what they go through to adopt and provide a good home for that child.

After his 1996 interview Britton Perry continued to pursue a career in teaching and acting in New York City. Then he decided to further his education and in 2004 received his master's degree in information technology from the Pratt Institute in New York City. At about that time he married a beautiful African American woman, Pamela, whom he met in New York. The Perrys and Pamela's family found striking commonalities and really enjoy each other, Brit's mother, Joyce, reports. After their wedding Brit and Pam moved to Washington, D.C., for jobs and because being in a racially and ethnically diverse community is important to them. Pam, a financial attorney, works as a senior manager for a mortgage company, and Brit is working as an information analyst for a think tank. In 2006 they became the proud parents of twins, a girl and a boy, Brooke and Quinn. All four grandparents play a proud and active role in their lives.

AUTHOR'S NOTE

AFTER A WORKSHOP session on adoption a middle-aged white man and his young black daughter came up to me. He asked if I would listen to his predicament and give him advice about how to handle it. He and his wife had been invited to a family reunion, quite a gala affair. There was just one problem: the man's brother, who was organizing the reunion, was a racist and had made it quite clear that his niece was not welcome.

The troubled man who stood before me, and his wife, both wanted to attend the reunion. Would it be okay, he wondered, if they got a babysitter for their daughter?

I looked at him for a moment in disbelief, pulled myself together, and pointed out that he now has a daughter who is African American and that, as her father, he must stand up for her and tell his brother that if she is not invited, he and his wife would not be attending.

On another occasion a parent shared with me the disillusionment he felt thirty years after Martin Luther King Jr. outlined his dream of an integrated and peaceful society. Such a society, the man said sadly, may not come to fruition. For this parent, like many other white parents I've met, King's dream was a major inspiration and no small factor in his decision to adopt transracially. Now the lack of societal progress was causing him, quite literally, to lose interest.

So when my editor asked me, after reading the interviews, "Why do you keep asking all these questions about the parents' continuing their relationships with their adoptive children? I don't understand that," I told her about both incidents in an effort to explain.

Transracial adoptees who were in the vanguard of this phenomenon—and I am one of them—were adopted domestically in the early to mid-1970s. Unfortunately, data on transracial adoption placements remain incomplete for this time period for a variety of reasons. What we do know is that from

1968 to 1975 approximately twelve thousand black and biracial children were placed with white families.[1] And, as the parents interviewed for this book attest, they were given little guidance or information by the agencies that handled the adoptions. The parents were on their own.

Much of the traditional empirical research done on transracial adoption was conducted by social scientists from the 1970s to early 1990s. It focused on the self-esteem and racial identity of children of color, like me, but mostly from the perspective of their white adoptive parents. Two things jumped out at me when I read those studies. One was that a large percentage of these first families lived in rural middle America. They were inspired by their church or Dr. King's "I Have a Dream" speech—or they simply wanted to adopt, and black and biracial children were *available*. But because of where their adoptive parents lived, the children often had no contact with the African American community because there was no African American community to speak of.

The other factor that jumped out at me was statements made by white adoptive parents, explaining that, in effect, they chose to be "color-blind" in how they viewed their black and biracial children. And, indeed, these studies concluded that love is crucial in raising transracial adoptees and predicted that these children would grow into productive people in society. But as I have traveled around the country speaking with adoptive parents—many of whom are quite amazing, I might add—I have met enough of their children to know that while love is certainly essential, these children need more.

Those statements about "color-blindness" are at the root of the problem: while it's wonderful, on the one hand, that their child's color did not matter to their loving parents, on the other hand, their child's color is *not* irrelevant and of course is a major component of identity. How could these children form healthy identities if their parents regarded one of their major characteristics as irrelevant?

One result was that some of these children grew up feeling like an experiment in racial harmony, disconnected from their ethnic community and not "a full voting member" (for lack of a better way to put it) of the white community in which they were raised. (Just who *do* you date in high school?)

Too often, then, as young adults, many of these children moved away and were shocked by the world they found outside their close-knit, nurturing hometowns. A certain element of disconnectedness entered their relationship with their parents. Probably, it was always there, shrouded by the demands of daily living and the challenges of raising any child in twentieth-century America.

Plenty of people in their twenties have a tough time renegotiating their relationship with their parents, but transracial adoptees, and their parents, are picking their way through a psychological, cultural, and emotional minefield. And if the parents are unable to understand the multiple quests on which their transracial adoptees find themselves embarked, their relationship may be ruptured. Sadly, some parents simply give up once their adoptive children are launched into adulthood. These parents are tired. Or, like the man I described earlier, completely disillusioned.

That's why we asked the parents represented in this book whether they have been able to maintain a relationship with their adult adoptive children. That's why we wanted to know how they have managed to do it (and most of them have). That's why we asked about their children's choice of marriage partner and how that has affected the parent-child relationship.

I think that the reasons behind most of the other questions we asked are fairly self-evident. But because my editor was so puzzled by the questions about the parent–adult child relationships, I wanted to offer a brief explanation for those readers who would have no way of knowing the answers, simply because this is a realm far beyond the experience of most people.

RHONDA M. ROORDA

NOTES

1. Rita J. Simon, Howard Altstein, and Marygold S. Melli, *The Case for Transracial Adoption* (Washington, D.C.: American University Press, 1994).

PART 2

THE PARENTS

JOHN AND MARIAN PELTON

WEST RUPERT, VERMONT
SEPTEMBER 2004

John Pelton is 65, and Marian Pelton is 62. They have one biological child, Peter, and three adopted children, Jay, Jessica, and Maria. Jay was 2 when he was adopted, Jessica was 3 weeks old, and Maria was 7 weeks old. The children were raised in rural Vermont. The Peltons are Protestant. John Pelton has a bachelor's degree and has done graduate work in economics; Marian Pelton has a bachelor's degree and has done graduate work in education. They are both retired general-store owners. They describe their economic status as middle class.

[It was important for me to learn about my ethnicity because] I always felt "half-baked." I mean I didn't feel completely done. It's very much a part of my personality.... I wonder how much it has to do with being black in a white family ... but I would strive and strive to get to some point and then I would get there and think there's so much more I still have to do. There's never a feeling of accomplishment or achievement or that it's all coming together for me. The piece that seems to be missing is my blackness.

—JESSICA PELTON, 24, DECEMBER 1997

INTERVIEW

RR: What encouraged you to create your family in the form of adoption in addition to having a biological son?

MP: We knew there was a need for people to adopt, and we knew that not everyone felt comfortable doing it, and we did. So we decided to do it.

RR: Where were you living at the time you adopted?

JP: Rupert, Vermont.

RR: Can you describe the community for us?

JP: In the whole town of Rupert there are six hundred people, and we live in West Rupert, where the population is maybe three hundred. The highway that goes through the village passes what used to be our general store, the center of West Rupert. A "T" intersection there leads to what we call "the hollow," and the road eventually turns to dirt and heads farther east. Anything west of us is New York State because we are right on the state line. If you head two miles north, you come to the village of Rupert. In the two small rural villages there are three churches, a firehouse-community building, library, historical society, town office, a small factory, several in-home businesses, three farms, and numerous residences. Our children attended elementary school in two 1- and 2-room schools. Several families had adopted children. Most junior high and high school kids from Rupert go to Salem, New York. A few go to Granville, New York, and a few go to private schools.

RR: What year did you adopt your children?

MP: We adopted Jay in 1973, Jess in 1975, and Maria in 1977.

RR: When you decided to adopt, what was the process like in making that decision and then working with the adoption agency?

MP: When we first started working with the agency, Vermont Children's Aid Society [VCAS] in Rutland, Vermont, about an hour from here, we were working with a much older woman than often is the case. It was quite a while ago now and I don't remember all the details, but she would give us time to think about different aspects of making the decision, of who we would feel comfortable accepting into our home as part of our family. She also, I believe, had some health problems, so we worked with her for a while, and then she was ill for a while and somebody else took over, a much younger person, with whom we finalized both our decisions and our adoption. So it took a little bit longer than it did with our next adoption.

RR: What is the sequence of order of your children?

MP: In 1969 our oldest child was born to us, a son, Peter, who is now 34, almost 35. The next one is Jay, age 33, whom we adopted as a Korean 2-year-old in 1973. Through VCAS connections were made for us to work with Holt Adoption Services on an overseas adoption. Our daughters, Jessica, almost 30, and Maria, 27, were adopted through the State of Vermont. These were in-country placements.

RR: After you adopted, did you believe at that time that Vermont would be where you wanted to raise your family?

JP: Yes.

RR: What were some of the most important factors that you both looked at in adopting your three kids?

MP: We concluded, eventually, that we didn't care whether we were adopting a boy or a girl, but we did choose that this child would be from another race or somebody who was more difficult to place, because we really wanted to help. Then we concluded that it would be better for us in our rural situation here, farther away from medical help, to choose somebody who was basically healthy.

RR: Did adopting children from different racial and ethnic backgrounds change either of you as an individual or as a family?

MP: I don't think it really did, although it did help us to grow from the point we already were at.

RR: Did you find, as you were raising your family, that race was ever an issue when your kids were on the playground or in their schools or community?

MP: I think basically we felt that the community and our family accepted us and our diversity very well. But we understood if someone was having a little difficulty with it at times. In fact, we realized there were probably more people struggling with this than was shown to us. We were close with an adoptive parents' support group at that time called Room for One More, in southern Vermont. There also was an active group in northern Vermont too. We had a great deal of support from people who had adopted transracially and those who were learning about adoption as an option for themselves. We were like one big family, often discussing how each of us was reacting, or thought we should react, following our decision of choosing transracial adoption. We all agreed that what we were doing was probably the best way to go for our own families—not going into it blindly but just expecting the best from people, and that's what we got. I think it turned out better for us than some of our friends, who shared personal stories, which were kind of upsetting. Yet our kids, too, must have absorbed our attitude because it was after the fact, years later, when we occasionally heard a little something from them that made us realize they went through more than we were aware of.

JP: Our parents had been here for years… . [My parents] were very well respected in town. I think that helped.

MP: John and I were born here, and we were friendly with everyone.

JP: We were respected, so that made it easier, I think.

RR: In your family and in the community, what were the values that you really focused on?

MP: We believed it was important to respect people, and care for people, and understand that everybody's a person, regardless of their race.

RR: With your two daughters, who are biracial, did you as a family struggle with hair?

MP: Yes, I think that we did. But we did the best we could, and we didn't get upset about everything having to be perfect. Sometimes that made it hard for our kids, and sometimes that made it easier—I don't know.

JP: There was a point where you took Jessica to Albany, New York, to the black community there to get her hair done, probably when she was in high school or starting college.

MP: Yes, definitely in high school or a little before that.

RR: What was it that encouraged you to seek help for your girls' hair needs?

MP: I didn't know that much about working with black hair, specifically, how to straighten it. [authors' note: Jessica says she was 12 or 13 when she got the idea to have her hair straightened to make it more manageable, and her sister, who is several years younger, wanted her hair straightened too.] When we brought Jess and Maria to the hair salon to have their hair straightened, it seemed to work quite well with Jess's hair, but afterward Maria's hair began to fall out because the chemicals apparently were too strong. The hair specialist had to stop treatment midway because Maria was really uncomfortable going through the process. It was a time of learning for all of us.

RR: How did you find out about this location and to bring your kids there?

MP: I can't remember exactly—I made some calls. There were a very few people of color in our area and within the school system. The girls spoke with them. It was a combination of both.

RR: After high school Jessica chose to go to a historically black college. What in your opinion led her to make that decision?

JP: In college I had a very good friend who was black. (I went to a small college and the percentage of black students there was very low.) I played sports with him and that is how we developed a relationship with one another. He was a great guy and he did a lot in the black community, and he really did well after college, and at some point we found out that he was on the board of trustees at this historically black college in the South. We learned of the school's excellent reputation.

MP: Over the years we had kept very loosely in touch with John's friend—like at Christmas time with those kinds of letters you exchange. Prior to Jess's applying to the college we never told him that she was interested in going there because we didn't want to take advantage of the fact that he was on the board of trustees.

MP: It turned out that she was put on the college's waiting list. In the meantime, for that year, she was accepted as a Rotary exchange student [Rotary
International sponsors an international student exchange program]. Our
college friend heard about Jess and was disappointed that we didn't let
him know sooner of her interest. The good news was that Jessica was
accepted to this wonderful college and graduated from there four years
later. We felt it was an awesome chance for her. She was a good student
and interested in learning.

JP: We thought she had lot of potential.

MP: Yes, in many areas. And we felt if she wanted to do this, it would be an
awesome experience for her to become acquainted with the black community or, as we soon learned, the range there is within the black community. It was good. It was difficult at times, but it was good.

RR: What were the expectations both of you had for your children growing up?

JP: I guess they were normal expectations that any parents would have. We
realized that it might be tougher for our adopted kids in some ways than
it would be for our natural-born child.

RR: Explain that.

JP: I think because there weren't more kids that looked like them in school,
so as far as dating and that sort of thing, it may not have been easy for
them. Also we were concerned in general about the prejudice shown to
minorities in society.

MP: We hoped for our kids to fit in, work hard, and be happy.

RR: What was the relationship like among your children?

MP: It was funny because one time in the grocery store—more than once—I
was asked how they got along, if they communicate with each other. Of
course they could and did communicate with each other, as siblings nor-
mally do.

JP: They've always been good friends. They enjoyed doing things together as
much as they liked doing things with anyone else.

MP: They've had their ups and downs but have become even closer as they've
gotten older, especially Jess and Maria.

RR: How would you describe your relationship now with your adult children?

JP: I think it is pretty close. We do a lot of things still as a family. Thanksgiv-
ing is big for us, and Christmas is too. And since they all live nearby—our
natural son lives only six miles away with his three children, and Maria
lives with us, and Jess is only thirty to forty miles away, and our son Jay
just moved home because he lost his apartment, so two of our kids are
living with us and the other two are very close.

MP: For a while both of our daughters were living in Washington, D.C., first one and then both of them; and Jay lived farther away too. Our kids come and go. Sometimes they need to come back until they make their next transition.

RR: What did you do to help each one of your children identify with her or his own racial group or ethnicity?

MP: We followed the same way of doing things as we learned growing up. We certainly were open to talk about issues affecting any of them. It's interesting: our kids have always given me a hard time because I was often pointing out people of color or things relating to them ethnically, but, no, we didn't go all the way as far as developing close friendships or opportunities with ethnically diverse people on a regular basis. Reflecting on that, it would have been a good idea.

RR: With all the thought and preparation that went into your decision in creating your family, what about the experience surprised you the most?

MP: I guess we weren't surprised.

RR: Looking back from the earliest time until today, what is your happiest memory of your relationship with Jessica?

MP: The happiest memories were when we received all of our kids. That is a moving experience every time you receive a child. With Jessica one of my happiest memories was when she finally decided three years ago to search for her birth family, and then when she went by herself to Indiana and was able to stay with the woman who had been her foster mother when she was a baby. John and I had traveled to her home and received Jess there. She had kept somewhat in contact with me, and then with Jess, and had always had her eyes and ears open for anything she might be able to fit together that would be valuable to Jess in her search. It was very exciting being on the phone with Jess so many times during those few days when she was in Indiana—her sharing with me her experiences [in] actually starting and then making connections with her biological mother's side and her biological father's side of her family. That was a very emotional time. Not so much that we were scared as that we were so excited for Jess. We cried a lot. Both sides were crying. Jess shared everything with us—we got so many phone calls.

RR: What would you say is the saddest memory?

MP: It goes along with that. Jess's birth mom, shortly after she had given Jess up for adoption, realized that she really wished she hadn't. She was given wrong information, and so her searching, which began right away, was always going in the wrong direction. She searched right up until her death from cancer, which was a couple years before Jess actually would have found her. And she was so much like Jess in so many ways, even though she was the white part of the couple that bore Jess—her ways of thinking, her ways of reacting, her ways of creatively expressing herself, both with people and with things she appreciated, and the way she looked so much like Jess.

RR: Did the position taken by the National Association of Black Social Workers affect your decision to adopt additional nonwhite children?

MP: No. We knew of their position while we were still adopting. No. We could see their side, but we felt that there still were needs that a loving family could meet.

RR: Did it affect how you related to your transracially adopted children in particular?

MP: I am sure it probably affected us to know—and it was important that we knew—that some people thought a white home was not the best. We didn't choose to change our town that we lived in; we didn't choose to live in a larger community.

RR: What, in your mind, was so effective in raising your kids in a smaller community?

JP: You know all your neighbors, you know just about everybody in town. Besides, we're in the store business, and our kids worked in the store so they became more outgoing than they might have been otherwise. Other people found out that our kids were just like their kids, and they were accepted.

RR: Do you know if any of your children experienced challenges in moving to another community where they may not have been treated as kindly?

MP: That is difficult to answer. But I don't believe there were any seriously negative situations. I still think, in looking back on it, that what we did was good for the community, good for us, and good for our kids, even though it was probably somewhat difficult for our adopted kids especially. Maybe more so with Jay in particular, who's had less contact with Korean people than our other kids have had with their race. He's also a much quieter individual. He's not outgoing like the other ones are, and it is difficult to know exactly what is going on. He continues to grow and move forward, even though it seems sometimes kind of slowly. It is a difficult situation when you talk about uprooting children from their birth family, even when it's a difficult situation that they were in initially. It is difficult—whoever takes them or wherever they end up. They always have baggage with them. That's what I've learned in the last few years. I just try to accept my kids as they are and love them and be there for them and yet not run their lives for them.

RR: Do you think the position taken by the National Association of Black Social Workers influenced your children's feelings about having been adopted or, for your son Peter, having siblings from different backgrounds?

JP: What is the position?

MP: The position is that this group believed in part that black children should be placed in black homes.

JP: Is that something that they've been advocating for a long time or just recently?

RR: In the early '70s is when they were really strong on that position. They didn't believe that black children in particular should be raised in white homes because it would affect their identity as black children and that they would not find a way back to the black community and they would grow up confused.

MP: Our daughters have certainly found their way back to the black community, but they have also found their way back to mixed communities and our own community. Which I think is awesome. It is what we strive for in this world of human beings.

JP: To me, it is almost humorous that they [the social workers] would take that position. I know these people have had a lot of experience in the field.

RR: Would you recommend that other families like your own adopt a child of a different race or culture?

MP: If their main goal is to parent children, and they really have some understanding for what a commitment that is, and they don't feel prejudice toward their child of color, and they've really searched themselves and are honest with themselves, then I think those kinds of parents are needed everywhere.

RR: Would you agree, John?

JP: Yes.

RR: What words of advice can you offer to parents who are looking to adopt transracially or are in the beginning stages of the adoption process?

JP: Talk to other parents who have gone through the process and find out.... One of the things that helped us the most was getting involved with Room for One More — the group that we were in with other parents, and a lot of them had adopted transracially, Korean children and so on. That was a big help to us, to hear what they were thinking about and how things were going with them.

RR: Is there anything you want to add that I did not ask?

MP: One thing that I have been thinking about lately is that I've realized how much we were affected by the civil rights movement. We were in college then, and that was a pretty formative time in our lives. We were young adults when Martin Luther King Jr. was assassinated. In the black community, you know what kind of a time that was. And we, as white people, having been touched by black people that we knew and those that we learned about, wanted to help people from different racial and ethnic backgrounds.

JIM AND ALICE BANDSTRA

BIG RAPIDS, MICHIGAN
FEBRUARY 2004

Jim Bandstra is 60, and Alice is 58. They have no biological children and adopted three: Jamie, Andrea, and Daniel. All the children were adopted before they were 6 months old. The children were reared in Silver Spring, Maryland, and later in Big Rapids, Michigan. The Bandstras are members of a Presbyterian/ United Church of Christ church. Jim Bandstra has an M.S. and Alice Bandstra an M.Ed.; he is a professor at Ferris State University, where she also teaches. They describe their economic status as middle class.

> *What you look like is not who you are. Self-identity is based on the degree of confidence you have in yourself, on what you do, your accomplishments, the goals you set for yourself and achieve—this is what shows on the outside. If you want to know about your ethnic background, go to the library, read books, hang out with people of your same race.*
>
> —ANDREA BANDSTRA, 23, MARCH 1997

INTERVIEW

RR: In 1972, over thirty years ago, both of you adopted your oldest son, Jamie, at 6 months old, and shortly after that your daughter, Andrea, and then your son Daniel, all under one year of age. What was the deciding factor in making those decisions?

JB: We were getting of an age where we wanted to have children. Our main motivating factor was our desire to have a family. After we adopted Jamie, we were happy with how things were going and wanted to adopt again, what turned out to be two more times.

RR: Did it matter to you or your wife if your children were biracial?

JB: No. We were anxious to have the adoption process to be as quick as possible. We knew that adopting Caucasian children would be quite a long process. I guess our lack of patience motivated us to adopt biracial children.

RR: In what state did you adopt your children?

JB: We lived in a suburb of Washington, D.C., at the time, but the agency we adopted our children from was located in New Jersey.

RR: Do either of you recall the experience of working with the social worker who handled your case?

JB: The social worker came to our home during the adoption process and visited us, I think once or twice.

AB: Yes, twice.

JB: I believe the social worker came one time when we adopted our son Jamie and then another time when we adopted our daughter, Andrea.

RR: Would you say that this social worker provided you with the information you needed in adopting specifically biracial children?

JB: Well, independently of that we joined a group called the Council of Adoptable Children and met with other people of like mind where we could talk about our experiences. I think also living in the Washington, D.C., area was a benefit to us, because it was ethnically diverse.

RR: Then, the two times meeting with your social worker and the steps you both put in place met your family's needs at that time?

JB: Yes.

RR: Looking back on that process, do you think that you would have done anything differently?

JB: No, I don't think so.

RR: Early on, what expectations did either of you anticipate about the relationships you would have with your children as they became adults?

AB: I think that our expectations for them were that they would grow up and become good citizens. We wanted them to have a good education, become profitably employed, and establish their own families.

JB: In our relationship with our children our expectations were that they would love and respect us like we love and respect them. I characterized it to the kids one time in this way: When they were younger, we told them what they had to do. When they became older, we were like fans in a stand at a sporting event to cheer them on, but we were not directly involved in their day-to-day activities.

RR: Your daughter, Andrea, was featured in *In Their Own Voices*, where she shared some of her experiences growing up within her family. From your perspective what were the dynamics between Andrea and her siblings growing up?

AB: I think that she had a normal relationship with her brothers.

JB: Andrea looked up to her brother Jamie. They were only two years apart, and Daniel was three years behind Andrea. It was a similar relationship that I had with my two oldest sisters, the two always picked on the third one [me]—so there was some of that. Daniel was a bit of a pest growing up so Andrea and Jamie dealt with him in that fashion some of the time too. It was typical sibling relationships within a family. We didn't look at it as "they were adopted." We looked at it as they were our kids and so we treated them that way. And they were brothers and sisters so we expected them to act in that fashion.

RR: You moved to Big Rapids in 1979—Andrea was 5—after living in Silver Spring, M.D. And you then spent time in England in 1983–85, when Andrea was 9. Given the contrast of living in an urban community in the Washington, D.C., area and then returning to a rural community, did you feel a difference?

JB/AB: Yes, there was a difference.

AB: Obviously, Big Rapids is more of a predominately white community … and rural. It is different than a community like Washington, D.C., where there are many ethnic groups, many nationalities.

RR: Yet it seems Andrea and your sons are confident about who they are as individuals. What did you do as parents, particularly when you moved to Big Rapids, that continued reinforcing your children's values?

AB: First, I think it was about the kids' being part of the community, part of their schools, and part of the church.

JB: When we moved to Big Rapids, we got Andrea and her brothers involved in a lot of activities like ballet, basketball, and other sports. So in Andrea's case she may have gained some of her confidence from that. Also Andrea had a very good friend who was African American and her same age that went to the same school as she did. The two of them spent time over at our home, and Andrea spent time with her family. It so happened that her friend's father, Gary Waters, was then a basketball coach in Big Rapids. [Gary Waters is now the head coach for the men's basketball team at Rutgers University.] Having that relationship was very important for Andrea (and us too).

RR: In addition to friendships, mentorship is a good thing?

AB: Yes. For Jamie, I think some of his athletic coaches, he felt, were good mentors. When kids are teenagers, obviously many of them do not want to talk to their parents about a lot of things. And so if there are other adults who are willing to talk with them or to help them, yes, I think that that is important.

RR: What would you say was your saddest memory you shared with Andrea?

JB: When she told us that she was going to be a single mother.

AB: That was a very difficult time for us.

JB: That experience was a bit scary, and we didn't know how it was going to come out.

RR: How did you work through that?

JB: We told her that we were not going to leave her. And that we were always going to be her parents, and she could count on us.

RR: What would you say is the happiest memory you have shared with your daughter?

JB/AB: Her wedding.

JB: It was a good experience for the whole family.

AB: She and I worked together in planning it. That was a good time. It was a beautiful wedding and a beautiful day. That would definitely be an example of a good time we had together.

JB: I remember that Andrea took a luxury car from the church to the reception site. The car had a sunroof, and she went through downtown Kalamazoo standing up and waving to everybody.

AB: It was quite interesting that, as they were going through the downtown area, they passed the Ku Klux Klan rally, as I recall—albeit a small rally.

RR: Your children are now in their midtwenties to early thirties. As your responsibilities and experiences as parents have evolved over the years, has your perspective on race relations also changed?

JB: My feeling is that it [the interaction with my children] made me more comfortable with people of other races because my kids were biracial. I think that living day to day with them was natural. And so when I interacted with people of other races, it felt like the same. It didn't feel different to me.

AB: Similar to Jim, it made me feel comfortable with people of different races. It allowed me to look outward, not be so ethnocentric or limited in my perspective; especially as it related to persons of different racial/ethnic backgrounds.

RR: Today, how would you describe your relationship with your children, now that they are adults?

JB: I think that it is a good relationship because we don't have issues that cause difficulties between us. If we have problems, we tell each other what they are. We communicate. We also visit our children fairly regularly, depending on our schedules.

RR: So Andrea, Jamie, and Daniel feel comfortable calling you on the phone and sharing things that they may be experiencing, good, bad, otherwise?

AB/JB: Yes.

JB: Alice pretty much talks with them all weekly by phone or via e-mail.

AB: For me, I think that the mother-daughter relationship is different from the relationship I have with my sons. I probably talk with Andrea more than the boys. I think that that is kind of a natural thing—for mothers and daughters to have a more intimate relationship. Andrea and I talk about a lot of what is going on in our lives.

RR: Parenting, it seems to me, has its ups and downs enough, adding to that the race factor. What has allowed you to remain engaged in your children's lives, given the tensions at times among persons of different cultures and ethnic backgrounds in this society?

JB: It goes back to the love and respect that we have for our children. We conveyed to our children from the very beginning that they were *our* kids, and we were their parents. We would never consider leaving them—

AB: Or not having a relationship with them. For us, I think that when our children became adults, the race thing became even less important than when they were kids.

RR: Your daughter married an African American man, and they have three children who are African American. Does the fact that your family is more blended racially make you any less comfortable, especially when you spend time with your daughter's now extended family and when they visit you in your environment in Big Rapids?

JB: No. Again, I think that that has to do with our relationship with our children. We don't feel uncomfortable when we go over to our son-in-law's, Antonio's, family home. His family treats us very nicely and we get along very well with them.

AB: Antonio's family always has big hugs for us. Talking about our community in Big Rapids, if you take our 9-year-old grandson, Latrelle, who has come here a lot since he was a little baby, I think that people think he belongs here, especially when he is with us at our church. The members of our church are very accepting of him. They make a fuss over him. They tell him how tall he is becoming; you know, the things that people say to kids. In response, I think that Latrelle likes to come to our church because he knows that people will talk with him. People also have accepted the fact that he is our grandson.

RR: Knowing the path that you as parents have taken with all of your children, would you have chosen this journey of transracial adoption again?

JB/AB: Yes.

RR: For adoptive parents who are now dealing with issues with their children like teen pregnancy, or issues about race and adoption, what can you share with them?

JB: My feeling is that you should consider them as *your children*, just as if they're your biological children. And it is important to develop an attachment with your children, in part by letting them know that you are not going to abandon them or be less involved in their lives because of any challenges they may have. You help your children in any way that you can.

AB: I can think of three examples of people who have asked us about our experience. We have been honest about our experience with our children but have always recommended to them that they should go on ahead and adopt, especially if they feel that transracial adoption is something that they can be comfortable with.

RR: What if these parents are not comfortable about the racial difference that they would encounter between them and their potential child?

AB: Yes, one would need to recognize that the child would have different color skin. And if that is uncomfortable to parents, then they shouldn't adopt cross-racially.

RR: Have you as a family experienced people looking at you awkwardly because you have such an ethnically diverse family?

AB: Well, people look at us funny all of the time.

RR: How have you dealt with that?

JB/AB: Ignore it!

JB: We always told our kids that if people had issues with them about their race, it was a problem of the other person. It was not their problem.

AB: When we as a family go out in public to restaurants or other places, there is quite a wide variety of people, ethnically speaking. Our son Daniel is married to a girl who is Indian from India, and they have two girls. And Jamie is married to a white woman, and they have five children. We just don't get worried about people who may be looking at us.

JB: After thirty years we have gotten used to it.

AB: The fact that people look at us weird has never kept us as a family from going where we wanted to go.

RR: Did the position taken by the National Association of Black Social Workers in the early 1970s make you rethink your decision to adopt cross-racially in any way?

AB: I know that their association did not accept our decision to adopt transracially. Their position was that it shouldn't be done. I understand. I think that it is a good thing for black children to be in black families. I don't have a problem with that. But I also think that if there are children that need homes, that these children should be placed in homes and be part of a family. I don't think that their position made us rethink our decision to adopt. We knew that we were right in doing what we did. They are entitled to a different opinion than we have.

RR: Can you see a difference in the way that you raised your children compared to your own parents?

JB: No, but I think that we may have extended it a bit.

AB: I agree. Our parents always accepted our kids as their grandchildren. But their communities were—

JB: Even whiter than Big Rapids.

AB: Their experiences were different. And they were from a different era, that is true. But I think that in a sense they were forced by circumstances to extend their opinions about race.

JB: In my family both of my sets of grandparents had adopted children. Each had one adopted child, including their biological children. It was a situation where they took them in when the need arose. I have an uncle and an aunt who have four adopted children.

AB: Adoption in Jim's family was a pretty normal thing.

JB: My parents were comfortable with adoption.

RR: How did you "extend it," the way you raised your children, compared to your parents?

JB: The fact that we adopted biracial children is what I was referring to there.

RR: To whom or to what do you attribute your reservoir of courage, love, and perseverance that you drew from when your kids where growing up and that you draw on today in maintaining such healthy, rewarding relationships with your children and now your extended family?

JB/AB: We attribute that to our faith in God.

JB: God loves us and we are his children. We extended that same belief to our children. With Christ we are not alone. We can succeed and do what we need to do through Christ, who strengthens us. That is also the response that we gave to the head guy of the social service agency where we adopted our children, when he asked us why we would make good parents.

RR: Finally, how would you like to see the face of adoption change?

JB: I would like to see not only social workers but also prospective adoptive parents go into this adoption process in an open and honest way so that there are not any surprises down the road. I hear about situations where parents feel the need to send the child back. That totally destroys me. I cannot imagine that. I just don't think that one should go into parent-hood and say, "I'll see how this works out, and if it does not work out, we will just send the child back."

AB: I also think that social workers should be open to transracial adoptions as good placements for children.

JIM AND KATHY STAPERT

GRAND RAPIDS, MICHIGAN
FEBRUARY 2005

Jim and Kathy Stapert are both 60. They have no biological children and have seven adopted children: Kim, Michael, Kara, Joe, Melissa, Chris, and Annie. Melissa was 2 when she was adopted, and the others were all adopted before their first birthday. The children were reared in Grand Rapids, Michigan. The Staperts are members of the Christian Reformed Church. Jim has an M.A. in education and is the principal of Grand Rapids Christian School; Kathy has an M.A. in early childhood education and is a kindergarten teacher. They describe their economic status as middle class.

> *I still believe that transracial adoption should be considered for the permanency of all abandoned children. But more attention should be given to training agencies to improve their work with parents before the adoption in order to prepare them to adopt transracially.*
>
> —KIMBERLY STAPERT, 27, MARCH 1997

INTERVIEW

RR: Going back thirty-some years ago, can you tell me what the process was that you two went through in determining how you were going to begin your family?

JS: I think we were fairly normal. We got married fairly young, Kathy was 19 and I was 20—that would be 1964 that we got married. We did not want children at that time because we needed to finish school. Kathy went to work so I could finish school, and then when I finished school, Kathy went back to school and I worked and so on and so forth. And so we tried to make sure we would not have children during that time. We were not financially prepared for it. But somewhere in our midtwenties we just kind of thought it was time to start a family. When Kathy did not become pregnant, we went for some tests, both of us, and found out that it might be difficult for us to have children. There were some possible medical things we could do, but by that time we were already talking about adoption, which was really not unfamiliar territory for us, in that while we were in high school—we were high school sweethearts by the way, and Kathy had babysat for one of our favorite teachers, and they had Native American children. Certainly, during that time in high school we were interested in things other than family and adoption. We were teenage lovers, you might say. But that family was intriguing to us, and we loved them and Kathy was especially close to them, so adoption was not unfamiliar. In fact, that teacher at one time gave a chapel talk about adoption that became very meaningful to us. By the midtwenties we were into the process with an adoption agency called Bethany Christian Services and decided that would be the route we would take. They acquainted us with the fact that ethnic minority children were in need of homes and that there were inadequate or not enough homes for these children. I think, to make a long story short, we looked at each other and said, "If not us, then who?" We had sensitivities from the '60s, we had formed our philosophical thoughts on race and racism, and war and everything during that turbulent time, and we were not doing this to be rebellious, but we were doing this because we had learned together, grown together philosophically in certain ways, and it did kind of boil down to "Why don't we do this?" And we couldn't find an answer so we went through rather extensive counseling with Bethany, to their credit, as to understanding that this was certainly a huge decision.

KS: At that time Jim was teaching at Oakdale Christian, which was an integrated Christian school, and we lived in this neighborhood, which is a multiracial neighborhood. We were attending Grace Church, which is an inner-city Grand Rapids church, and we felt that we would have the support for our children as well as ourselves within the community, and we have had.

RR: When you made the decision to adopt transracially, did you get any feedback from your family members? Was that something that was OK with them?

KS: It was positive with them from the beginning. They all accepted it and nurtured and supported us with our decision.

JS: Yes. That's fair. I think now that we are the age we are, I am sure they had senses of "Do you know what you're getting into?" And you worry about your children all your life, and do-they-know-what-they-are-doing-here sort of thing. And I am sure that was part of our parents' thinking, but we have been blessed with wonderful parents who loved us dearly, and we love them dearly. We were confident that they would be accepting and nurturing, as Kathy said, and that they would be wonderful grandparents for our children regardless of race.

KS: During that time, as well as after that time, they were involved in inner-city work in Kalamazoo, Michigan, so they had some relationships with people other than the normal Dutch Christian Reformed Church, which is pretty typical of most parents of people our age.

RR: So in the early 1970s, when you first adopted Kim, what was the adoption process like?

JS: It was very extensive in terms of our counseling and, again to the agency's credit, I am glad they didn't treat it cheaply like, Hey, here's somebody—they really worked hard, I think, to help us realize what a major step this was in our life, maybe a life-changing event for us, not only having children but crossing racial walls that have been built in this society and what that would mean. I don't remember exactly how long the process was, but I think it was a good nine months from beginning to end.

KS: We laughed about it because it took *nine months* to get our precious little bundle. We did have a lot of help from Bethany, especially trying to help us find other families who were doing this, which was unusual. There were not a lot of families adopting transracially, so [they were] checking on different things about us and seeing where we plugged in. We had to read books, articles, talk with them about our reasons for wanting to adopt transracially and our views on parenting. Subsequent to that, I don't know that Bethany required potential adoptive parents to be as knowledgeable about making a choice like this.

JS: We got irritated and impatient about parts of the process, but looking back on that now, it was wonderful and healthy, and I think that kind of intensive criteria ought to exist in all adoption agencies. In [our] later adoptions some of them went so quickly [because] we were already an integrated family. Obviously, it became much, much less in-depth. We were well known then as to how we were doing as parents. But that first round was rather intense.

RR: At the point at which you began to adopt, can you tell me what your views were about black people and about race issues?

KS: We lived through, like Jim said, some of the upheavals and the problems and the unknown things of the '60s and into the '70s, and so we were aware of the poor treatment of African Americans in this country. We were not out to save the world, that's not why we adopted our family.

JS: We wanted children.

KS: We adopted our kids because we wanted children. And we felt that with the community and the place that we lived, that could happen. I worked at Baxter Community Center [in the urban area of Grand Rapids]for a short time when I went back to school, and we just really felt that this was something that we could do. There were people we lived with, we lived with neighbors who were Taiwanese, African American, mixed race.

JS: You can't understand us unless you understand the history in which we grew when we were in our late teens and twenties, and the history of the turbulence in the United States, in this case having to do with racial tensions. We were raised very sheltered and unknowing about what was really going on in the broader world. We had a wonderful life. It was a protected life in a way. As we became educated about what things really were, we were determined that we would not be a part of the problem, and again we did not adopt children to try to prove something. We wanted children. The decade of learning was a huge change for us personally, a huge change for what our priorities were in life, a huge change in our understanding of American civilization.

RR: The decade of learning, meaning prior to your adopting? Or when you were adopting?

JS: Prior to, primarily. In other words, as the '60s rolled along we learned a lot about what this world was really like, as opposed to the '50s. We thought *everybody* was cozy and warm and happy. I am exaggerating a little bit, but understanding that decade and that we were at the peak of forming our adult commitments, adoption became part of that—and again, not to save the world, not to prove a point. We wanted children. But I am back to looking around and saying, when Bethany confronted us or educated us with this option, Why not us? Didn't we just say that this is what we believe in? this is the dream? this is what ought to be? Why not us?

RR: What feelings did you experience when you finally received your first baby in your home, and what dreams did you have for this child?

KS: It was wonderful. And I was blessed to be able to stay home and raise her and some of our other ones. It was absolutely wonderful. We did all the things that the African American, that the Caucasian parents did in our community. I made meals at home, and when my younger kids were growing up, they had their snack when they got home from school. I volunteered at school and did different activities with her and for her. She went to a preschool, and our friends from our church and from our community were of different races. Bethany did encourage some kind of interaction with other adopted families at that point, and that was positive.

JS: We had our picnics and all that fun stuff.

KS: And I did babysitting, and some of the children I cared for were white, some were black, some were Asian, and so that brought other children into our home right from the beginning.

JS: I think the major thing is that race was not a feature. Our reactions were normal. In front of that fireplace there, I have a picture of me holding Kim for the first time in our home in a rocking chair in front of the fireplace there. And it didn't have anything to do with anything but I'm a dad. She made me a dad. I'm rocking her right there.

KS: She made us parents.

RR: And after Kim you adopted six other children. Why did you choose to adopt six more?

JS: We had no grand design—let's have a great big family. We had no design. We had no design as to any gender of the kid, the boy/girl thing—

KS: Ethnicity, even. It didn't matter to us if the child was biracial, black, or white.

JS: And in every case the child[ren] came to us one at a time. We both come from families of three kids. And three seemed kind of normal. Two is where we started. That was really a family now. We were young and could do all the stuff. And then, kind of one by one, and in some cases Bethany approached us as to whether there would be room for one more. I think the only happening that sort of made us take another jump was that our fourth child fell out of the van on 28th Street and was hit by a pickup truck and broke his leg, and it's a terrible story. But it all turned out good. And somehow it struck us like, wow! What a miracle! And then we saw pictures in the paper and said, you know, again we didn't adopt the next one because we wanted to—but there was a sense that the Lord saved this child, if there is another child in need. And that's when we adopted our older child, at 3 years old, and then beyond that, I don't remember. We really thought four was it until that happening in our life.

KS: There were various circumstances in our life that we felt this child maybe needed a younger sibling to see the way babies need to be treated and cared for, so there were different proceedings. Our last little child, dear wonderful daughter that she is, was a very difficult baby, and I think that kind of ended things for us.

JS: That was the conclusion.

JS: I think another factor was that at that time I was diagnosed with a tumor in my head, and that was a watershed for us, I must have been 42 years old. In the sense that before that we were young, could do anything, nothing was going to happen, we were going to live forever, and we'd raise all the kids that were directed to us by the Lord and by our own initiative. That event, which was, if not life threatening, was also life changing—how I would come out of that head surgery a different person. There were huge risks involved, and here we had these seven children— actually, our last one wasn't even [ours] legally, we hadn't had the year wait with the court. That changed our philosophy [of] "we're going to live forever and can do anything" to "wait a minute, we are getting older. There are going to be limitations on what we do."

KS: And that's when I went back to school to get my master's degree because we thought, well, if anything should happen—

JS: It was like insurance.

RR: So now all of your kids are biracial—African American?

JS: Yes. They are both African American and white.

RR: Was it that you asked for biracial children or that they were presented to you?

JS: I think the last two were presented to us. I remember our friend Harold at a basketball game one time kind of sidling up to me and saying, "I know you've got a big family and a lot of responsibilities, but have you ever considered another—?"

RR: Were either of you concerned that some people may not approve of your decision to adopt transracially?

JS: In those seventeen years the attitudes about white parents' adopting black children went up and down. The black social workers' organization was against it, but by that time we understood the issues involved and we were just busy raising our family. We had already done all this stuff to prepare ourselves for this, so it didn't really matter what other peoples' philosophy about it was. We're in it, that's who we were. So, again, we didn't ignore it, but we didn't allow ourselves to be hurt or get upset about it. Or argue the point. We just tried to raise our kids.

RR: One of the things Kim talks about in *In Their Own Voices* is how she had such a good relationship with the two of you and felt comfortable in talking with you about some of the issues that she was facing in elementary school, high school, and even college. How did you develop that relationship with her and with the rest of your kids?

KS: We were always very open and caring with all of our children. We communicated regularly. That time for us was very special. As a family we had devotions at our supper table where everybody would share. Now, when our grandchildren are here, we do the same thing. It was a time where they would get a chance to tell and say what their day was like. They'd come home from school, sometimes happy, sometimes sad. I was here with the oldest four when they got home from school—well, really more than that, I was home with all of them up to a certain point—when they got home from school, when they had all of this stuff to talk about and to share. We did a lot of reading; we enjoyed many family outings, like going to parks, going to playgrounds together.

JS: We came from strong families, and we raised our kids in a similar way in terms of family structure. I think maybe an underlying theme in our family, simply put, is, when it came to adoption and racial issues we sought very hard to help our kids to understand that that was a good story. Good stories are not necessarily stories without problems, but underlying that, *they made us parents*, which we wanted. They have a home, which they didn't have—that is a wonderful story in spite of the bumps along the way. It is part of the religious view of the perfect Creation and the Fall: we are here to repair what is broken. There was brokenness in our life—we never preached this to the kids, but I think underlying that's who we are. There's brokenness here and we're repairing it, guys. Again, we don't say those words.

JS: We did not hide anything about adoption, we never said, you know, let's not talk about that. We said why not, this is a good story. We made books about each child's adoption. And on their placement days, we'd look at it and say, "Look at this, look how funny Mommy is."

RR: There were two things in particular in Kim's interview that I thought were interesting. One, she expressed warmly the times when she had her special placement day celebration and how she was uniquely honored on that day. And, two, she expressed fondly the times the two of you read books that valued her as a person. One of them was called *Black Is Brown Is Tan*. She talks about that as being a wonderful highlight in her childhood. What gave you the creativity to incorporate those traditions into your family culture, and why did you think it was important?

JS: The credit goes to Kathy. She's a wonderful teacher.

KS: Thank you. I've had friends for a long time who are other than white. A very dear friend of mine is a biracial woman, not adopted, who has a wealth of wisdom to share with people, and she does in various ways. She helped me appreciate the special uniqueness of being a biracial child because she is a marvelous person. She's been around for our kids; they called her Aunty Jan forever. And she is still a dear friend of mine. We have a strong connection in many ways. It is in my makeup to be inclusive in the books and stories I read to my children. I would hope if I had a child who is white, I would be the same way, that I would also include literature that celebrated people of other races and ethnicities too.

RR: Did you specifically have to think about how you wanted to create a family and church support system for your kids?

KS: No, because we were already doing it. Yes, there were ways where we would look for more ways to include it. For example, when Kim worked at Bethany and formed a Kwaza project that was marvelous.

RR: Please describe the Kwaza project.

KS: That was a program for minority children who had been adopted, and it was a marvelous program. They had an Easter program, and our kids filled these Easter eggs and hid them all over Bethany, and ministers came in to preach and our son Joe was the Easter Bunny, and it was this really great program to bring together these children who had transracial adoption in common. Sadly, there isn't a program like that, to my knowledge, anymore. I think that was a three-year experimental or grant kind of a program. It was great. And that was a way our younger children could plug in to the community. Kim also became a part of the inner-city Santa Claus parade where the rest of our kids were involved. But our whole life was that way. When we had people come and visit, they could be black as well as white. It wasn't that we had to go out and search for ways to help these kids find their racial identity. When we adopted Kim, a big thing with the white social workers was how are you going to learn how to do that black hair—and I was like, I don't know. Is that really a big deal? My friend Jan, who is biracial, said, "Look, anytime you need help with anything with your children, let me know." Well, as a young parent I went to the hair shops with my children, and then a friend of mine who also had a biracial child and a black child said, "Let's go and take this class at *Ebony* to learn more about black hair." So we did, we took this class on cornrowing and different things to do with black hair. Another friend of mine and I also wrote to Johnson & Johnson and said you need to put black children on that commercial because we're using this product in their hair. So there were things we had to learn about. We had a marvelous pediatrician with all of our children as babies, Dr. Miller, who helped us with skin care, hair care. He also volunteered his services at Bethany. One of our children has very dry skin [so] he told us what to do—it was a mess in our bathtub, but we did it, and people are still doing that. Our youngest child was recommended to do the same things that we were recommended to do with Kim thirty-five years ago by our pediatrician.

RR: Kim mentions in *In Their Own* Voices that when she was in elementary school, she was playing on the playground, and somebody blurted out a racial slur toward her, and said, "You look like the color of poop," and she felt comfortable to share something that hurtful with you. How did you, given your expertise as educators, and of course as parents, handle that?

KS: This is a situation at an integrated Christian school at that point. She had negative experiences also from black kids within our neighborhood, because she was a pretty biracial young woman. She handled things very uniquely, her own style, as she still does. To me brown is the color of chocolate, and there is nothing better than chocolate. So it's a person who doesn't know "what's up." If you want to look around you, there are a lot of things of different colors that are beautiful and a lot that are not. We have books around; *Shades of Black* is one of my favorites, and it is a beautiful story. So to look at those books and those stories shows a whole other side that maybe these other children are ignorant of. They don't know.

JS: I think we tried very hard not to fly into rage and say we are going get that person and call the mother out of anger, et cetera, but show willingness to confront it, to bring it to the school, to bring it to the parents appropriately. I hope the kids saw our strength in saying we're not just going to ignore this; we will stand by [you on] this. I think it is more of an attitude. Instead of wanting to go after the parents in rage, we took the mind-set, rather, isn't it too bad that there are people who have such notions in their mind? The more we confront this type of thing, we do it using this approach, not only because we may be offended but the offender has the opportunity to learn too.

KS: They have to learn to cope.

JS: It is not our problem, it is their problem, and we may feel hurt about it, and hurt for our children, and we did feel hurt for our children, but on the other hand, help our children understand the name callers are the ones with the issue, and even if they never straighten out, you go on with your life. That's the way it is going to be.

KS: And at the library there was a little boy who continually harassed Kim, and she spent a lot of time on this block with children of a variety of skin colors. Anyway, Kim would go to the library, and this one child would relentlessly harass her about her skin color. At one time he had yelled at her, even as far as our house. He said something about, well, you're adopted. And she said, right straight back at him, "My parents want me! Yours don't want you." And that was the last we ever heard from him.

RR: So she had a comeback.

JS: I think the harassment of our kids, to whatever extent, has been as much about adoption when they were little as a racial thing. The racial thing played into it because it made them obvious—you know, is that your dad? And [a] what-went-wrong-here sort of attitude.

RR: And then we get into high school and college. You get into the dating and the being a little more serious about our relationships with others. How, in your eyes, did she maneuver that situation?

KS: Very well to the outward eye. Inside it is hard to know what her feelings were about everything. But we laughed that at one year she went to six or seven senior proms with all these different guys. And they ranged from East Grand Rapids black to inner-city black to white.

JS: But I think we agreed that the teenaged years were the most troubling, and maybe most parents would say that in some shape, manner, and form. Troubling about their own identity related to their own adoption, troubling about their own racial mix and where they belong in a world that has separated people by race. Those years have been the most challenging times for them.

KS: Through the church and the school and the community, we can name—we aren't going to—friends that our kids had, good friends, who were of a different background than they were. Some were white, some were black, and some were Asian. They formed good friendships with a variety of people. It is like trying on clothes. In high school you try on friendships, and some you can keep, and some you put in the closet and you might pull out from time to time. But high school is a hard time for forming friendships.

JS: It is for so many kids, but adoption and race is another overlay.

RR: It really is. I don't know if you can offer some insight here, but what do children who are biracial or black or Hispanic, who are adopted in white families and go to these predominately white schools, what do they do when it comes to dating? Do you become the third wheel?

JS: I think they figure out in such a setting what kids are receptive to their dating friendship and what kids are not. I think they get a sense of that's not going to work because that kid and his family—The dangerous thing is that they may be used by a kid who wants to show his parents something about himself: "You can't stop me from dating who I want," or "You might not believe in this interracial thing, but I do." Well, they ought not to be used for kid-parent wars.

KS: When our kids did things with a whole group, it was pretty interracial. I think of Kim's going out with a group of her friends. The group of friends she chose to hang out with was rather interracial through high school; our son Michael chose the same type of group of friends. Although Michael moved maybe a little bit more toward minority groups, including Hispanic, and the same with most of our other kids.

JS: One dynamic that is different [from] when Kathy and I were growing up, way back when, [is that] dating was kind of the way you did things socially. And in some ways we are getting somewhat back to that, but our kids went through a phase where dating didn't happen nearly as much as just gangs of kids going places. So therefore that one-on-one stigma of black-on-white was shoved aside a little more than it would have been in our day. But things are going back to a little more dating, I think.

RR: Do you think, as educators and as adoptive parents, that parents who have black and biracial children in predominately white schools should be concerned for their children because of the problems that could arise because of this kind of environment?

JS: I think the parents have to know it is an issue. It is another overlay in these kids' lives. It is one more facet parents have to pay attention to.

KS: And you certainly have to be aware, even from the time you pick up that precious little bundle, that that child may turn toward a different culture than yours. That child may connect with a different group of people than what you are. That child is your child, but that child is God's child, and that child is going to have his or her own feelings, which are not ours, are not the birth parents', they're nobody's except that child's. These children are, in my view, especially blessed, because they can move in circles that everybody else can't. Kim can do some things professionally that a white social worker cannot do; she can do some things that a black social worker cannot do. The same is true for my daughter Kara as a nurse. Michael is working in a black community as an entrepreneur in his society. He owns Wing Heaven in Grand Rapids, and it is expanding. He can deal with white people, black people, Asian people, and Hispanic people with his tax business. He can move all over. He can talk the talk of the ghetto, he can talk the talk of white upper-middle-class people, and in his business he does that. He has to deal with people from a primarily white establishment, and he works in the inner city in a black establishment. I have a lot of black friends through my work, and they'll say, "I didn't know that was your son who works there." And I jokingly say, "Oh, you don't think we look alike?" And he comes to school, and the interesting thing is the majority of my children in school are African American, and he'll come in and say stuff, and they will get like "that can't be your son." One year one child said, "That can't be your son." And I said to Michael,

I thought you were my son. "Hey, Mom." He put his arm around my shoulder. And I thought, "I'm going to let it be and see if they bring it up again later," which they never did. However, in my class we do talk about adoption because I always have some children in foster care or adoptive care in my classes. So it is a natural kind of thing for us. But getting back to it, the kids basically have to make their own choices, and the parents need to know from the beginning that they might not choose to go to your church, they might not choose to be a part of your group, but that doesn't mean they don't love you or that they're not accepting you.

RR: Where did you get that confidence that it's OK to allow your children to grow wings and soar as they grow up?

JS: We learned it.

KS: You learn it with your children, you learn it from the time they are little. You are open to it.

JS: I think that this is a little tangential to it, but as we got into this—and now I'm talking about the learning—we thought we could create an environment that would guarantee that our kids would turn out the way we wanted them to. As we grew with our children, we realized what a huge factor genetics plays into their personalities, abilities, and interests. I think that we reached a point where we were open to learning and admitting that our parenting style and expectations needed to be modified a bit, because they are not what we may have figured we could make them into, and so we haven't tried to—well, all parents try to make and shape their children somewhat. My point here is that we became open to understanding that our children are very uniquely created like every child and that our job is to discover what that is and in a sense go with the flow on that.

KS: For parents, parents must know that these children are, as all children, they are connected to you, but from the first time they take a step away, they are moving in their own direction. The most important thing to us is that our children are Christian and that through the church and through the experiences in the family that God is the center of our life and of their life. And that happens in different ways, maybe in personal conversations, maybe during bedtime prayers, maybe in conversations [while] driving a child to school, maybe they come home from school with something and you build on what that is, but that is the most important thing. Issues relating to skin color and gender are definitely important pieces in their growing up, but the most important thing in their life is that this is a journey, this isn't the end of life; this is a journey through. How can we make it? How can we find our place, and it has to be with God.

KS: Interestingly, my husband and I talk about the commonalities in our life—we were both from three-child families, we were both from white, Christian Reformed families, but our ethnic backgrounds are not the same. I don't know my ethnic background; I know some of it but not a lot of it. It just wasn't that important in my mother's family, or maybe there were things in my mother's family that they didn't feel they wanted to share. But it was never a huge issue to me. But with our children, their ethnic background is important to us, if for no other reason because of their appearance. As biracial children they are not just black or white, [and] they need to find their way along what that means.

RR: Reflecting on these past thirty-five years as a family with joys and disappointments, do you think that you would do it again, transracially adopt? And what memorable event with your children comes to mind that you want to share?

JS: Oh, yes. It is a wonderful story. It is a good story. Would we do it again? There is not a child that is ours here that in any way we haven't been blessed in learning to know them and to be loved by them and to love them. We would do everything over again. I think a bigger question than the transracial issue would be whether we would adopt the number of children we adopted. And, again, don't misunderstand what I am saying. When we were young, we could overcome everything, we could live forever and all that. We didn't understand the complexity of what we were doing. We didn't understand the financial implications of what we were doing or the time and energy of what we were doing. But I think we'd both say that, of course, we would do it over again, because who would you not have wanted to touch?

KS: As far as a day, or a special occasion, in our family that was quite memorable, I would say it was each placement day, which was so marvelous, the last one being Annie's, who came to our home seventeen years ago.

JS: —with six kids joining in on a placement day.

KS: These times were amazing, the many wonderful people it brought into our home. Even to look at the pictures now, it brought in our immediate families, Jim's and mine, who are primarily white, although his family has developed into a much bigger family because he has a niece who has adopted two black children and a son who has married an Hispanic woman, and so the families have evolved from that, but opening the house and having all these people come to celebrate the bringing of each child into this family have been wonderful.

JS: To see our families pulled together was a huge joy for us.

KS: Just to have our special friends and family come—and Annie will graduate from high school this year, and it will be like that again. It will be another group of people coming here.

KS: And they will see each other and say, "Why are you here?" And they'll say, "Well, I'm Kathy's friend from Henry's school." "Oh, we've been in the Staperts' family for all these years." "Oh, well, I was their teacher in high school." "Oh, well, I was the coach on this team."

With the time and everything that has been involved in raising our large family, one of the things that we've realized is that you don't accumulate a wealth of material things. If Jim and I had children by birth, I wouldn't spend as much time planning and investing in what sport they would plug into. Jim and I are not athletic people, but our kids may well be, they may well have that within them. They may have great musical talent. All of our children from the get-go took lessons, piano lessons, violin lessons, singing lessons—they were a part of this big Suzuki violin program, two of them. They were part of Anton Armstrong's, a nationally known choir director, choral group when he was in Michigan. Michael, Kara, and Joe were all a part of that. All of the girls and a couple of the boys took piano lessons. We've had strings, we've had drums (that's Chris's thing), we had clarinets, so you bring all that in because maybe that is an area they might excel in. You don't know, or an area they might enjoy for a while or an area where they might meet people that will help them appreciate things, that particular skill. Our kids played in middle school every sport that came up. Who knows what they could excel at? Annie, our youngest, is a competitive cheerleader. We've had football players, basketball players, and track runners. But you'd want your kids to have all this wealth of possibilities so that they can pick and choose what they might be good at, where they might meet friends who will be good for them, where they might meet people from whole other areas who are interested in their music or their singing or their sports, and maybe some of the children will be interested in that.

RR: Do you think adoptive parents need to try harder in many cases than non-adoptive parents in raising their children because of the racial differences?

KS: Yes. Adoptive parents have to try harder. We have to try harder. We have to find connections for our kids, and we were blessed in that we have that already, but yet you still seek to find that for them. You have to find where is going to be their area to excel. We have some daughters that are drama queens, and I am not kidding. And granddaughters who are already beginning to find their interests, and you hope they'll find it. All of our kids had opportunities to be in plays in school and see if that's an area that they want to be interested in or an area they wanted to excel at.

And I see Kim as being a very outgoing, capable, social woman because she's had a lot of ways to find that ability in herself. And we can say maybe we started her on that path, but she's the one who pursued those interests.

RR: Do you think that transracial adoption is an option that other families should pursue?

KS: Yes, I think definitely they should, and I think our world is becoming more of a brown world. We will always have African American people, we will always have white people, we will always have Hispanic people, and we will always have Middle Eastern people... . The smaller our world becomes with transportation and the media, the more people connect and the more interracial marriages or interracial relationships there are going be. So I believe our children, they will find more people like themselves in the world. And if there are children whose parents are unable to raise them, there need to be people who are willing to accept them.

JS: Well, it's kind of a strange dilemma, isn't it? In the sense that, first of all, I'd answer the question [by saying that] people should not back away from transracial adoption if that is what they want to do and if there is a need. On one hand, it probably has some merit that if everything is even, for every available child there is a like parent, children should be matched with ethnically like people. On the other hand, strange as it is, racial mixing has a huge purpose in our society. If we make the ethnic match the big thing, we haven't really built the bridges that we all hope to build. So I won't sit here and say, "Let's make all adoptions to mix the world all up," to say the least, but on the other hand, there is something missing if our goal is to go like with like with like, and all we're doing is perpetuating the world as it exists, that we hope we can do better with, that is more reflective of God's kingdom.

RR: Do you think, from the policy side of transracial adoption and from the actual process that social workers go through in connecting families with kids, is it adequate or does it need to be improved, in your opinion?

KS: I think it needs to be better. When we adopted Kim, a good process was followed. However, now it would be helpful if prospective parents knew the steps that need to be taken when a minority child is placed in a majority home. I think that should be explained more clearly. I don't think agencies should say, well, these white people want a child, and this child is available, so let's place this child in that family. The parents have to be educated and trained to know what that entails.

RR: Why do you say that?

KS: Because I think in this case ... potential adoptive parents need to know.
I don't think that a huge part of white society knows what it is like to be
black in this society. I don't know what it is like to be black, but I do know
that these children need to have connections with a black world. I don't
think a brown or black child should be raised in an all-white community
unless there is *no* other home for the child. I think that that family has
to be drawn in and be shown that they have to make some more connections so that the child will feel comfortable and won't feel out of it,
because there will be comments, as you have suggested, and the parents
have to know how to handle that. And parents can do that, they can reach
out, but I think they have to know that they *need* to do that. That there are
issues that they need to read about, know about, that will relate to their
children of color. You can't say, well, you have to have a black friend, that
is absolutely ridiculous, but you can say you need to move in a world that
is bigger than this little tiny white community. You have to move somewhere else. I don't mean you have to move your home. But you have to,
yourself, make some connections so that this child won't see his color/
ethnicity as unnatural. And with us, because we already had that piece in
place, we would look at some of that and say we don't have to read that
book; we already read that. Or we don't have to do this—it was good that
we talked about it—we'd read things and we'd talk about it. That's not to
say that a [white] family cannot adopt a biracial or a child who is black. I
would also like to see more black families adopt across the lines as well.
Now, if there is a black child and a white child, and they both need a
home, I think the natural thing would be to put the black child with the
black home and the white child with the white home, and that's not bad.
But when we adopted one of our kids, there was a black family who did
cross the line and adopt a white child who had some physical problems.

JS: She was a medical doctor and maybe they were both doctors, but because
of that child's condition, what a beautiful placement for that child.
Because these parents had expertise in that area.

KS: They were loving, caring people and wanted to adopt a child. What if
they had wanted to adopt a healthy white child? Would that have been
allowed? Or was it because of the situation that happened? Regardless,
theirs was beautiful adoption. And we did meet with them at some of the
adoption dinners we attended and saw the child for a number of years
being raised. I have to say that that child will always have a white connection because look at the media—it is saturated with white positive
images. That child will see white people on TV, white people in the
malls. No matter where you live, you are going to be able to see white

people and be able to buy white dolls and be able to participate in activities and opportunities afforded to white people. But if you are in a white community raising a child of color, you have to reach out and make more of an effort because it is not all over the place.

JS: The priority in adoption is to place children in good homes, and transracial adoption ought not to be denied if it is appropriate to find a good home for a child.

Jim Stapert died in 2005.

RON AND DOROTHY

WEST LAFAYETTE, INDIANA
JULY 2005

Ron is 71 and Dorothy is 66. They have ten biological children and one adopted child. Shecara, who was adopted when she was 4 days old, is the only biracial child in the family. The children were all reared in West Lafayette, Indiana. The family is Roman Catholic. Ron has a master's degree from Purdue University, and Dorothy completed two years of college at Purdue. Ron is retired and Dorothy is a homemaker and an artisan.

I feel like I'm the go-between for the black and white sides. I know lots of black people who think white people are a certain way; I also know white people who believe all blacks are a certain way. They have stereotypes of white people that do not fit my experience with white people. The issue is not just black and white; it extends to people's views about Mexicans and Puerto Ricans.

—SHECARA (A PSEUDONYM), 28, MAY 1998

INTERVIEW

RR: Please go back to 1957 when you decided to begin your family. How did you decide on beginning a family, where were you living at this time?

D: I think we were planning on a large family when we got married. We were living in West Lafayette in an apartment. (The building just got torn down.) We got married in '57, and we bought this house in 1958 and moved here. All the kids have been raised in this house.

R: We've added on to the house a couple of times, as you can imagine.

RR: Tell me about the community back then. What was it like?

D: It has always been a college community, which makes it different than a big city or even a suburb. Because we have the college influence in general, West Lafayette is known to have schools where the children score better than all the other surrounding communities, and the schools like to take credit for it, but I think it is because all the parents are professors at the university. They push them, and there is a certain amount of inherited ability there too.

R: Genetic pool!

D: Therefore, for anybody who doesn't fit into that kind of mind-set, it becomes difficult.

R: West Lafayette is not an industrial town. The largest industry in Lafayette and West Lafayette is an auto-manufacturing firm that is way on the east side of Lafayette, which is across the river from West Lafayette, so quite a distance away. There tends to be a separation between Lafayette and West Lafayette that started very early on and has continued all through time. The prices for housing are slightly higher in West Lafayette than they are in Lafayette; the schools definitely rate higher in terms of the standardized Indiana testing, et cetera. There is a difference that divides two different cities.

RR: Racially, what are the demographics of West Lafayette?

D: That has changed. Back when Shecara was little, as she said, there were very few blacks. However, because Purdue has a tremendous number of international students—almost 50 percent of the names at the graduation from high school are of Asian background. Whether or not the kids were born here, I don't know. But the names are Japanese, Chinese, Indian, Korean, and they are very smart, and they are the ones who get the best grades. We have a high percentage of Asians in our community now.

R: Africans are not as highly represented as Asians here.

RR: What brought you to West Lafayette?

D: We were students at Purdue University.

RR: And then you decided to stay there?

D: Yes.

RR: You have eleven children. You had seven biological children before you chose to adopt transracially, a biracial child. Walk me through that process in making your decision to adopt.

D: It was one of those nonintellectual things. I was reading a mission magazine, I believe, and they were talking about the plight of the American Indian children, orphans, and it just hit me. I called up Ron and told him about it, and he said, well… OK. So we started looking into it, and the Indian tribes at that time had just decided they weren't going to let their babies be adopted outside the tribe.

RR: Was this in 1969?

R: Yes.… There was a strong feeling from their view that their ethnic community would be absorbed if they allowed these babies to be adopted by white outsiders.

D: So the social worker then said, well, are you interested in a black baby instead? And we said OK. There was no intellectual reasoning behind it. It was strictly emotional.

RR: So when you went through the adoption process, what was that like?

D: We worked with our local county.

R: A lot easier than it is now, I know that.

D: It was extremely easy.

RR: What did you have to do?

D: I don't remember very much. I think they came to the house here once or twice. And that was it.

R: The social worker verified whether the place was clean, you know, that sort of thing.

D: They finally called us up one day and said, "We are bringing your baby tomorrow."

RR: So there was no discussion about the racial difference of your baby and how you must raise a black child?

R: That was a long time ago—1970 is a long time ago.

D: There was none. I can remember we had to have a medical physical. And our family doctor said, "You're doing WHAT? You're crazy!" That was about it.

RR: And how did you handle that?

R: Like we do most doctors' comments—

D: Smiled.

RR: What were the dynamics like during your children's childhood? What activities were you interested in as a family?

R: Did you come from a large family yourself?

RR: No. I have one brother and one sister, and they are biologically related.

R: It will be a little bit difficult to understand, but it operates more like a bus station.

RR: Yes. I think your daughter alluded to that in her [interview].

R: You know, people were coming, people were going all the time. We had regular meals at a set time. Our kids very much had to be here for the meals.

D: And just from the sheer amount of work there was to be done to run this household, everybody had their daily assignments, and they traded around.

R: So it was a rotating kind of schedule, you didn't stay on doing floors or dishes or something all of the time. And nobody got stuck with something they didn't like because it was on a rotating basis.

RR: What were the values you taught your children?

R: I think probably the same as all the cultural values were at that time. The culture has changed dramatically since the 1970s, but at that time, it was all those cultural things: honesty, not trying to cheat other people, taking care of other people rather than ignoring them. Those were common cultural values in the '70s. So we didn't do anything different.

D: One thing that is different now is that children today have such an organized life with sports and all the various organizations that children are in, and that they have to be driven to. And that didn't exist then and especially in this household, because I had babies, I could not take one child to a sports event.

R: We didn't know what soccer was.

D: Well, it wasn't here. No, actually, we saw some international students playing soccer once, and we couldn't figure out what it was.

RR: Now I am focusing more on your daughter Shecara and your relationship with her. She was raised in a somewhat affluent neighborhood and had access to the university, to a lot of richness around her, and had a wonderful family she was living in. Can you recall the first time when she questioned her racial difference, given that she had ten siblings who were white and parents who were white?

D: We never particularly mentioned the racial difference. One thing that we did tell her from the very beginning, so that it wouldn't come as a shock, was that she was adopted, and nobody else was.

RR: How did you explain that to her?

D: We just started out when she was a baby, before the words mean anything, [so] it never was a surprise. We told her, you're adopted; we picked you, that sort of thing—but we never brought race into it. We re-read your first book this morning just to remember what Shecara had said. And in there she said that the first time she realized her racial difference was when, in her fifth grade, a boy called her the n-word. And she said until then she wasn't aware of it.

RR: Do you recall when that incident happened, and if she came to you?

D: Yes. She came home from school and told me, and I think she was aware of what it meant, but she complained that she'd been called that. I called up her teacher, who was a jagged coach kind of guy, and told him about it. And he said, OK—goodbye. And it never happened again.

RR: So she felt, in your opinion, comfortable to talk to you about things going on in her life, including issues that may be affected by race?

D: Oh, yes.

R: When we get to her teenage years, now we get all kind of angst, and it doesn't make any difference what color the kid is.

D: I have a grandson going through it right now. And being black and being adopted, you probably understand this too: you don't know how much of it is due to race and how much is due to being a teenager.

RR: Did you have at the time friends that were black or acquaintances that you could touch base with?

R: There are not a lot of blacks in this community. There are a lot of Asians. Throughout the high school, through the smaller elementary schools, and all the way through Purdue, there is a lot of Asian influence, including influence from India.

D: But practically no blacks. There is no reason we wouldn't have, but they just aren't here. We live a very kind of stay-at-home life, even now. We don't go out and socialize a whole lot; we don't travel very much, so therefore we didn't make a point of going out and seeking many friendships outside of the home.

R: It was tough to do with that many kids.

RR: Did your other children recognize the physical differences with their sister?

D: It was never mentioned. I'm sure that they knew.

RR: So you didn't necessarily talk about adoption as a family?

D: No, there were so many other things going on that that wasn't a big issue.

R: There was just always some new person coming into the family.

D: And she was only 4 days old, so that makes a big difference. If you adopt somebody who is 5 or 6 years old, it's a change for everybody in the family. But this was just another new baby in the family.

RR: Did your neighbors question why there was this black child in your family, and did any of your own family members—your parents— question?

D: There was no sense of segregation here—no, there was no problem.

RR: As you indicated, you read your daughter's interview in the first book. She had a journey where she had identity struggles.

D: Yes, that was in high school.

RR: Starting in high school where she was able to even articulate it more.

D: That's when she first started feeling problems, in high school.

RR: How did you see that? When it came to your attention, was it a shock?

D: I don't know how to answer that.

R: The teenage years are just tough years. We had all these various kids going through their own version of identity issues. So it was just a little different version for Shecara. But it was still "Who am I?" "Why am I here?" "What can I do different?" "How can I get out?" It was kind of one struggle after the next, after the next. It didn't stand out as being—it was her version of this kind of angst.

RR: Your daughter made a decision to associate with a specific type of group within the black community.

D: She found some black friends in high school, yes.

RR: Did she talk to you about why those friendships in particular were important to her?

D: Let's back up. In junior high school Shecara joined this—what she refers to as a black youth group, [but] what that is, is a community center in Lafayette. It was called the Hanna Community Center, and they had all sorts of activities for the black community. Since then the local hospital has bought up a lot of the land down there, so it is now just a community center for black and white, both. But at that time it was mainly black. Then there was one lady there who kind of took Shecara under her wing and taught her a lot about being black and was very, very good for her. We managed to get her over to the center weekly.

RR: Did Shecara bring friends home with her that were black?

D: Oh, yes.

RR: Did that affect your comfort zone any or was that OK?

R: It was like a bus station, all kinds of people coming and going [at] all hours.

RR: So you'd just wave and say hi?

D: They were just another kid—Turn out the lights when you leave. There was one little boy in her first-grade class, she referred to him there in her writing, and his mother was going to Purdue trying to get her degree, and she didn't have place for him to go at lunch so she asked if he could come home for lunch with Shecara, so we did that for a year—he was black. And that was the one she referred to as "like a brother... a friend," so she couldn't date him in high school because they were friends the whole time they were growing up. That was one black connection that I just happened to think of. But, no, her friends, in fact, they still come around here when she's back here in town, and we see them occasionally.

RR: In her interview Shecara talks about the transition she made in her early twenties where she did identify primarily with the black community, and she even moved for a period of time into a black community.

D: Yes, when she ran away and left a note for us.

RR: When was this?

D: That was when she realized that it is not just the color of skin, but it is also a cultural difference. And she had to go learn the culture, and that's when she went to Indianapolis. We didn't hear from her for months on end.

R: We had a couple of times when she would call with various kinds of problems, and we would send one of the older kids down to pick her up and bring her back home, and she lost her little car down there and never could find it.

RR: Was it a shock?

D: Yes. But she was old enough at that point that we figured she's got her life to lead. She's got to figure it out. We couldn't put any constraints on her. She had to experiment.

R: Everybody does. Everybody has their own path.

RR: When she came back from Indianapolis, what did she share with you about that experience?

D: Not a whole lot. She had spent some time with her boyfriend's family, and she told us about them, but we really didn't know where she was living or how bad it was. She didn't really tell us.

R: We learned more from her interview in your book than what we got from her. Those were years when she was doing this exploration, and everybody does it.

RR: Now she's married. Tell me about her family, her husband, her children, and whether, earlier on, you were able to see the path that led her to where she is now.

D: I think Shecara felt the need to be in the black culture because I think she was afraid she wouldn't be accepted in the white culture. And that's the way this country is. At one time weren't you considered black if you have one-eighth in your blood? She always went after the black football players, the black basketball players, living here in this community. She would go over and watch the practice and things like that. When she finally did meet Arsale, then she was happy.

R: There was a suicide attempt back in the middle of all this.

RR: When was this?

D: It was her senior year of high school, because she didn't quite graduate. She went through the ceremony, but she had one class she flunked so she had to take it over in the summertime. It was just before graduation. She came and told us.... She said, "I just took a bottle of pills."

RR: What was she going through that made her feel that that was the only option?

D: We thought she was depressed, but we learned from your book that she had a boyfriend who now had a girlfriend, and we didn't know that was behind it. We learned that from your book. We also later learned of undiagnosed thyroid problems.

RR: When did she get married?

D: I think 1998 or 1999.

RR: Tell me about your son-in-law.

D: He's great. He is very, very quiet. I don't think he feels at ease in a white community because he grew up in the black community completely. She can switch back and forth, but I think it is a little harder for him. He gets along great with her brothers. No problem there. But he is just not the communicative type. So we don't talk much.

R: She complains about that too.

D: It is just his personality.

RR: Shecara and her husband Arsale have four children now?

D: Yes.

RR: Tell me the similarities and differences between how you raised your children and how she is raising her children.

D: As she pointed out in the book, there is a difference between the black culture and the white culture, as she has experienced it. Arsale's family was always in the St. Louis area, which is highly black, and the one thing that we have discovered is that St. Louis is also very southern. There's a difference between North and South as to how you raise your child. I think part of what she thinks is the difference between black and white, I think is influenced by North and South. He was brought up by the "spare the rod, spoil the child" philosophy, and we don't do that. They had a little bit of a hard time at the beginning, especially since India, her first daughter, was used to expressing her opinions.

R: But she [India] is very smart, so she sees through something that's going on, and she analyzes it immediately in her head, and she is ready to comment on that analysis. Well, that can be seen as "talking back," especially if you are in the South.

D: But India's approach is the same way as her mother's approach would have been here. Our kids were allowed to say whatever they analyzed, and India was brought up that same way, and then Arsale was brought up as the child has to be quiet when he is around adults. When they got married, they lived with Arsale's mother for a while, and she just complained about India to no end. She [India] was mouthing off to her all the time. And India said, "I was just talking." So you understand.

RR: Right now, do you have a good relationship with your son-in-law?

D: Yes. He has gradually come around, especially since India is a teenager now, and he is a little more talkative. And he has come around to the fact that you don't have to hit the kids too. They are working that out.

RR: Do they also have a son?

R: Yes, his name is Asante.

RR: Do you see the differences in how your daughter and your son-in-law raise a black male as opposed to how you raised your white males?

R: Remember that we are a long distance from each other, so we don't get to see up close. We only get to see them when they are here. That may be only two or three times a year.

D: I would think the main difference would be the sports aspect. Because Arsale is a football and track coach, that is what Asante admires, and now Asante at first grade is playing football and participating in other athletic activities. That's more of a difference than anything.

RR: Looking back at just the experience in adopting your daughter and raising her and seeing her as a mother, when you reflect on that, what comes to mind?

R: Every experience in life is broadening.

D: I am glad we did it, if that is what you are asking.

RR: So you're glad you did it. Are there surprises, are there wonderful things that you got out of it that you didn't even expect?

D: Oh, yes. It is the same way when you have a baby biologically. You don't know what is going to happen when they grow up. And it wasn't really different than any of the others. They all come out different.

RR: What is something that you just are very pleased about with your daughter?

D: She is a wonderful person. She is very caring.

R: She is wonderful. She'd make a wonderful nurse if she could find a position down in St. Louis where she could get back into that field.

D: But she feels that St. Louis is one of the most prejudiced places she has ever been in. And that because of discrimination, she believes that the blacks keep themselves separate from the whites and the whites keep themselves separate from the blacks, and they are rude to each other. And she just doesn't understand it.

RR: You can imagine for her, growing up in a family where she learned how to cross racial boundaries, that it must be frustrating when she loves you as her family and as her parents, and she's living also in the black community. I can imagine, and I am sure you can, too, the frustration that not everybody is where she is.

R: Yes. Why can't we get along?

D: People like her and you understand better than the rest of us the need to get along.

RR: Absolutely. Because when you have people you love in both communities, you love deeply, you want for the sake of your children, for the sake of yourself, to get along. So I understand what she is going through. Tell me what you would say is the most exciting experience you had with your daughter.

D: You mean besides the suicide attempt?

RR: Well, that would probably be the saddest. But the happiest?

R: It is hard to sort out because there are so many of them. And each one of them has got their own special path that they're going down. So you feel excitement for each one depending on whatever path it is that they take. I don't know that one stands out from any others.

D: I don't know a particular incident, but she is a wonderful person now, and we are real happy with her.

R: She's done some work with Greater Lafayette Area Special Services programs just a couple of blocks away from here, when she was living here and Arsale was still going to school, and she was greatly loved by all the other nurses in that program, and when she came back this last time, she tried to make some contact with them, and I know that she would be particularly warm and loved if she could get back into that kind of thing. So I think that is probably her strength.

D: When her kids get older, we know she wants to get back into nursing, but she is presently staying home with them.

RR: Then your saddest memory?

D: The suicide [attempt].

R: That's hard to go through, because you've got to reassure the kid that, no matter what it is, how bad the situation, we've got a large enough group, and there's enough talent in this group, we can solve anything. And you have to get that across somehow, and you know that you haven't, obviously, because here's a girl who's trying to end her life, and somehow or other you've failed to get across the idea that we got enough talent here that we can solve anything for us. It is sad to realize that somehow or other that didn't come across. That's the way life is.

RR: After that incident, when you talked about it with her, did she understand that then?

R: She seemed to.

RR: And sometimes I think we in our minds realize that our families love us and we know in our heart, but sometimes it doesn't always click in our heart until something happens and then we see how our parents actually handle it.

D: I don't think it was a 100 percent serious attempt because she came and told us immediately.

R: Look at all the research being done right now. Even *Time* magazine, about a year ago, had a huge article on what makes the teenage mind tick. And all these MRI studies being done by the National Institute of Mental Health, this one guy has studied whatever it is—eighteen hundred or two thousand teenage brains using MRI scans for many years, and people are just barely starting to understand that the brain is going through all kinds of changes, some of which are the result of hormone changes, but some of which aren't, and it is so complex that it is awfully hard to figure out what to do or how to do it, because the physiological changes are happening at the same time as all of this other stuff is going on—getting to know boys, getting to know other cultures, et cetera. It is complicated.

RR: It is amazing any of us gets through our teenage years.

D: A lot of our kids say, "I don't know why they keep saying school was so wonderful. I hated it."

RR: Looking back on your own experience, your adoption journey, is there anything that you would have done differently, and what are the things you are glad you did do?

R: We are glad we adopted.

D: I think it was easier on Shecara, being adopted into a larger family than, say, if she had been the only child, and all the focus would have been on black versus white, whereas this way it was just ignored. She was just one person of the group. So I think that way it gave her a good solid childhood time, but the reverse of that is that then, maybe, we didn't pay enough attention to getting her introduced to the black society early enough. That would be about the only thing that I would change maybe. And I don't know how we could have done that for her.

RR: Ron, would you agree?

R: Oh, yes. The black experience around here is around the university, that's where the sort of center in West Lafayette is. There is a black cultural center. There is that group of students from the university who are all the time putting on various kinds of musical performances, shows, dance, all the rest of it, for the university. That really didn't exist in very deep form at the time she was growing up. It does now. They got a new building in the last ten years, they've got a director who is an outgoing person, and a lot of that has happened since she grew up here.

D: About the only blacks who were here at that time were football players and basketball players.

RR: So that was her window of blackness?

D: Yes. She did meet a few of the black people who live in Lafayette during her high school years, but, with a few exceptions, the blacks who lived in Lafayette are of lower economic class, and therefore you know what that [could] lead to—drugs. So I can remember we were talking with a black man who worked at Purdue, we just knew him a little tiny bit, and he asked about Shecara, and we said that she was trying to hang around with the football players—well, why? [he asked]. And we said, well, she has a choice—footfall players at Purdue or druggies in Lafayette; there isn't anything else.

RR: Were you familiar with the stance that the National Association of Black Social Workers made about the time you adopted your daughter?

D: No.

R: No. What was it?

RR: It was a position that the National Association of Black Social Workers announced in 1972. They were concerned in part, much like Native Americans in this country, that these children, their children, black children, would be pulled from the black community, sort of like a brain drain, academically speaking, and that these children wouldn't grow up with a strong sense of their self, their understanding that they were black, understanding that they were part of a black heritage; rather, these children would grow up confused, that they would struggle [with] not knowing who they were and where they would fit in.

D: That was 1972—so that would be a couple of years after we got her, because she was born in 1970. As we told you before, nothing was said to us, nothing at all, so I can see why they [NABSW] came up with this statement.

RR: If you were adopting now, hypothetically, would you want your social worker to say more about the race piece, given what you know about your daughter's journey?

D: I don't know. If something had been said to us, I don't think we would have done anything differently. For one thing, as Shecara pointed out in your first book, she doesn't even know if she is black. She could be Mexican, Puerto Rican. Therefore it is kind of hard to respond.

RR: Did she feel, then, that she needed to possibly explore her Mexican or Puerto Rican roots?

D: No. She worked as a nurse at the community health center, and we have a fair number of Mexican workers; they've settled here. She says that the older grandmas would start talking to her in Spanish, and she would say no, I don't speak Spanish. And then they would bawl her out for not maintaining her heritage. She got that a number of times.

RR: You're not sure 100 percent what all of her heritage is.

D: No. Her father was light black—that's all they told us, and her mother was white.

R: And, as she said in your first book, she tried several times to get interested in trying to run down to see where her parents might have gone or who they were, and she would go about so far and then she would quit.

D: And we knew she was doing this and encouraged her and everything. But she never really quite—but it was a one-night stand as far as we could tell. The mother was a Lafayette resident.

RR: You could understand the concern that the National Association of Black Social Workers had?

D: Yes.

R: But she was in a unique category. Was she black? I don't know.

D: And then, again, as you brought out in your first book: Would you rather be in a white family or be in foster care? It's a question. At that time, I don't know what it is like now, there were more black babies than there were black families willing to adopt.

RR: There are still many children of color that need homes.

D: I feel that the difference between black and white is not as big as the economic differences. If you get somebody who has had a hard-scrap life and you bring them into West Lafayette, there is a big, big difference.

RR: Could you see your daughter moving to West Lafayette?

D: She'd like to move here. But he [Arsale] wouldn't. He likes St. Louis.

R: She'd like to be a little closer to West Lafayette, just because there is a lot of camaraderie that goes on between the various kids in our family. We have a family Web site where anybody in the family whose kid did something, they take a photo of it and put in on this family circle site so everybody gets that same picture all at once. So we're taking pictures when they come here, and we put it on that little circle site, and we got Shecara a camera so that she could contribute to that circle also, and she communicates very well with some of the kids more than others of the kids—so she'd kind of like to be closer so that there could be more interaction between her kids and the other cousins. But we're saying that isn't going to suit Arsale. Maybe you should pick a place like Indianapolis—that's only sixty miles away, but it has a lot more blacks and black culture that you can get there that you just can't get here. So far that doesn't seem to be in the cards.

RR: Would you recommend [to] other young families to adopt transracially?

R: Well, we don't try to influence other people on these kinds of things. Everybody has got their own path to follow. But if somebody had asked specifically, was that a satisfactory experience, we would say sure. We learned things that we'd never learn any other way unless you just do it. But I don't know if we would try to influence anybody to adopt.

D: If somebody is interested in adopting, then I would tell them fine, go ahead. If there is a baby that needs you, fine. It wouldn't matter to me if it is transracial or not. It would be better for a child to be in a family of its own color but that versus foster care—well!

RR: Looking at your transracial adoption experience compared with societal issues of race and economics, what would you like to see social work, as a profession, do to address some of these concerns?

R: I am not sure it is one that would be shared by anybody else—we haven't talked about this between ourselves. But I feel if we make the adoption process too restrictive, then you cause other kinds of problems in the culture. It pushes the abortion rate up, it causes child protection services to be overloaded. So I view with a certain amount of skepticism this present trend that I read in magazines about the adopting family has to meet such rigid criteria for adopting, that it is really tough to get adoptable kids into families.

D: Like they have to have a bedroom of their own?

R: This kind of thing discourages people from what I feel is kind of a human response to a need, and I think it is going to be counterproductive in the long run.

RR: Is there anything I haven't asked that you would like to add?

D: That almost goes back to the question of the national group that recommends adopting within your own color. I am wondering if, for the world's sake, that is not the best thing. It might be the best thing for the individual child, but from a global perspective, it almost seems like mixing cultures would lead to greater understanding of people. And therefore I wonder if maybe people like you and Shecara are fulfilling a role of mixing cultures that supersedes the individual.

PAUL GOFF

WASHINGTON STATE

FEBRUARY 2004

Paul Goff, 64, was widowed in 1995 and remarried two years later. He and his first wife had two biological children, Michael and Adam, and one adopted child, Laurie. She was adopted when she was 1 month old. The Goffs raised their children in Seattle, Sierra Leone, Ivory Coast, Panama, Bangladesh, Washington, D.C., and New Orleans. Paul Goff is Jewish and a physician. He describes his economic status as upper middle class.

> *Discriminating against a child because of the color of her skin is disallowing a child a life. I have been more places, done and seen more things, and received an amazing education more than people twice my age have done or will ever do because I was adopted into my family, which happens to be white.*

—LAURIE GOFF, 27, JUNE 1997

INTERVIEW

RR: In 1970 you adopted your daughter, Laurie, in Washington State. One, what was the climate socially and politically in your community then for white parents adopting black children, and, two, what was the mental process that both you and your wife at the time went through when adopting, given those conditions?

PG: Well, it was a time when there had been a tightening up of adoptions, and if you wanted to adopt, you needed to decide how rigid you wanted to be in terms of the criteria. People who wanted white children from similar backgrounds stood almost no chance of adopting in a reasonable time frame. And so we thought about other options. My wife Ellen had had difficulty with pregnancies. We had lost two babies before having our two children, and they were both boys, and she wanted a little girl—we both wanted a little girl—so we decided to adopt, and we went through the process. We thought about interracial adoption. We lived in a nice area of Seattle. It was a very lovely place to live to raise a family. It didn't seem like there were any real issues to us in terms of adoption, especially interracial adoption. Our backgrounds were very open to that notion. I had gone to Howard University for medical school. Race was not a big issue with us. So we went for interracial adoption, in part because it was happening in society and in part to try to do anything else, we probably wouldn't have been able to do it in the time frame we had in mind.

RR: In making the decision to adopt a biracial child, were either of you concerned about how society might view you?

PG: That was not an issue for us. It was interesting, though, the mind-set of the agency we went through. We adopted Laurie through a Jewish adoption agency in Seattle. When we began the process, we put down on the application that we would be open to interracial adoption. It took a year or two for the agency to agree to place a biracial child in our home. Basically, this agency did not pay attention to our initial decision or indication that we wanted to choose this type of adoption. Then, a year or two later, the agency had a major meeting, including other potential adoptive parents, because adoptions were very slow. There we indicated again that we were open to interracial adoption, and they seemed surprised.

RR: Why do you believe the agency was surprised that the two of you were interested in adopting interracially?

PG: Apparently, not many professionals within the agency had much experience with interracial placements. In fact, then it was not something that they had done before. (Maybe we should have realized that, going through a Jewish adoption agency for this kind of adoption, would be difficult.)

RR: After adopting your daughter did you feel that you needed to adjust your lifestyle because you were a blended family?

PG: No. That was not a problem. We had thought about [it] but our lifestyle was already such that we were committed to being in situations where there was ethnic and cultural diversity.

RR: What was your lifestyle?

PG: When we adopted Laurie, I was in training in Seattle, and we lived in an interracial community and had quite a large support group there. A number of people from the same area had done interracial adoption, and there was a group of us who had monthly get-togethers, so Laurie was not at all isolated. The fact that our daughter was African American was not an issue for us. There were other African American people around so she did not stand out.

RR: What were the values that you taught your children?

PG: We came from a liberal Jewish background. We essentially taught our kids to respect others who are different than them and emphasized in our home the importance of learning about others' ethnic/cultural backgrounds and finding richness in that.

RR: As your children were being raised, what were some of the places that you lived due to your professional career?

PG: The first place we traveled was Sierra Leone, which is in West Africa. That was a really interesting experience. It opened my eyes. It was probably the most wonderful overseas experience that we had. At various times people encountered Laurie and our family and they tried to figure out what happened. My secretary in Sierra Leone figured that my wife had made a mistake and I had forgiven her. This came out afterward. But essentially, we lived fairly normal lives for that type of lifestyle. There was never any question of our blended family's being accepted into these communities. People were always interested and accepting and open. I can't really recall any overt discrimination.

RR: What was it like for Laurie and her two white brothers to live in an African country?

PG: Let me say, when you bring an African American kid into a white family, it is not a question of whether you tell the child that they are adopted or not. It's obvious. Laurie's standard line to people was, "Don't you know that I'm adopted?" And that was started when she was 2 or 3 years old. Michael and Adam fully accepted her being in the family. They were a little older than she. When we lived in Sierra Leone, Laurie was 18 months and her brothers were a few years older. So obviously, they were more independent than she [was] then. The two boys went out regularly into the community where we lived. My parents tell the story of visiting us in Sierra Leone and having Michael and Adam take them for a walk down to the little village that was just below us on the hill, and all the villagers would greet them, and my mother tells the story of topless women. It was really a different culture than ours. But the kids had friends who came up from the village, and we were fortunate to be able to pay school fees for a few kids in the village so they could attend school. Our family enjoyed living in Sierra Leone very much.

RR: After Sierra Leone you traveled to many other locations. Can you name and describe a few of the other places?

PG: When Laurie was about 7 or 8 years old, we lived in the Ivory Coast, which is located on the western coast of Africa slightly south of Sierra Leone. The Ivory Coast was a much more urban, developed community compared to Freetown, the capital of Sierra Leone, where we had previously lived, which was more of a quaint community. So clearly, that was a different experience for our family. And there, there was less interaction with local kids, although there was some. Our kids went to an American school in the city where they made good friends, and some of their friendships at these schools, Laurie can talk to that, were lasting friendships.

RR: After the Ivory Coast where else did you go?

PG: To New Orleans for a year.

RR: Now describe New Orleans.

PG: We were in New Orleans from 1979 to 1980. It was the year they canceled Mardi Gras because of the police strike. That was our claim to fame. During that time it was a miserable place. For example, there were shootings in supermarket parking lots. It was the only place I've ever lived (including all of the places we lived overseas) where, when our kids went out, we asked them to call us when they arrived to their destination to tell us they got there safely. New Orleans seemed like a very unsafe, strange place. There didn't appear to be much of a middle class left in New Orleans. Either people were very rich or economically very poor.

RR: Would you agree that the schools in New Orleans then were still racially segregated in many ways, even after the *Brown vs. Board of Education* decision in 1954?

PG: Yes, not legally, but you're right—there was de facto segregation. Mostly, the schools had been integrated, but they were not well supported. We were fortunate enough to get Laurie into an exceptional school right by Tulane University, which had a lot of faculty members' kids in it and strong community support. So in that sense she went to a good academic and somewhat ethnically diverse school.

RR: How did you as a family reconcile the fact that the communities in New Orleans were so visibly segregated?

PG: We just lived our lives. We were there for only a year, so we didn't have much chance to get into the politics of it. Laurie had many friends from school, and it was an eye-opener for her to see how they lived. She had lived a very privileged existence in many ways, and being in a community where there was a fair amount of poverty was quite different for her.

There, was the first time Laurie had a friend whose mother was a single parent. New Orleans was an eye-opener for all of us.

RR: One of the admirable points I think that came out in *In Their Own Voices* when we spoke with Laurie was that she talked about how wonderful her parents were and how much in particular her mother advocated for her in the school system, in the communities in which she lived. How did you as parents learn how to advocate for Laurie specifically?

PG: I think it just comes from a long background in education. My wife had originally been a teacher, her parents were teachers, and she had a very strong feeling as to what she wanted for her kids. And there were certain schools that just wouldn't work for our kids, we thought. In the New Orleans situation we had to get the school to agree to accept her. I remember Laurie's mother and I went into the school and pleaded with the administration to take her in, knowing the school at the time was looking for only white kids to enroll. It turns out the school accepted her sight unseen. She was basically crossing the district and color line. Essentially she went there a little bit under false pretenses, but we wanted to get her into this particular school because we had heard a great deal about the quality of education there. It was in New Orleans that it became evident that Laurie needed some tutoring, and Ellen was very proactive in recognizing Laurie's obstacles and working out how she could teach Laurie how to overcome them. Ellen was a very dedicated mother and then also was a stay-at-home mom.

RR: I think that it was also remarkable how she was especially attentive about taking care of Laurie's hair and skin needs.

PG: We had many friends who advised us and who taught Ellen how to maintain Laurie's skin and hair. (I didn't really ever get very good at it.) But she worked very hard at trying to make Laurie feel comfortable with her hair, particularly. It was hard, working with Laurie's hair, but Ellen figured out how to go about it. We had next-door neighbors in Seattle who were very helpful and friends elsewhere who had ideas, et cetera.

RR: When it related to your daughter, what were the expectations you had for her when she became an adult?

PG: There were no stated expectations, but I think there was an understanding that she would go to college. Earning a college degree was assumed for all of our kids, no questions asked. In terms of expectation of what she would do after college, we wanted her to decide how she was going to lead her own life.

RR: It seems as though her interest was and is in social justice issues.

PG: I think it has been ingrained in her family for some generations. Her grandparents were always very active in promoting certain social-political issues, and her mother, in particular, was active in college in similar ways. I can remember Ellen did sit-ins when she was a freshman during the '60s; I participated in some social events, but I was too busy trying to survive in medical school. Certainly, it was an interesting time to be at Howard University in the early [to] midsixties. During my freshman year, the first week before orientation, I went to the March on Washington, stumbled into it not understanding fully at the time what its significance would be. And my classmates were, many of them were people who had never had an equal relationship with a Caucasian. Either they had been in communities where there was no contact or the relationship was not of equals. So it was a very interesting experience for both my classmates and me.

Yes, we all, the entire family, had exposure and strong feelings about many social issues.

RR: When you look at now the thirty-plus years in which you raised your daughter and your sons, but particularly your daughter, what about the adoption experience surprised you the most?

PG: That is a difficult question for me to answer. I know it wasn't easy for Laurie, in many respects, because in the end, as she leaves home and goes to college, her background is so different that it is hard for her to find real peers and people who can really understand where she's been. And part of that has to do with our background, and part of it has to do with the fact that we're a blended family, and part of it has to do just with adoption in general. Families with adopted kids, if you look at outcomes of adopted kids, I think you would find that they're not the same as other, nonadoptive families.

RR: Do, then, adoptive families play out better or worse compared to other families, in your opinion?

PG: I'm not sure I would put a value on it, but I think that there is more dissonance, I don't know if that's the correct word, but there's cultural tension and it doesn't necessarily mean black-white, it's just having people of different backgrounds in many instances, there's a higher instance of difficulties. In general, I think we were pleased with the adoption experience. We thought it was good for Laurie, we thought it was good for us, but there are difficulties that arise as you go through this that make it different than a nonadopted kid.

PG: [pause] It's hard for me to talk about this right now.

RR: Can you think back to what your happiest moments with Laurie were?

PG: College graduation. She did some performing in high school that was quite lovely. Just watching her achieve as she's gone through life is a great joy.

RR: What is a sad point?

PG: I think that we've had some difficulties in recent years. A lot of it has to do with the death of my wife—not that that is the issue but Laurie lost a great supporter and it has been very difficult at times.

RR: Knowing your background and your experience in this adoption process, would you say that the position taken by the National Association of Black Social Workers impacted you at all?

PG: No.

RR: Their stance against transracial adoption didn't [move] you one way or the other?

PG: Actually, it was not well known at the time we were doing the adoption what their feelings were. We had some very close neighbors who were skeptical about this type of adoption. I had a medical school friend, who we met after medical school, after we adopted Laurie, who was very negative about the whole idea. He was a black guy. But he wasn't negative in the sense that he was angry at us or anything like that, but he was skeptical that this would turn out OK. But in terms of their [NABSW] announcements, it didn't particularly affect us at the time.

RR: How do you maintain a relationship with Laurie as an adult since the dynamics have recently changed?

PG: She is my daughter. Just like my other kids, I do my best to support and cheer for them.

RR: For the many parents who are now starting the process, which you did now some thirty years ago, do you have any words of wisdom that you could share with these young families?

PG: I think adopting cross-culturally is an adventure. It's the same but different, if you follow what I am saying. It is the same as having your own children, but it is different. And we always felt that by adopting Laurie, we made a commitment to have a diverse life, not necessarily do all the crazy things we did but to have a life in which there was color, and it was part of our obligation to our family to expose them to different people and communities.

RR: How have you been able to do that?

PG: We always lived in places where there were other people from a variety of ethnic backgrounds.

RR: Do you think that is important in general?

PG: I really do. I think it would be very hard to do this in a community that didn't have some ethnic and cultural diversity. It is nice for kids to have other kids who look like them. They don't have to be their best friends, and they don't have to hang out with them, but just not to be the only person, that would be very difficult for the child.

RR: I really applaud you and Laurie and your two sons for just the conscious effort in building and maintaining a beautiful family. All families have of course their ups and downs, but nonetheless you're continuing on the journey. It is remarkable.

BARBARA TREMITIERE

YORK, PENNSYLVANIA
FEBRUARY 2004

Barbara Tremitiere, who was divorced in 1986, has three biological children, Michelle, Steven, and Scott, and twelve adopted children, Laura, Kristine, Robert, Kevin, Douglas, Marc and Monique (twins), Nicolle, Chantel, Andrew, Daniel, and Michael. The age of the children at adoption ranged from 2 months to 15 years. The children were reared in York, Pennsylvania. Barbara Tremitiere is Protestant. She has a Ph.D. in social work (adoption emphasis) and is a professor at York College of Pennsylvania. She is the founder of the One Another Adoption Program in Pennsylvania and is a therapist. She describes her economic status as middle class.

The biggest thing you can give a kid is time. A lot of people are running everywhere, throwing their kids on nannies, raising them on computers and television. Just give them time and love. That's what they need.

—CHANTEL TREMITIERE, 29, FEBRUARY 1998

I dispelled all the myths and stereotypes of black people. I realized that I needed to be proud of who I am and stop hiding behind being biracial. I learned to stand up and say, "I am who I am, a beautiful black woman. God made me and He 'don't make junk.'"

—NICOLLE TREMITIERE YATES, 28, DECEMBER 1997

INTERVIEW

RR: When you began your adoption process, you and your husband were married, is that correct?

BT: Yes.

RR: What decisions did you make when you decided you wanted to adopt? What thought process did you go through?

BT: I always knew I was going to do this, and we agreed when we got married that we were going to have three kids born to us and adopt three, if that was the way it worked out. We got married in the 1960s and had three kids in four years, which was quite a lot, and then he got a vasectomy. At that point I was working in the field of adoption. We first heard about our son Doug through his social worker, who gave me a flier with his description and a photo of him attached. Back in those days, if a social worker wanted to place a child, she had to make fliers on the child and send them out all over the place and hope that somebody answered. You didn't have copy machines then, so you had to manually glue together these fliers with pictures of children available for adoption. Anyway, I really became interested in Doug because he sounded so like a child that we could certainly take.

As far as the actual adoption process, we put our name in for him and were approved by the agency to adopt him. We had to go all the way out to Pittsburgh and back several times to get our home study completed, which was an interesting arrangement. So in 1968 we officially adopted our son Doug. He was a 1-year-old black little boy.

RR: What were the social ramifications of white parents adopting a black child in 1968?

BT: We were disowned by our parents, communicated with by the Ku Klux Klan, to name a few, which was all kinds of fun. Other parents who adopted like we did experienced similar occurrences. The 1960s was a time when society did not condone transracial adoptions.

RR: What were some of the concerns expressed by your family members about your decision to adopt transracially?

BT: Our families didn't think this was a good idea. The idea of adding a black person to their family tree was not something either of our families wanted to have happen. In the first place, having a black person in their family had never occurred to them in their lifetime. Our parents adamantly tried to talk us out of it, tried to scare us out of it, tried everything that they could, but it didn't work.

RR: So why did you adopt?

BT: We felt that this was something we could do. We didn't have any problem with adopting black kids; and they were the ones who were waiting in the foster care system to be adopted. I knew that, because they were the ones in my caseload still waiting for long-term placement. To us it seemed like the natural thing to do. So we did it.

RR: When you blended your family, where did you and your husband at the time choose to live?

BT: We had lived in San Antonio when he was in the service but moved to York, Pennsylvania. It was there where we decided to adopt.

RR: Can you describe the type of community York, Pennsylvania, was?

BT: It is an interesting community because there are a lot of Lutherans here—actually one out of every three people in York is Lutheran. And at that time the Lutheran Church was doing a lot of work with refugees, so in addition there were a significant number of people in our area who had taken in refugees in their church, et cetera. As a result there was quite a mix in the City of York as far as different kinds of people. Never, in all the time that we had our kids, did I feel that I was different than anybody else, because if I went to school and I was picking up my black kids, there were a whole lot of other people picking up kids that didn't match them, too, so it wasn't that big a deal. However, just as we were a real integrated community, we were also in southern Pennsylvania, which was in KKK territory. As my kids were growing up, we received notes from the Ku Klux Klan telling us they didn't like what we were doing. In those days the FBI kept the notes because they had no way to copy them. Now I wish I had copies of the notes to be able to show people all the idiocy that went on. But the FBI kept the infamous notes. We learned to keep an eye open for the Klan and hoped that they would not burn us down.

RR: Your family ultimately consisted of three biological children and twelve adopted children who were of mixed races, including black, Korean, and Vietnamese. What was the time period in which you adopted all of your children?

BT: We started in 1968, and Andy came in 1975, and Laura came during Three-Mile Island—I think that was 1977—and she was the last one. I think it was within ten years.

RR: How did you explain to your children their ethnic and racial differences in relation to the way society may look at them and their family?

BT: We just kind of *were*. The kids would experience things, and then we would talk to them about it. When they said, "I'm different," we would talk to them about that. It just seemed very natural. It wasn't like it was anything that was forced. As the questions came up, we answered them.

They went to integrated schools; they had an integrated church, so pretty much that was their life. When the questions came up, we just answered them, so it never was like a big deal, like we had to really make a big point of their racial and ethnic differences.

RR: Was it important for you and your husband to discuss each child's ethnic makeup?

BT: With who?

RR: Within your family. Did you embrace their unique cultures?

BT: We joined a church that had blended with an African American church (this was unusual in those days) so the church population was very integrated. We were very focused on being sure that we had a community around us that they could fit into, could identify with, et cetera. So their friends all the way through their lives to this point have been of a very mixed nature. They have always gone to schools that were integrated. So it was always part of their life. When we started adopting, our birth children were 4, 3, and 1, so this, too, was a part of their lives.

RR: Do you feel that you grew as an individual with your children?

BT: Oh, yes, definitely. Naive us. I guess I realized that there was a lot I didn't know about taking care of my children's hair and skin needs. But I didn't know how much until I had to learn and actually do it. It was good that we had friends who we could (and did) approach and say, "Can I throw you money to help my kids with their hair?" Sadly, I think early on I assumed that all that vital information came to you by osmosis. The truth is, it doesn't. So after I kind of blew it and realized that I didn't know, then our friends helped us out on that. All the things we didn't know, we would ask those who did know and learned from them. But, no, it was never uncomfortable for us parenting our kids, not ever.

RR: Chantel and Nicolle were in the first book, *In Their Own Voices*. So I am speaking in reference to that. What would you say would be the highest point that you experienced with them in this process?

BT: That's hard to say because they are just our kids. I do think watching each one of them become their own person and achieve what they wanted to achieve and to have them actually, like the two of them, as you well know, have very different ideas on topics like adoption and just very different viewpoints in general, has been great. This is something that we've always prized, encouraging them to be able to develop their own viewpoints, and they did. We discovered that about each one of them. Each one of them is totally unique, totally different from all the others. Not even the twins are similar—in relation to their choice of occupation or having the same viewpoints on issues. Yes, I feel very good that we were able to allow them and enable them to find their niche in this world. I believe it makes them much stronger human beings.

RR: What was it that you did to enable them to do that?

BT: We deliberately exposed our kids to a lot of different interests to see what they would want to do, what they would like to do, et cetera, and then helped them to become whatever it was that they decided they wanted to become. For each one of them it was a totally different ballpark. And we'd fight the battles as we had to, if they wanted to become something that maybe was not seen as appropriate for them to do. Our expectations were high for all of our children. For example, I always had in my mind that if they had some major talent that took major kinds of training, that they would get the best so they'd have the best shot at the world. Doug, who is a brilliant person, is a linguist and always wanted to work with the government. It became necessary for him to go to a college like Georgetown University so that he would be prepared for that profession. We were able to help him get there, and he's a Georgetown graduate. That was very important for him. Marc is an artist, and it was very important for him to go to a school that would allow him to do the best he could in that area so he ended up at Syracuse University, and now he is a professional artist in New York City. Chantel achieved in basketball, and we were able to help her get a scholarship for that, and she went on (after she earned her college degree) to play professional basketball with the WNBA. Each one of them was totally unique, and so our focus became helping them to get the best possible training. Being African American kids, minority kids, they needed to have that extra push in order to get into the careers that they chose.

RR: Would you agree that, for those parents who adopt across racial lines, there is an extra effort on their part that should be put forth on behalf of their child?

BT: I always thought so. I really believe that African American kids in particular do need to have that edge. Other people might believe differently. I certainly wanted my kids to have that edge, and it has worked well for all of them. That's what I fought for, so they could do that. Unfortunately, when we got divorced, I had six kids in college, so we had to really fight for all the student aid available to them, and do everything that we possibly could in order to get them through. In the end all the ones who were in college finished. With all the challenges we went through, they came out the other end alright.

RR: What would you say is your relationship with your children today?

BT: I believe I am very close to all of my children but one. And that's her choice. That doesn't mean that I in any way, shape, or form ignore her or do anything differently for her than I do for the other kids. This is her choice.

RR: Do you feel that the type of parenting you gave your children did indeed help prepare them to live in this global economy that we now live in?

BT: Yes. I certainly believe so. In our family we have always been very opinionated, and some of them really are. We differ greatly as to political perspectives and other kinds of things, and that's fine too. We sometimes have to agree to disagree, but it has become more interesting as they have grown older because each one of them has felt very free about being able to speak confidently about what he/she believes and to make his/her own way in the world. Sometimes their brothers and sisters don't appreciate it when they send them e-mails all the time, but—oh, well, it is a free country. I think they definitely have been able to develop in different ways, ways that they needed to. I feel very good about how that has gone.

If there is anything we did right, that is definitely it.

RR: Looking at the social work profession as it relates specifically to transracial adoption, do you see progress since the late '60s?

BT: I've been around for this whole discussion on transracial adoption. When we first adopted in 1968, the following year there was a conference held in Canada on adoption. Then they didn't use the term *transracial adoption*. I forget what they called it then, but anyway I went to this conference. I'll never forget the experience because the man who gave the keynote address, his name was Leyton Hudson, started off by saying, "Welcome, brothers and sisters, and those who have joined us by choice." To me it was a very interesting choice of words. There were quite a number of us who had adopted across racial lines, and it was an OK thing for us—obviously not for the rest of the world. But for those of us who had done this, we were pretty much our own supporters. About five or six years later the next major adoption conference was in St. Louis, and that was the conference to end all conferences. That was the North American Council on Adoptable Children conference in which the black social workers took over absolutely every session there was in the conference and disrupted it. They told us we had done the most terrible thing in the whole wide world. There were white parents walking up and down the hallways crying, and actually some parents gave their kids back to adoption agencies after that conference. It was horrible. Then it became more interesting because about ten years after that, back in St. Louis again, some of the black social workers apologized for what happened the first time around. They had finally said, essentially, these kids are already in placements, so we might as well help the white parents who are raising these children. The mood changed. The social workers were more supportive, and we were not yelling at each other anymore. There were, of course, still philosophical differences on the issue, and still are, but for the most part in the profession we kind of decided to agree to disagree through the years. I have always, as an adoption worker, placed transracially, always. From the time I began in the field, all the way up to today, most of the children I place are placed transracially. The children available tend to be older black kids. There aren't a thousand people lined up to adopt them. I always believed that if there were in-race families for them, then of course they should go there, but for the kids who are lingering in foster care, yes, I want them to be placed transracially.

RR: You talked about how both you and your husband struggled to fight for your children and to make sure that they had the best opportunities possible, ethnically, culturally, and professionally. How can you share the importance of that or the value of that with other families?

BT: First, many families adopt kids across racial lines, and they don't really think about what that entails, especially long term. Some parents tell me, "I don't have any problems with my kids," and do very little to prepare them for *their* lives. It is necessary to realize that the kids have to live in a very real society, and therefore it becomes the parents' business to be advocates for them and to realize that the opportunities are not always the same for them as for their white family members. Parents need to be there and fight the battles to ensure that their kids are getting the best education they can, so that they get the best chance that they can in this world. Second, I think it is important to live in an integrated area so that transracially adopted kids are not the only kids in the community that look like them. In racially and ethnically isolated communities, these kids can get left out of things, like going to dances and other social activities, because of the difference of their skin color. This was the way it was when my kids were in school. They were, though, in an environment where that wasn't a problem. But a lot of the kids I placed lived in environments where that was a serious problem, so these kids would be put in a position where they either snuck around or dated who they weren't supposed to date or did not date at all, and that was unfair. I've always explained to the parents that they needed to get these kids in a community or a place where they felt OK about themselves and in an environment where they didn't have to fight never-ending battles because they were different than everybody else.

RR: Do you think it is OK to raise a black child or a Korean child in an all-white community or predominately white community?

BT: In general, with Koreans and other Asian kids they tend to be more acceptable from the perspective of the white community, in contrast to black kids, because it's just the way the world works, unfortunately. Interestingly, I find that if Asian kids are raised in an area that is integrated, they will date minority. And if they're in an area where it is predominately white, that makes a difference too. With my Korean daughters, one had a black husband and one married a Puerto Rican man, so in both cases that was true.

RR: In the search for identity does race actually matter?

BT: Yes, race matters. I think it becomes even more important to people who don't live in multicultural families like ours where everybody is different. Once you are in an environment where everybody is different, then you realize that it doesn't have all the importance in the world, for sure. Race is important only because it is important in our world. So if we are going to raise these kids, we need to be able to help them adjust to the very real world they live in. Interestingly enough, my kids talk about this question a lot. My son Marc, who lives in New York City (he's the artist), believes differently. He says that, of all of his friends who are black males and have hugely succeeded, [they] are the ones who were either raised in areas that were mostly white or who were raised by white people. So is the message that kids are more likely to succeed when they're raised by white parents as opposed to parents in communities of color? Or does the transracial adoptee see life through the same eyes as his/her white parents so that it equips him/her better for the very real world that we live in? My son is very philosophical, and he's studying this question. By and large my kids enjoy and benefit from interacting with people cross-culturally and internationally. My son Doug is over in Europe working on his master's degree now, and he's just been a "world" person all of his life. He is very comfortable in many different cultures/community settings. I would never use transracial adoption just to break down the racial barriers, but it does seem to do that.

RR: For people who are looking to adopt, when we go through the adoption process, what are things that we need to ask social workers as far as adopting children cross-culturally, and what are the roles that social workers should play to make sure there is a good fit between the parent and child?

BT: You are obviously aware of the Multi-Ethnic Placement Act that, unfortunately when it is played out, makes it difficult sometimes for social workers to make good decisions about the homes or families they place children in. By law, as it currently stands, social workers cannot prevent a family from adopting across racial lines, no matter even if they are ill prepared to raise a racially different child.

RR: But can these parents prepare to raise children of color before they adopt them?

BT: That is what I try to do professionally, to help prepare potential parents for issues they may face as they raise their adopted children. Truthfully, that's what they need to be doing too. And for the most part they do that, but there are some factors working against them, particularly in the public arena, so I continue to do a lot of educating with these parents. Still today it is amazing how much I am asked to talk about this topic. I've been talking about transracial adoption since the 1960s. And sometimes I think, isn't this a done deal? Obviously not. Families are still struggling with issues affected by race and adoption. The guidelines I set for parents adopting cross-culturally are the following: *First*, the importance for families to live in an integrated area and for their kids to be in integrated settings. In my opinion it is unreasonable for parents to think they can stick their children of color in a racially white and isolated community and expect them not to have some kinds of problems. We have to be really careful that our kids are comfortable in their family and community, too, and that they are not going to be put into situations where it is intolerable for them. I feel very, very strongly about that. *Number two*, it is essential that the parents ensure that their own lifestyles are as integrated as their children's lifestyle. The key is that the parent is not just dropping their kids off someplace for only the child's benefit, but that this is something that is normal and natural for the entire family. *Number three*, I encourage families to engage in discussions with their children about issues like race and adoption and simply talk with them about what is going on in their lives daily. I believe it will prepare the children better for life situations before they run into them. I know you can't prepare them for everything, but you can be there for them—and that's the most important point anyway.

RR: For the cases where children are in rural or suburban communities where they don't come in contact with that many persons of color, what can the parents do?

BT: I think they need to see that somehow their kids do come in contact with people from a variety of different ethnic backgrounds. If they have to go to church in a different area or be sure the kids get into sports in a different area, et cetera. Parents can do a variety of things to include ethnic diversity in their child's life and theirs. Understand the suggestions I just mentioned are secondary; actually moving their bodies to a more ethnically diverse environment is the best thing. This needs to be their commitment to their children. I know it is not always easy to hear that, especially if you are parents who have adopted interracially and live in a predominately white "comfortable" suburb.

Interestingly, I ask my college students occasionally to write on this topic. And what I ask them to do is to talk about their high school experience and what things happened to the kids that were ethnically isolated. It is horrible what they tell me. It's horrible what kids have to suffer in their high schools because of their racial and ethnic differences. In my opinion it is a whole lot better not to put kids through that if you don't have to. Why not move into an area where they—black, biracial, Asian, and Native American children—at least have a good shake at a positive existence and are able to attend a high school where there are other minority kids?

RR: The civil rights movement ended in the late 1960s, and many parents did feel that the world was going to change, where it would be an integrated society.

BT: Oh, right—we were going to walk hand in hand.

RR: That has not happened. So how do we move forward instead of losing steam?

BT: I don't think we're losing steam, and I think that there are so many changes happening, because, as I said, I teach and I am trying to keep in touch with where the kids are, too, so I can see how much things are changing—it just takes a long time. The concern is that we can't get complacent and think that we've done it, we've arrived. My son Marc in New York speaks to this. He lives in Brooklyn, and he's on some community projects in his area. And while he's doing that, he is also able to educate some of the people in his community on issues of race and culture. Marc is in a neighborhood where most of the people are black. His wife is white. So what he does is he takes it upon himself to work with his neighbors, from the other angle, on the acceptance of white people living in the community. He is always conscious of his responsibility to do that, and I think we all need to be conscious of what we are doing and the kinds of examples we're modeling. We cannot afford to be complacent.

RR: I have talked with parents in my own travels who have adopted transracially and years later have just stopped fighting for racial and cultural integrity. They're tired. They raised their kids. My concern is that for every transracial adoptee, they cannot afford to stop—they must continue on this journey. What is your view on that?

BT: Absolutely! When I speak to groups and get an opportunity to speak to parents, I stress that same point. It is never over until it is over for everybody. Just because we've raised our kids, it doesn't mean we should become complacent. We've still got grandchildren. Even if that is all you fight for, you've got to make a better place for your grandchildren. Our society needs to get a grip—get it together here—and realize how insane racial intolerance is. From the time my kids were little, it would enrage me that when I would go into a bathroom in a public place with them, and when I closed the bathroom door stall, my kids would often be treated poorly by people when they saw them out there all by themselves. Then, when I came out of the stall, and they saw that I was with them, their attitudes would change from shock to uncomfortable politeness. That's when we see that racial prejudice still goes on.

RR: So where do you get your strength?

BT: From my kids, I guess.

RR: For the parents who are struggling with just getting a network in place to get the kind of support that you've had, what can they do?

BT: They can do that too. They can even integrate an area if they want to. They just have to work hard enough at it. We lived out in the suburban area when we first were going to adopt, and then we deliberately moved into the city, developed a support network. I don't let the parents off the hook when they make all kinds of noises about that. From my point of view, if you're going to adopt these kids, this is what you need to do.

One day I was speaking in Vermont about transracial adoption. And there was this gentleman there, and while I was speaking, I was noticing him out of the corner of my eye. He was leaning against the door, and he had a dark brown baby in a pack on his back, obviously his kid. As I was talking, I continued to watch him and suddenly he disappeared. So I thought, well, there goes another upset parent. Later on that day he came up to me and he said, "I was in your session this morning and I had to leave, I suppose you probably noticed." And I said yes, I did. He said, yes, but you don't know what I left for. He continued by saying that when he was listening to what I had to say, he got very upset and went and got his wife out of another session and took her to lunch so that they could talk. In his words he said to his wife, "When we moved to Vermont, our idea was that we were going to have this farm, and it was going to have kids on it, and they were going to be all different races, and we were just going to have this happy family, but I realize now that we are only looking through our eyes." Rhonda, then this gentleman looked at me and said that when he was listening to me talk, he realized that it was their dream, and not their children's dream, and that they would instead choose to move to a more ethnically diverse environment for the best interest of the entire family.

RR: Where would you like to see adoption be in the next twenty years?

BT: I would like to see us being realistic about the concerns I have high-lighted in this interview—still having transracial adoptions but not going back to just letting people get away with thinking that there are not any differences, et cetera. Obviously, I would like to move all of the kids out of the system. Realistically, there are as many coming in as are going out. What I want, I want kids in families, but I also want them in families where they are going to be OK growing up and where it is going to be healthy for them. And that's what I'll spend my lifetime working on, try-ing to make that possible.

RR: What final words would you like to leave us with?

BT: Whenever people talk about transracial adoption, like it's something strange, foreign, or weird, I never can understand that because, to me, with my kids, it has been the most normal, natural thing in the world. And I think when people see it as parenting kids, with building in some special reinforcements, it becomes more doable. Actually, when we par-ent our kids, we all should be doing these kinds of things. We all should be working for the benefit of each child to be in the best situation they can. What I am proposing shouldn't be all that unheard-of. But unfortu-nately, it is. Sadly, I think that a lot of people in today's world just don't take parenting itself very seriously. If we're going to parent, we need to really take it seriously and realize that the choices we make are choices that affect our kids' lives.

RR: As far as thinking about adopting transracially, what should the mind-set be?

BT: First, we must look at adoption, period, and certainly adoption across racial lines, and recognize that we are providing a family *for a child.* This child is a child who needs a family. Two, we must focus on encour-aging the child to find his/her niche in this world, rather than expecting this child to live up to something we may want him/her to be for our own egos. For my children I don't expect them to be forever grateful to me because I adopted them. This is something I chose to do because I wanted to parent a very real child who exists. It is my task as their parent to allow them to be a very real person with strong identities too. Adoption is not going in and selecting this perfect kid that is going to fit into your family like a kid you think you would have produced. You are there to provide a family for a waiting child. Not to bring them in and attempt to manipulate them to meet unrealistic expectations that you may have.

RR: What are realistic expectations to have when adopting children?

BT: That when a child comes into your home, your job is to discover what that child is all about and then help them become the best that they can be. That is it.

RR: What if an extended family member doesn't approve of your adoption? How do you advocate on behalf of the child, or is that even necessary?

BT: We were disowned when we adopted in the first place. So we simply told our parents, after we cried, that until they could accept our kids as our kids, that we would always act toward them as we always had but that they were not coming into our home until they could accept our children and relate to them as grandparents. It took them about six months.

RR: They learned quickly.

BT: They learned quickly. But you have to be that clear because obviously there are a lot of transracially adopted kids out there who are very hurt by how relatives act toward them and the things that relatives do, and you just can't let that be. You have to set the parameters—this is your child.

NORA ANKER

SOUTH HOLLAND, ILLINOIS
MAY 2004

Nora Anker is 74 and her husband, Harvey Anker, is 75. They have three bio-logical children, Kathy, Mary Ann, and Lynn, and two adopted children, Kim and Rachel. Kim was 5 years old when her adoption was finalized, and Rachel joined the family at 2 days old. The children were reared in South Holland, Illinois. The Ankers are Protestant. Both are high school graduates. Harvey Anker is a carpenter, and Nora Anker is a homemaker. They describe their economic status as middle class.

Sometimes transracial adoption is a good thing. A lot of children of different ethnic backgrounds are in the foster care system without any possible adoptive homes for them. And if white people want to adopt them, that's great. But I think they need to make sure that the children stay in touch with their roots. It's essential that they know the history and background of their people. I feel as though I've lost touch with who I am.

—RACHEL ANKER, 22, SEPTEMBER 1997

INTERVIEW

RR: Tell me where you and your husband settled after you were married.

NA: My husband and I settled in Lansing, Illinois, in 1951 and lived there for ten years, and then we moved to South Holland. Originally, my husband was from South Holland, and I was from the Lansing area.

RR: Where is Lansing in proximity to South Holland?

NA: Lansing is adjacent to South Holland. Lansing, like South Holland, is a suburb of Chicago.

RR: Did you start your family when you were living in South Holland?

NA: Actually, we had all three of our biological girls when we were living still in Lansing. We didn't move to South Holland until 1961.

RR: How did you become interested in foster care and adoption?

NA: I had two miscarriages, and I did not want to go through the pain of that again. Shortly after my miscarriages I read in the newspaper about the need for foster families to care for babies who were abandoned in the hospital. These babies didn't have enough stimulation, love, or attention. I believed I could foster at least one of these babies. I always did want more kids. My husband and I talked about it, and I looked into it more. It seemed like within a short period of time, we went downtown, to Chicago, and had an interview with Chicago Child Care Services to move forward in the process. It was a real blessing; our dream of fostering babies became a reality through this organization. In fact, we experienced a wonderful relationship with Chicago Child Care Services for the next twenty-some years and fostered many children through this organization.

RR: In addition to being foster care parents, you also chose to adopt.

NA: Yes. After we had our three biological children, we cared for (and later adopted) our first little girl, Kim, who was 2 years old when she entered our home. We had her for only three months before we went through the process of adopting our second child, Rachel.

Our daughter Kim is deaf, and we found that out a couple of days after we received her. She was considered "unadoptable." It turned out Kim was up for adoption, but by the time she was three or four, she had to start school and still was not adopted. We knew that we could and wanted to adopt her. In our situation we believed you do not keep a child in your home for three years and not have her become part of the family. The thought of a 3-year-old's leaving us was just heartbreaking. I couldn't stand it. Kim's adoption was finalized when she was 5 years old.

RR: After Kim you adopted Rachel.

NA: Yes, although we fostered a lot of babies in between. We had about twenty-six foster babies altogether.

RR: So when you adopted Rachel, was she a foster child at first?

NA: Yes, Rachel was a foster baby. We brought her in our home when she was 2 days old. Rachel was up for adoption, and then at one month, she became ill and we found out she had osteomylitis, a staph infection that settled in her hip—the doctors said it was a scourge at the nursery at that time, referring to the cause of her staph infection. So at 15 months she had surgery. Consequently, the agency decided not to move her to another home. Instead they wanted us to keep her through the walking and talking stages to make sure she developed well. After that period Rachel's picture was featured in the *Chicago Sun Times* one Sunday with other children that were available for adoption. They'd run a picture and a story on these children. I was outraged by this. To me they were advertising *my* baby. Interestingly, after that advertisement ran with Rachel's picture on it, I was told by the *Sun Times* that it was the first time since they had been running ads like this one that they had no response. And I thought, thank you, Lord!

RR: Was the intent to run stories like these to recruit families for these children?

NA: Yes, as I think back on that, maybe they felt they had to do that because there were so many kids in need of homes. The way I felt, because it was our baby they were picturing, and that I had to submit a picture, was sick and upsetting. Of course I didn't want to do that, because I knew it was such a cute picture of Rachel and I feared that someone else might want to adopt her. But this reminded me of those stories you read in the local paper. There'll be a picture of a cute puppy and it says, "Fido needs a home," that kind of thing. You've seen that too? I haven't seen this in any papers since then, but that was done here in Chicago for a while.

RR: Were you then able to adopt Rachel at that point, after no one responded to her picture in the newspaper?

NA: Well, we planned to adopt her at that point, but there unexpectedly was an edict imposed on the West Side of Chicago prohibiting case workers from placing black children into white homes. It was not a law but it was an edict. The case workers at Chicago Child Care were going along with that, so there was a lot of time that went by before we could officially adopt Rachel. In the meantime she needed surgery again.

We had a friend whose daughter Kelly went on to become a social worker after college. She happened to be working for Bethany Christian Services here in Chicago, and they were telling her about this family who was waiting to adopt this little African American girl, and Kelly knew right away who it was. She said, "Oh, I know that family, I know Rachel." We were the only ones on the whole southwest side of Chicago who were able, in spite of the edict, to adopt transracially. I guess because of the circumstances, and because Rachel had been with us by that time for three years. As far as I was concerned, wild animals weren't going to drag her out of this house.

RR: Can you describe for us the community of South Holland in the early 1960s where you and your husband spent most of your child-rearing days?

NA: South Holland was an all-white community at that time. When Rachel was in sixth grade, an African American family moved in about a block away from us, and after that, a couple of more African American families moved to our community. These families were leaving Chicago because they wanted a stable community with quality schools and places to worship that they could be a part of, and they believed that South Holland was that type of community. One little black girl was in Rachel's class at school. Before that, Rachel was the only little nonwhite girl in the school.

RR: What were the values that both you and your husband instilled in your children?

NA: We taught our children all the Christian values, of course. I need to go back. When we were hoping to adopt Rachel, I didn't know if it was right—not for us but for Rachel—if it would be fair to her to be adopted by us, a white couple. I talked with three good friends of mine, who could look at this objectively, to find out what they thought about it. I talked to my husband's sister and she said, "By all means, if you can (we didn't know if we'd be allowed to adopt her yet) you must, because otherwise she might not be raised in a Christian home," and that was important. Then I talked to a friend who was in the same situation and thinking about adopting an African American child. She understood our situation and thought we too should adopt Rachel. Another friend said, "By all means adopt her." And I thought, sometimes we don't get handwriting on the wall but we can go by answers from friends and family whose opinions we value. As far as we were concerned, we had no problem adopting a black child. And as far as Rachel was concerned, if we could adopt her, our family and friends looked at the whole situation objectively and without hesitation they all agreed that it would be good for her too.

RR: Was Rachel the only African American raised in your family?

NA: Oh, no. I would say maybe two-thirds of the babies we had in our home came from different nationalities. We had twins who were African American, and some we had for two weeks, some for two months, some for six months, but more than half were African American.

RR: What is your daughter Kim's racial and ethnic background?

NA: We know that Kim is part Lithuanian. Her birth mother once said she was both Lithuanian and German. But she is not African American.

RR: In looking at how Rachel was raised, she had mentioned in her interview that she valued her Christian upbringing. However, she also stated that she felt at a disadvantage because she wasn't exposed to the African American community.

NA: Back then I wondered where I would have gone for that, her ethnic heritage and culture. I knew Chicago could have provided her with a rich cultural experience, but I also knew you don't just drive into Chicago and find it. Our priority then was to care also for the other babies in our home, babies that were 2 weeks old, babies with problems. When you are into foster care, you don't take on a lot of other activities. Back then, how on rarth would I have done it? Today there are many more resources available about black history. In fact, our church has had, for the last couple of years, special exhibits and projects celebrating Black History Month. But that just wasn't there in the '70s. As far as searching for my kids' biological families, I offered to do that at one time for both Kim and for Rachel, to go back through the agency and see what we could find. I enjoy dabbling in genealogy anyway. Kim was not interested in locating her biological family, and Rachel expressed the same sentiment as well. I thought, if my roots are interesting to me, why wouldn't theirs be to them? They both said no, so I didn't pursue that again.

RR: Was the community in South Holland supportive of your blended family?

NA: Absolutely—never was there a problem with that.

RR: How did the community show its support?

NA: South Holland was and still is a close community. Here, there were a lot of relatives around. Rachel was always part of our extended family, too, the same way our biological children, Kathy and Mary Ann and Lynn, were part of it, she was too. There was no special, singling out of anybody.

RR: Did adopting a child of a different race change you as an individual or family?

NA: Maybe it did, but I don't know how if it did. See, that wasn't a problem with me.

RR: What wasn't a problem?

NA: The fact that our adopted children were from different nationalities, different races was not a problem for me or my husband. To me a baby is a baby, and when we took care of these babies, it couldn't have mattered less what nationality or race they were. I strongly believe you take care of a child regardless of his/her race or ethnicity. And after Kim, too, was here for three years, well, of course you don't give them up, unless you have to. And we didn't have to in this case, and because we wanted to keep her, we wanted to adopt her, that's why the case workers went to bat for us. So I don't know if the adoption experience changed me.

RR: Within the school system or community, did you ever need to advocate for your family or children because of their skin color?

NA: No.

RR: So race was not an issue as you were raising your children?

NA: No, I didn't know about it if it was. Although one time a church member said something somewhat derogatory to me in reference to my fostering children. He said [fostering these kids] was just supporting hanky-panky. And I quickly stated, "It is never, ever, the baby's fault." This same member said to me about my family "There are so many!" I responded, "It is one more than none and it is never the baby's fault." Fostering babies was something that we could do to make a difference. But to answer your question, that was the only time that I can remember where we were confronted with a negative situation involving my kids, where I needed to advocate for them. I believe it boils down to, if you're doing what the Lord wants you to be doing, you go ahead and do it, and let the chips fall where they may. If there were any chips that fell, so to speak, after that incident, I never saw them.

RR: As Rachel was growing up, what were the expectations that you had for her?

NA: I don't know if we had any expectations for her that were different from the ones we had for our other kids.

RR: What type of relationship did you want your children to have with both you and your husband?

NA: We expected to have a good giving-taking family relationship. It was important to us that our kids grew to love each other and that my husband and I loved each other and our kids. To earn a respect for each other was very important to us. Today we are still all one big family, now with the grandchildren.

RR: What would you say were the happiest moments raising your daughter Rachel?

NA: Some of my happiest moments with Rachel were during some of our family vacations, our camping trips. Also, I enjoyed watching Rachel with her friends. She had so many friends while growing up. Just watching them interact was always a pleasure because she got along well with, it seemed, everybody. It made me very thankful to see her experience, with wonderful friends, fun activities like having slumber parties at each other's houses. I would say that her school years were good years.

RR: What are some difficult moments you shared?

NA: Oh, when she was in the hospital, so long—forty-five days out of her senior high school year. That was tough. She missed a lot of school, she needed special tutoring, and that didn't always come through on time in the hospital. The tutors would have come, but the school didn't always arrange it in time, and that was difficult. Then to see her go through another surgery—that was especially difficult for us. The good news is that Rachel did make it and did graduate with her class.

RR: What is it that has helped both you and your husband to go through, like any family does, the good times and the bad times?

NA: Well, our faith, of course, and praying through every situation and looking for guidance in everything we had to do. That's the only factor that carries us through. So many people were praying for this kid as she was going through all those difficult physical problems. We were so blessed by the support of her doctor and our friends and family. Following one of her surgeries she had to go back three times into surgery to have that hipbone scraped, and the support of friends and family was just amazing. We couldn't have gotten along without that support. Our church was always there for us.

RR: When you and your husband decided to adopt your children and blend your family, so to speak, what surprised you the most in this entire process of raising your children?

NA: In regards to Rachel, it would be everybody's acceptance of our family just the way it was. But I don't know if there were *surprises* along the way. I think we just sort of went into each challenge one step at a time. We had had all these foster babies; we kept some for six months, some for two months, some for a couple days, and we were also an emergency foster home for another agency. Then Rachel had one problem after another with her physical problems, so we learned to wait each time for months until her problems were addressed. Life sort of happened. The blessing with Rachel was that she became legally ours. There was nothing different from the day she came and we were taking care of her until she was legally ours when she was 5 years old and we went downtown to court to legalize that.

RR: The National Association of Black Social Workers took a stance in the early '70s essentially against transracial adoption.

NA: Did they take the position that they did not believe black children should be placed into white homes?

RR: Yes, they did because of their concern for the racial identity and psychological development of the black child. Their concern was that, specifically, if black children were placed in white homes, that they may grow up with not having a strong sense of who they are as black men and women, and may not have a connection to their ethnic community. Did that position affect you in any way?

NA: No. I think I just led with my heart and not my head. I wanted to keep Rachel. We had had her for three years. You don't just walk away or give her up easily. I could not stand the thought of that, and I just didn't think through those issues addressed by this group.

RR: Do you feel that Rachel's identity was impacted somewhat because she wasn't exposed to the black community?

NA: I didn't think so. Now, when I was reading over her answers in *In Their Own Voices*, I thought, well, maybe it was, to a degree. But it was never a big problem because she did not bring it up while she was growing up in our home. We would see black people here and there, but it is true we had no friends or families that we associated with who were African American. There were none to associate with. When I went to high school in the late 1940s, one of my good friends was a black girl, but she did not live here in South Holland.

RR: Do you think the fact that Rachel did not see many African American people impacted her in a negative way?

NA: I didn't think so at the time, but maybe it did (from reading her answers). Did she tell you that she has had contact with her birth mother? A couple of years ago Rachel saw an ad in the paper that said this agency would help you find your birth family. So Rachel wrote the letter, then they contacted her birth mother, and she said she wanted to meet Rachel too. Rachel went downtown to meet her, and since then her birth mother and sister have been out to our house. (I haven't yet met Rachel's younger birth brother, but I have met her older birth brother.) The older brother is a policeman in Chicago. And just the last time when she went to visit her birth family, her mother nonchalantly handed her a picture and said, "This is your father." There's a name on it, but she doesn't know where he is or anything about him. So that was kind of a plus, to at least have the picture, to have some information about her biological father. I don't know if she'll ever meet him, but a lot of times I have to push her into even calling her birth mother, Pat. I think Rachel should keep that relationship going. For her sake, she's not that interested in it, but Pat is, so she should do it for her sake too. Her birth mother let her go for adoption because she couldn't take care of any more children at the time (at least that's what the case worker told me). I've never asked Pat what the situation was. That's not my place to do that. But I think that it's good that Rachel knows her birth sister too. Her half-sister has two little boys, the brother has none, and there's a younger brother, but I don't know where he lives now—he's in Chicago someplace. I am happy Rachel met her biological family. I would want to know a little bit about my roots, and I think it is good that she does.

RR: Would you recommend that families like your own adopt cross-culturally?

NA: I never thought about that. There's a family in our church now who has adopted two children from China, and it is a beautiful family. And my daughter's friend went to Russia and adopted a baby. It seems there are more international adoptions now than there were twenty, thirty years ago. I think that if we had never had children and if that was a possibility, to adopt cross-culturally, I would prefer to adopt domestically first before adopting internationally because we have so many available children here in the States that are in need of homes. If adopting internationally or domestically is what people feel led to do, then I think they should follow their heart and do it.

RR: What words of advice can you offer to parents who are looking to adopt transracially or are in the beginning stages of the adoption process?

NA: I don't think I have any. I really don't because our situation was different. We didn't have to adopt to have a family, so I never came at it from that angle.

For me, for us, as I expressed earlier in our discussion, a baby was a baby was a baby, no matter what the nationality or race of the child. It was and is the child you are taking care of. When my husband and I made the decision to adopt, neither the race nor the nationality of the child entered into our decision-making process. It was the baby that needed the care and the love, and that's what we provided.

RR: What do you think has influenced you as a mother and a wife to be so open to adopt and foster children of different cultures and backgrounds?

NA: Maybe what I just said and also my interest in missions, and because I have always been interested, especially, in Africa. I don't know if that had any influence or not on my decision to want to adopt.

RR: Have you traveled to Africa?

NA: Three years ago we went to Africa. Two weeks ago I came back from another trip to Africa, Malawi this time. The people that we met were just wonderful, beautiful, gracious, and hospitable people. The country of Malawi, where we visited, is the third-poorest country in the world, but those people are just wonderful, even though they are economically impoverished. Thinking on it, maybe that's where my interest in helping others less fortunate than myself came from.

RR: Growing up as a child, did you experience an event that nurtured this spirit of giving in you?

NA: Reading about the work of missionary Johanna Veenstra and hearing about missions around the world in our church were definitely key events in my childhood that, as you say, nurtured my spirit of giving. I went to the Munster Christian Reformed Church, and I was always interested when a missionary would come to speak, and especially reading about them and hearing about them in Sunday school. I guess just something about their life and work had an influence on me. It may have influenced me in my thinking. How do we really know, though, what influences us all along? All our contacts, all our relationships, influence us to some degree, and I know that just hearing Johanna Veenstra's African story about her work and what she was doing was always of interest to me, so that probably influenced me even when I was young.

RR: What are the demographics in South Holland today?

NA: I think it is 55 percent African American now. But in the schools, like in the grade school where we do the mentoring program, I think it is 98 percent African American. When Rachel went to school she was the only African American then, up until sixth grade.

RR: Finally, tell me today how your family is doing. What are they doing, where do they live?

NA: Kathy moved to Arizona; Mary Ann is the artist in the family, she's teaching art, she does beautiful work, they live in Indiana. Our Lynn works in Chicago, and Kim just told me she was the number one recruiter for Affordable Luxuries [a direct sales company], surpassing the challenges of being deaf in this world. Kim is married and has four children of her own. Rachel is pursuing her college degree and hopes to graduate soon, after all these bouts with hip problems. Once she completes her studies, she will go into teaching. She is also in a steady and good relationship with a wonderful young African American man.

MARJORIE GRAY

GREENBELT, MARYLAND
FEBRUARY 2004

Marjorie Gray is 57 and has two biological children, Christopher and Jean, and one adopted child, Rhonda M. Roorda. Rhonda was 2 years old when she was adopted. All were raised in the Washington, D.C., area. Marjorie Gray was divorced from Rhonda's father in 1990 and remarried in 1998. She is a member of the Christian Reformed Church. She holds a master's degree from the University of Maryland and at the time of the interview was volunteering as an English tutor and at her church, where she had been employed as the director of a senior center. She describes her economic status as middle class.

> *Transracial adoption can work. This avenue can give hope to a child and the possibility for the child to develop into a positive, productive, and inspiring person. I've experienced the commitment of white parents to their adopted child; I've also experienced the commitment of those in the black community, such as godparents and mentors, to an African American child who was raised in a white family. And when it happens ... this joint effort to raise a child ... it is real and it is powerful for everyone involved!*
>
> —RHONDA ROORDA, 27, JUNE 1997

INTERVIEW

RJS: When were you and Rhonda's father divorced?
MG: We separated in 1989; the divorce was final in 1990.
RJS: And when did you remarry?

MG: 1998.

RJS: Do you have any birth children?

MG: Yes. Two. I have a son who is a year older than Rhonda, and a daughter who is eight years younger than Rhonda.

RJS: So, roughly, Rhonda is what?

MG: Rhonda is 34 now, Christopher is 35, and Jean is 26.

RJS: And you don't have any other adopted children?

MG: Correct. I do have a stepson, though, who is a year older than Jean.

RJS: How did you come to adopt? What was most important in your decision to adopt?

MG: I think that right after my son was born, I, we, already had decided to adopt. I had a very difficult delivery, and I had always been interested in adoption, I think because of the idea of family's going beyond the idea of blood family—I got that idea, I think, from the church. Being in the church, and even in the Bible, the idea that the Jewish people were God's own bloodline, but the Christians were adopted into the family, which is a biblical thing. And my father was a minister, and we grew up in a lot of different small churches, but always the people in the church felt like my family. I felt like I was adopted into that family. And yet I wasn't that close to my blood relatives, my brothers and sisters. I was the oldest of five. Also, the idea of interracial [adoption] was always appealing to me because I grew up in Michigan mostly, some other states, but mainly Michigan, and there were no blacks around, but yet I was fascinated. Missionaries would come from Africa, and my mother even told me that when I was 3 or 4, a missionary came and showed slides of small African children, and I just loved it. She said that I said a prayer when I went to sleep to bless those little black children. One of the favorite songs that my parents would always sing was "Red and yellow, black and white, they are precious in God's sight." So I was drawn to that. I did have relatives who were missionaries in China, actually. I think also because of reading. As I got older, one of my favorite books was *Black Like Me* and so I just totally identified with that. When I was 19 or 20 I went on a summer mission program to Harlem, and I also had an aunt who lived in New York City and befriended several young people from Harlem, and especially one young girl. She was sort of a godmother to this girl. It was just always preparing the way, and then my husband also, when he was in college, worked in the inner cities in Michigan with a black church and became very involved in that. But at the time when we adopted Rhonda, we were living in upstate New York, and it was very separate, I think. We didn't see blacks there, either. And it was a small town, but we had decided to adopt. We also wanted our son to have a sibling, and yet I thought I did not want to have any more children biologically. It was very difficult, and I just felt like I didn't want to go that route. I knew that it would have been better to maybe adopt first because, I don't know, I had some second thoughts. Maybe it's too late to adopt, since I've already had one, because I knew that most people that adopted were infertile. Anyway, so we did it, and that's about how it came to be.

RJS: How did you get to Rhonda, specifically?

MG: We went to the county. We couldn't afford any private adoption. The county at that time, the first thing they asked was, would you be willing to take a hard-to-place child? We said, what's that? They said, well, either black and/or handicapped in some way, disabled, or an older child. So I said, and he agreed too, race is no issue, but handicapped is an issue. We just didn't feel that we could deal with that. We felt that that would be kind of a thing where we would feel sorry for the child, and we just felt with our son that wasn't a good thing. But older we also had no objection to because our son was already three by that time and, another thing, having a small baby at that time, I couldn't—I don't know why, being the oldest of five children I had always babysat, but never—I preferred an older child. So she was 2, they showed us two pictures. They showed us a picture of Rhonda who was about to be 2, and of a baby who was about 9 months and who was a boy. And since our son was a boy we thought we would go for a girl. And since she was a little older, we just thought it would be good, and it was.

RJS: Do you think that adopting a child of a different race, did it change you as an individual or did it change your family in any way?

MG: I think it changed me because I think that I thought that I was very progressive, open minded, and everything, but I think that this really was the hands-on. I realized that thinking you are and actually living in the situation where people are going to question this, including some of my own relatives, or act in a very condescending way, that was a whole new thing. So I think it really helped me to mature politically, psychologically, spiritually. And to question my own motives and not just take these things for granted.

RJS: Did it change your family life in any way, do you think, bringing a child of a different race into your family?

MG: You mean the nuclear family?

RJS: Yes.

MG: After a year we moved. We adopted her, and my husband had to fill out his teaching contract for that year, because we adopted her in September so he had already signed a contract, but we decided to move and we applied for VISTA, which is similar to Peace Corps. We had previously applied to the Peace Corps, but then I was pregnant, so we couldn't go in the Peace Corps. So we applied to VISTA and were accepted by them and decided that that would be a good thing to do. But then they told us to come to Washington, D.C., and that they would place us, but then when they realized—I don't know if they didn't realize it before—they thought they could find a place for a family of four, but they couldn't. So we were in D.C. and no placement, even though we were accepted. So then we just got jobs, teaching jobs and other part-time jobs in the D.C. area. We really thought that it was a godsend that we were here because in this area not only were there a lot of blacks but there were wealthy blacks, there were educated blacks, and the church that we went to of our denomination was in D.C., and there were other families who were biracial.

RJS: What is the denomination of your church?

MG: Christian Reformed, which is Protestant.

RJS: As Rhonda was growing up, what expectations did you have about the kind of relationship you would have with her as she became an adult?

MG: That's a good question. I think that at the beginning I had a lot of fears about that. I think I thought, well, we're close now, but I think I felt a little bit leery, that I thought maybe when she was an adult, she would want to live in a more racially segregated area, even. Actually, I thought about that quite a bit because of her close relationship with her brother. I thought for a while that she would maybe marry a white person because she was very close with her brother, and her brother dated blacks almost exclusively at first, although now—he's not married yet—but that's a whole other story. But I think I had mixed expectations about that. I hoped we would be close. And another change it made in me is that many more of my friends were blacks, and I started working with blacks as I got into gerontology. I was fascinated with, I don't know, the whole maternal aspect of the black family and everything. And I had very close women friends that were black.

RJS: Did you purposely seek them out?

MG: It just seemed like my work and where I lived—it seemed like I would get along with them better. I don't know why. I felt like I was actually black on the inside and white on the outside, a reverse Oreo or something. I could identify so much.

RJS: You hinted at this before, but how about Rhonda growing up, how did she get along with her older brother and her younger sister?

MG: Well, growing up, I think the two sisters were in rivalry for the attention of the brother. So they didn't get along that well. And the family itself was splitting because of the marriage. I can't remember details other than the general spirit of rivalry because the brother and sister were together, of course, eight years before the other one came along. And I remember when I was pregnant with Jean, we told them and they were very happy. And Rhonda said I hope it's a girl, and Christopher said I hope it's a boy. But then after she was born, I think maybe Rhonda had some second thoughts about maybe it should have been a boy, because then I would at least be unique. And being the middle child is hard anyway, and then being the adopted child and being of a different race—I think I was worried about that and maybe for a good reason.

RJS: What about Rhonda's relationship with her siblings now?

MG: It's very good. I think she's still probably closer to her brother, but that's partly because her sister lives in Hawaii and has a son, and so it's like she's in a different world.

RJS: Where does her brother live?

MG: Here, in this area. They call each other often, e-mail, and she's his marriage counselor, even though he's not married, if he ever gets married.

RJS: What about your relationship with Rhonda today?

MG: Excellent. It is more of a sister relationship. I have the feeling that twenty years after I adopted her, she started adopting me. Which was around the time she did her first book, I think. It was like she decided, OK, this is the mother that I'm choosing. Part of it is that she didn't even search for her birth mother, at least not much. I was amazed. She even seemed to choose me over her godmother, who she was very close to, who's black, from our church. And it was very good. The whole marriage thing, I got married; the next year, I think, she got married; and we were just like sisters, and we talk at least twice a week.

RJS: Does she like your husband?

MG: Oh, yes. That's another thing. She's adopting him as a father. She called us on our honeymoon—they do get along. He has a son who is several years younger than she, but she gets along very well with him, treats him like a brother.

RJS: And I take it you like Rhonda's husband?

MG: Oh, yes. Very much. They stayed in our home for several days one time. He is quite a bit older than she is, maybe twelve years or something, but I am amazed because I am so grateful that they met because at the time she met him, she was actually on the rebound from a guy who's white. I don't want all this in there—but she already knew Floyd, they were already good friends, they had played chess together, he was her banker, and then they gradually—it's a perfect balance because she is so outgoing and he is more reserved. But she has brought him out and he has balanced some of her effervescence. And I'm just so glad. Because my black friends say, where did she find him? Because black men who are well-to-do and single are scarce.

RJS: As Rhonda was growing up, what, if anything, did you do to help her with her own racial identity, to help her when she came home, or seemed to be confused about who she was racially?

MG: We didn't really do it in a way that was crisis oriented. We didn't wait for her to come home, because I don't remember her coming home saying things very much. But it more often happened at the grocery store, that sort of thing. People would say, "Oh, what a cute little girl, are you baby-sitting?" That kind of thing. I think we just always took them together, our son and Rhonda, to plays, museums, bought books about African American history, associated with people who were black or who had adopted like we had.

RJS: You had friends who had adopted?

MG: We did, which helped. At the church we had two families, it is not a lot, but that was some, and we just—I don't know, clothes, everything— we tried to be aware of it. We just explored that whole history and everything, Martin Luther King Jr., and we saw a play down at the Kennedy Center in the Theater Lab, which was for children, and the folklife festival, we always went down to that. We just always did things as a family, all the music, we went to concerts, festivals. Being in this area was ideal, and being in Takoma Park, which was where she lived from about the age of twelve until she went to college.

RJS: And then she lived with you?

MG: She lived with me her first year out of college—before she went to graduate school in Michigan—she lived with me and worked down in D.C.

RJS: With all the thought and preparation that went into your decision to adopt, what about the experience surprised you the most?

MG: I would say that when we very first adopted her, she was a lady, at the age of 2. She had her second birthday, and the foster family had given her—she came with all these dresses, about ten dresses for a 2 year old, and maybe one pair of slacks. And I'm quite a tomboy myself and then of course having a son—but I put the dresses on her all the time at first, but I remember we had a sandbox and I put her in the sandbox, and she took her hands and brushed the sand off, as if to say, "I don't touch this stuff." But what is even more surprising is how fast she changed when she started associating with my son and with us. And soon she would not wear dresses when she had her choice. She would only wear slacks. I think some of that is still in her, and it is wonderful. Now she has a really beautiful femininity, that she can be comfortable in dresses, and it is very good for her in her business and her position.

RJS: Looking back to earlier times, what's your happiest memory of your relationship with her?

MG: It would probably be recent, because since, as she mentioned in her first book, going through all my own issues with the marriage and everything, I didn't have that many happy ones at the beginning. But recently, probably when I first heard she was going to write the book, because I sent her an article from *Parade* magazine in which someone talked about transracial adoption, and I sent her that and I said, "Rhonda, that's an idea, maybe you ought to—" so I don't know if it was me alone, I think she had the idea herself, too, of writing about it. But then when I heard she was going to write the book, and I heard that it was going to be published, we were so happy. I was happy with her and for her. I thought it was such an affirmation of my whole life. In a way, that adoption to me is more lasting than my relationship with my husband, because I got divorced. But it's a very big thing.

RJS: And what about your saddest moments?

MG: Probably the time when she was in high school and she was being [sexually molested] by this white teacher, and I really don't think I knew how bad it was. Her father did.

RJS: When did you know?

MG: Oh, I knew when her father started taking action about it, and they brought it to the school board, and so I did know and then I felt bad and sad, because I hadn't been more involved in the beginning. Maybe it was easier for her to confide in her father, but I still felt bad.

RJS: It was her geometry teacher?

MG: Yes. He kept calling [the house] and [making] her stay late.

RJS: Did the position that the National Association of Black Social Workers took on transracial adoption's being racial genocide—did it affect how you related to Rhonda or did it make you rethink your decision in any way?

MG: I don't think I knew about it until much later. I did know about it but probably not until after the divorce, when Rhonda was in college. I probably found out about it when I was actually getting my degree, because I went back and got my degree in gerontology, and I was reading some more sociology books and things, and I think that's when I found out about it. I didn't let it bother me because I totally understood it. I had many black friends, and I think that some of them maybe wished that they could have afforded to adopt. I didn't let it bother me.

RJS: Well, now with the new law, they can't prevent the adoption. Do you think it affected Rhonda?

MG: I don't know. Maybe she went through a time that it did. Maybe then she had some doubts. Maybe she thought she would be a traitor if she spoke up for transracial adoption, but now she seems to be pretty fine with it, I think. And one interesting thing is that she goes to a different church than her husband. Her husband goes to a black church, and she goes to a basically white church, where there are only a few blacks. She says that she just likes it better, because it was more like the ones she was in as a child; or because the people are more educated—the people that happen to go there. She's in Michigan, she's basically in a small town in Michigan, where there's not going to be that many educated blacks. But her husband doesn't mind. She says they come home and tell each other what happened.

RJS: Thinking back, with all your knowledge and hindsight and the experiences accumulated, would you have done it again? Would you have adopted a child of a different race, knowing what you know and all your experiences and everything?

MG: Yes, I would have.

RJS: Would you recommend that families like your own adopt a child of a different race?

MG: Yes, but I think they should know that they have a stable marriage, which I should have known, but I didn't. And they should make sure that they are prepared to live in a mixed area and to become, so to speak, one of that community.

RJS: What about Rhonda's relationship with her father?

MG: It has been deteriorating, evidently, recently. But then it has its ups and downs. I do feel a little bad about that. She says it is partly because of his new wife.

RJS: She's from Vietnam.

MG: Exactly. And then it's got something to do about her marriage, too, because neither of us were there, and I did not take offense at that because I was talking with her right along and understood that it was going to be at a time that his family could come and that we couldn't come, because it was at a distance and everything. And we had already met him, and it just didn't work out. But my ex-husband, her father, was quite offended, and also his wife, and they wanted to throw a big party.

But I think that she was closer to him at some times, and that could happen again, but I don't think so. I think it is also because her husband is kind of recycling that kind of looking up to a man, which in a sense

is good, whereas a mother and daughter kind of thing can change into a sister relationship, but I don't think a father-daughter can change into a brother-sister that much. It would be awkward.

RJS: What words of advice would you offer to families who are thinking of adopting transracially, who are in the beginning phases?

MG: I basically would ask them why? Why are you singling out a transracial child, or are you doing it because they are hard to place? I don't know if that is the case anymore. It was the case then, it might be, or because you want to be on a great mission to unite the races, because you can't do that with one. But yet it is a step if you have that vision of a society where people are more integrated. I would basically say talk about it for a long time. Don't rush into it. And then, too, the things I said before about living in an area where there are role models of that race and being prepared for—understand institutional racism, which is still with us.

RJS: When you adopted Rhonda, did you talk to your parents, members of your family, not necessarily to get their approval but just to—

MG: Yes, my parents were very much alive, in fact they still are. They are 82 and 81 and quite close to Rhonda. Although over the years they—especially my father—were quite condescending, and some of his brothers and sisters and quite—maybe even thinking it was not a good idea. So they have come a long way. And my ex-husband's mother was alive, not his father. And they were very close also. She was from the Netherlands. She was very close to Rhonda. She has died since Rhonda's book was published, but, yes, we were very much in with the family. And with my siblings—she is still very close with her aunts and uncles. In fact, one of my sisters has adopted a Korean girl and she is very close.

RJS: What else should I ask you? What would you like to say?

MG: One thing about Rhonda's and my relationship, I think she has influenced me to dare to become a writer myself. I have always kept journals, I've always written poetry, and now I have started to publish my poetry, and she knows I credit her partly for that. So now what I'm doing—because I've written not only poetry, but I've written a nonfiction book I'd like to get published, so I am like her, looking for a coauthor who is already published, because she found you!

RJS: What is the book?

MG: Well, it is a survey of the Bible, actually. It is something that has been done before, but I think I have a new slant on it. So I'm taking writing classes and I'm studying how to do query letters and all that.

EDSON AND JUDITH BIGELOW

ESSEX JUNCTION, VERMONT

MAY 2004

Ed and Judy Bigelow are 65 and 66, respectively. They have three biological children, Ed, Brian, and Hilary, and three adopted children, Susan, Keith, and Khai.
The children were reared in Essex Junction, Vermont. The Bigelows are members
of the American Baptist Church. He has a B.S. and did graduate work in both
engineering and business; Ed Bigelow is retired from IBM and the Vermont Air
National Guard. Judy Bigelow, a retired school counselor, has a master's degree
and did additional graduate work in elementary education and counseling. They
describe their economic status as middle class.

*You've listened to the Old Negro Spiritual, "Ain't Gonna Let Nobody Turn
Me Around"? And you see black people who are on welfare or in a perpetual
state of being dependent on somebody and saying that, "because this white
person has put me here, I can't get any further."... Don't tell me that they
are remembering their history. Don't tell me that they are celebrating their
"blackness."... We need to give our people the knowledge to be successful, not
the message that they are in bondage.*

—REV. KEITH J. BIGELOW, 28, OCTOBER 1996

INTERVIEW

RR: When did you adopt your first child?
JB: We adopted our first child in 1968.
RR: Did you adopt in order to start your family?

EB: No, we already had a family.

JB: Yes, we had three biological children.

RR: Why did you adopt?

JB: Well, it's kind of a long story, but I have relatives who are adopted, and I grew up near a home for unwed mothers, and adoption was always a recognizable way of adding to a family. And then we had three kids who were very healthy and we felt very lucky. This goes way back now to the '6os; in addition to [our] being interested in civil rights there was something called "zero population growth," and we figured since we already had three children, if we wanted more, then we really shouldn't add to the world's population, so we started considering adoption. We went to the home in Burlington, Vermont, and applied with an adoption agency there. Since we already had three children, the agency asked us would we be interested in some child who was "hard to place?" So it was this agency that encouraged us to start thinking about the fact that there were some children who would be waiting longer than others for a home.

RR: You decided to adopt across racial and ethnic lines. Can you tell me about that process, and why you adopted transracially?

JB: We started the process for Susan's adoption, the first one. She wasn't born yet, but the agency knew which children were on the way, and they told us that there was one child who was part Hawaiian (who was considered "hard to place" in the '6os). It didn't seem particularly difficult for us to adopt this baby. We imagined a child who looked Filipino. We didn't really have a clear sense of what "Hawaiian" meant, ethnically speaking. That was Suzy. So we already had our toe in the water. We had started thinking about children who needed placement. Then, after adopting Suzy, we met with our social worker and other parents who had adopted across racial lines and formed a group called Room for One More. We participated in this group for quite a few years. Through this group we would see lists and pictures of children who were waiting. And when Suzy was about two and a half, we decided that we still had room for one more as a family. And we started looking, and that was when we found out about Keith, who was African American [and] in a foster care home in the Washington, D.C., area.

EB: To give you a little overview on this, as we learned by starting and going through the process and paying attention, or having things beat into us over the head there, we were discovering there were kids who needed homes. So our home was not vacant of kids—we had three—but our motivation was more in response to kids who needed homes.

RR: After Keith you adopted Khai.

JB: Yes. And she is Vietnamese. And by now it was 1971, but she didn't come home until 1973. So Keith and Suzy were now 5, and we decided we could do this at least one more time, and at that point the Vietnamese War was going on, and there were baby lists and everything else. We became involved with a group in Canada through which we eventually adopted Khai.

RR: Can you tell me about the community of Essex Junction, Vermont, where you decided to raise your family?

JB: It has grown. It is kind of a classic suburb, I think, now. But when we came back here in 1965, it was not a suburb yet. We bought an old farmhouse because that was pretty much what there was on the market. There weren't housing developments and all of that, which there are now. The population at that time was about ten thousand people. And it is eight miles from Burlington, where I grew up. Burlington has several colleges; it is the largest city in Vermont. It has whatever large cities have, both good and bad.

RR: Ethnically, what were the demographics of Essex Junction when you were raising your kids?

JB: There weren't very many people of different backgrounds. It was pretty white. There were a few black families and other adopted children whom we knew from church, which was one reason we kept going in to Burlington to church.

RR: When you were raising your kids, what were the most important priorities that you focused on?

EB: We focused on food, clothing, and shelter.

RR: What values or what ideals did you want for your kids?

EB: I think the Baptist Church coincided with the ideals that we already had, and that was a way for the kids to get some additional support in the same vein that they heard from Judy and me.

JB: For one thing, we wanted them to feel good about who they were as individuals and also be accepting of other people.

RR: Did race ever enter into the picture as you were raising your kids, from people in the community or your own family?

JB: I think our own families were surprised that we adopted to begin with, and then we surprised them again because we adopted a couple of more times. Certainly, all of our kids were appreciated and loved by their grandparents. One time, when Keith's grandfather was patting Keith on the head, Keith was 4 or 5, he said he didn't like that, so we suggested that Keith could pat Grandpa back—on his balding head.

RR: Would you say that the community you raised your kids in was conducive to achieving the goals that you wanted to achieve?

EB: Yes. And maybe because the folks we interacted with within the community were of that mind.

JB: There were a few other families that we met that were black families or families from India, something like that. Also, that adoptive parent group was ongoing through all of this. Many of the people that we socialized with, we also met quarterly for parties and monthly for meetings to talk about issues pertinent to our situation. For instance, I remember reading the book *How to Raise a Black Child*, which was very helpful to us. We met the author, from Harvard Medical School, when he spoke at an annual conference on adoption in Boston.

RR: As Keith was growing, what were your expectations of him, about the quality of the relationship he would have with his siblings, or with you?

JB: Well, one of things we did with all of our kids, because we had the three older and the three younger, we used to travel quite a bit in the summertime, and we matched them up, an older with a younger, and Keith was lucky. He got Brian as his big buddy and that worked out really well. They were a good pair.

EB: Yeah. We had four hands, and there were six kids so we had to do something creative. So we used the buddy system. As far as expectations, I don't think the expectations were any different for the three that are adopted and the three that were born to us. We expected our kids to be a comfortable member of society, and contribute, and at some point pay their own way.

JB: And of the six children, Keith is the one who has done the best at that. Not the only one—but not all of them have gotten there yet—and he has.

EB: Sometimes I still feel this way: the general question of differences between adopted and birth children—my sense has been that there is more variation between the children born to us than between the adopted ones.

JB: We laugh about it. We say one of the reasons we felt free to adopt is that our firstborn had dark hair, dark eyes, the next one is blond and blue-eyed, and they were both so different.

RR: How would you describe your relationship with your children today?

JB: We just got back from visiting two of them in Maryland and Virginia, Khai and Hilary. Suzy lives up the street, and we just got off the phone with her. Keith is the farthest away. The oldest is coming over to do his laundry tomorrow. Brian, the second son, needed backup last night, so we helped his wife to pick up her car, and it took us four hours. So the ones that are nearby we see as often as we can, and the ones that are away we take the trips whenever we can. And it is always good to see them. It is easier now that they are grown up.

RR: What is your relationship with Keith and his family?

JB: Good. They live far away in Michigan, but we are going to see them in June.

EB: We intend to stay in Lansing three or four nights when we get there. Our granddaughter is in a dance recital and we are going to a birthday party for our grandson, age 3.

RR: When you were raising your children, was race important to you as far as helping each one of your kids to identify with their ethnic background or heritage?

JB: One of the things that I came across while I was doing parent groups with Room for One More was a curriculum put together by a group of parents that emphasized *appreciation of differences* instead of *accepting differences*. The wording is something I've tried to be conscious of throughout the raising of my children. People have differences, and you learn to appreciate those differences.

The first day of school Keith was a little jittery, and he might have been an early ADHD [attention deficit, hyperactivity disorder], but his first-grade teacher said he's such a lovely child, he's always singing. The next time she said, "He can't keep still." One of the differences with Keith was that he had a lot of energy as a little boy. As he's gotten older and more settled, he's found ways to use that. He still has a lot of energy. I have to chuckle—in your book he answered that question, "Did your parents do anything special." He said no. I laughed and when I called him, well, first I said, "OK, I'm going to take that as a compliment," because he thinks whatever we did, we would have done for any and all of the kids. I'd like to think he was right. I'm not sure he was. But I had to ask him, "Don't you remember that I made you a dashiki, and you went to camp with counselors from all over the world, et cetera, et cetera?" And he said, "Oh, yeah." Again, it was part of that adoptive group, that we worked really hard to find ways for kids to see their race in positive ways. We got *Ebony* magazine—and I'm sitting here looking at the piano, and over the piano is the biggest piece of artwork we have in the house, and it's of a black family. I told Keith he'd better take it for his own home now [that] we are moving into smaller quarters.

RR: When you look back at your experience of raising your kids, particularly the adoption experience, what part of that experience surprised you the most?

JB: I think we were pretty well prepared by our social worker and the group experience. One of the things people said they didn't like is that people look at the family all of the time. Well, people looked at our family, too, but I figured part of it was that there were six kids, and maybe they were very attractive kids—not all the same color, but they were very attractive children. We went to Montreal, partly because there was a Vietnamese community up there, and there were also more people of other races up there so people didn't stare at us as much.

RR: What would you say were some of your happiest memories with your children?

JB: I would say traveling with them.

EB: We took tent trailers and did some camping, and we did that to travel as much as we did to camp. One year we went to the West Coast and came back through Calgary. That was neat.

RR: Do you have any memories with Keith that stand out in your mind as far as points where you bonded?

JB: We went to Montgomery, Alabama, together for a couple of weeks for a military school for Ed's Air National Guard duty. We stopped in Plains, Georgia, just after Jimmy Carter had been president, and also Tuskegee. Keith might have been 6 when we did that. I think that was one of the first times that he saw black people as a majority somewhere, and he saw black people of all ages—little children and grandparents, not just children his age with parents our age. I think there was a whole spectrum that was really good for him to see, and for everybody to see, because he didn't have that much exposure to people of color in Vermont.

EB: For a good number of years we kept cattle here, beef cattle, and we raised hay and sold hay, and delivered it with a truck. And Keith was very helpful, and as far as I was concerned, he was a member of our "A team."

JB: His work ethic is very good.

RR: What would you say is your saddest memory with Keith?

JB: When he was a young man and got married and moved to Michigan; because Keith and Magda [Francoise] had lived right next door to us for two years, including the birth of their daughter and her early months.

RR: Would you say that the position taken by the National Association of Black Social Workers affected your decision to adopt?

EB: What position is that?

RR: Essentially, that black children could be harmed psychologically being raised in white homes.

EB: Compared to what?

JB: If there are places within black homes where these children are able to be placed, then that's probably the first option for everybody. But as Ed said, "Compared to what?" I think we both felt defensive and offended by that. We ran into it at a national adoption conference in 1973 when we were in Washington, D.C., and that's when it first hit the consciousness of those of us who were in the middle of adoption.

JB: I can tell you we weren't very happy with hearing that.

EB: I think that they [NABSW] didn't consider the options. Being bounced from foster home to foster home is crap.

JB: We were told Keith was in seven foster homes before we adopted him at age 3. That doesn't sound optimal. I think you lose people in those systems too. If there are homes, children should be there.

RR: So you would say that it did not affect your decision to continue to adopt or the way that you raised your family?

JB: No, it didn't. In fact, well, Khai—her adoption was in process at that time that we were in Washington, D.C., at the adoption conference. We had asked at the agency we were working with in Montreal, I think that was the Open Door Society. We had said that we would like part American, part Vietnamese—whatever that kind of combination of child was possible because they said that the children who were part American were going to have a particularly difficult time in Vietnam. Anyway, we ended up with a child who was part French and Vietnamese. But our original request had not been that.

RR: Do you think that those sentiments addressed by the National Association of Black Social Workers impacted Keith's perception of who he was as a black person in your family?

JB: I don't think Keith thought about the black social workers one way or another. I guess maybe I do not understand the question. As you can see from some of his inaccuracies [in his interview in the first volume in the series] in details of his original move into adoption, it hasn't been something he's spent much time thinking about.

RR: Do you think that the whole sentiment [that he could be harmed psychologically] affected him while he was growing up?

JB: I think he felt pretty comfortable at home, and he's the kind of person who might be comfortable wherever he is. I don't think he was aware of their position. And it certainly wasn't something we discussed.

RR: Would you recommend, thirty-some years later, transracial adoption to other families?

JB: That's something that's very interesting, because once you have been involved in it, you're kind of keyed to look for it, and whether we recommend it or not, I think this area is particularly fertile ground for that to be happening. We know quite a few younger families who have adopted children, and who have adopted across racial lines, where there are children from China, lots of children from Korea, and more and more you see families who have American children of color.

RR: What do you want to share, finally, about adoption and what you've learned, or where would you like to see the social work profession develop in the future?

JB: The three agencies we've worked with have done really good work, and we only know about it because we've helped with it in the past with all three agencies. But they continue to do good work, and we're long out of it. They help support families and kids after they've adopted, with whatever challenges these families may face.

RR: How has adoption expanded your life and your worldview?

JB: We wouldn't be going to New Alpha Church every once in a while, or the gospel fest, or we wouldn't be visiting a Buddhist temple in LA when we visit our young man from Vietnam that we sponsored after we adopted Khai. And we wouldn't have grandchildren of color to enjoy. Yes, definitely.

RR: Is there anything that you wanted to say about the profession of social work or where you would like to see it develop?

JB: I think that the profession of social work is one of the hardest and most challenging professions anyone can do. It is desperately needed. The social workers that we worked with were wonderful. I am sure that the people who have made this their profession have big hearts and are doing their best to encourage adoption within the races, as well as, hopefully, encouraging the opportunity for cross-racial adoption. I feel that one of the things that may have been missed by social workers generally (and hopefully I am wrong) is the support for African American families to officially adopt within the system. I think that unofficially it's been done within black families forever. But I think they need support, whether it's a financial arrangement or whatever. I think there are families of all races who would benefit from adoption, both the families and the children.

EB: In our situation it seemed to be that there were more adoption issues than there were racial issues. They are wondering about gee, where did I come from, and whatever happened to my family and things of that nature, more than the fact that they are from different racial backgrounds than we were. Then the other one, I did read the write-up of Keith's in the book, and there was reference at least once, and maybe more than once, that we're conservative. I do not think we are conservative, but the use of the word has gone on and on. I think it has basically opposite meanings, so it's a word that doesn't mean anything anymore.

JB: Well, we're very conservative with the way we spend money—and what we'll go out and buy. To get back to the adoptions, we were definitely at an advantage at having not just one adopted child. That really helped form some identity within the family—that they are not the only one adopted. And I think it would have been nice—well, two of them are children of color. The part-Hawaiian child you have to really be told that she is part Hawaiian. If people do adopt and are able to adopt more than one, I think it is nice for the adopted child so they don't feel alone in whatever that situation is.

AALDERT AND ELISABETH MENNEGA

SIOUX CENTER, IOWA

OCTOBER 2004

Aaldert Mennega is 75 and his wife, Elisabeth, is 73. They have three biological children, Yvonne, Annette, and Michelle, and two adopted children, Rene and Dan. Rene was 3 months old and Dan was 1 month old when they were adopted; Yvonne was nine years old, which meant that she was no longer living at home during the formative years of her siblings. The children were reared in Sioux Center, Iowa. The Mennegas are members of the Christian Reformed denomination. Aaldert Mennega has a Ph.D. in biology and retired as biology professor at Dordt College; Elisabeth Mennega is a retired nurse-homemaker and a retired employee of a Christian bookstore. They describe their economic status as middle class.

At my worst, I resent the community that demands I deny either side. The truth is, the white community has generally done its part to allow me (sometimes forcing me, through prejudice) to explore my identity as a black person. It is the black community that resents me for exploring my white ethnic heritage but then turns away because I'm different.

—DANIEL MENNEGA, 29, APRIL 1998

INTERVIEW

RR: Tell me a little bit about what motivated you to raise a blended family.

AM: We like children, so when we were in Grand Rapids in the early 1970s we contacted Bethany Christian Services, which places children in homes.

In fact, that was the time we adopted our daughter Rene. We called Bethany and asked if they had any child available. They said, "Yes, but it is a biracial child." We said, "Hey, no problem. Can we come out and meet the child?" So we went there, and she was a gorgeous little girl and right there we fell in love with her.

RR: Did your social worker discuss with you what that would mean for you to bring a biracial child into your Dutch white home?

AM: I don't think they said much about that. We just found out after we brought her home. A year later we adopted Daniel, who was also biracial.

RR: Was it with the same adoption agency?

AM: Yes.

RR: Where did you raise your family?

AM: In Sioux Center, Iowa.

RR: Please describe that community.

AM: Sioux Center is a community that is related to the agriculture around here. It is a small town; I think at that time about 5,700 people lived here, and now it is closer to 7,000. [authors' note: The 2005 U.S. Census estimate was 6,500.] Most people went to church at that time. The community was quite conservative and made up of a lot of Dutch and German people. Basically, it was all white at that time but not anymore.

EM: Bethany asked us, "Are there any other biracial children in your community?" They did not want to place children in our home if there weren't. At the time there was another professor who had Korean children, so that helped our case. But that was one stipulation I remember.

RR: What would you say were the priorities that you had within your own family, as far as what was important to you and your children?

EM: The most important thing was to instill in them the love of God and raise them as good citizens. We gave them a Christian education, and though we all make mistakes, God knows our greatest desires were that they would become good citizens and assets to the community and to this country.

RR: Did either of you feel that by adopting two biracial children that that would impact you as a family?

AM: It wasn't a big deal to us. They were just wonderful kids, and so they were just our kids and that was it. We weren't trumpeting around here, "Hey, we have different kids." They weren't different to us, they were just our kids.

RR: How did the siblings interact with each other?

AM: They quibbled like all kids do—but there was no such thing as, "You're black/you're white." They never said anything like that that I know of.

RR: Do you remember at all, during the time that your children were growing up, where there might have been a race issue, where somebody in the community may have said something to any of your children in a derogatory way?

AM: Oh, yes, yes. I remember definitely one time that our daughter Rene was sitting at the dinner table, and she was quietly crying. I said, "What's the matter, sweetie?" And she said, "Oh, nothing." I kept coaxing her. Finally, she told me that somebody called her a nigger. So we talked about it. I remember telling her that God made her and that she was a beautiful, black young girl, and there was nothing wrong with her, and that she was as good as anybody else. And she felt much better after our talk. That is the only racial incident that I remember happened to Rene. Dan, though, had a couple of run-ins. I think he was a third-grader and a handful of fourth-graders in the school surrounded him. One of them held him down, and the others started to attack him. He started spitting and kicking, and pretty soon a teacher came along and separated them. And when he was in high school, one time some of the guys didn't like him—I think it was a racial thing. So after school they surrounded him, and one guy says, " OK, we'll have it out. We don't like you and here goes." Well, before he knew it, the guy hit his eye, and he had a bloody eye. So they fought until Dan couldn't see because of his bloody eye, and he said, "OK, I give up, I can't see."

RR: How did you as a family deal with that?

EM: I called the social worker at Unity [Christian High School]. I explained why Dan was wearing sunglasses. I said, "You know, I would appreciate it if you take care of this immediately," because those were kids that went to his school. And they did. And I don't think anything ever happened again. I always told the children, "If you are bugged, just ignore it, unless they touch you. If you start reacting, there's a challenge. Ignore it because you yourself know who you are."

RR: What are your personal views toward others with different ethnic backgrounds?

EM: In the Netherlands I think there wasn't this racial prejudice. There wasn't such a thing. Holland owned Indonesia, and we thought those people were beautiful. And we never thought about the fact that there was a difference.

AM: We had never seen black people until 1945 when the Canadians and Americans came to liberate us. We hadn't seen a black person before then. There was no problem. But now there is a problem in Holland with a number of black people having immigrated into Holland, but that was after we left.

RR: So your views on the black community here in America were what?

AM: We had nothing to do with black people because we were living in a white Dutch community in Grand Rapids. But when I was inducted into the army in 1951, then, of course, I mixed with black people. They were just people. Some of them had a strong accent if they were from Georgia or Alabama, so they were hard to understand. But so were the whites from down there. My view is that black is fine and Korean is fine, Chinese is fine. All people are people!

RR: When you were living in Sioux Center and raising your family, were you ever concerned that there weren't many African American families for your children to interact with?

AM: No, not really. We just brought up our kids, and they played with other kids. No, I don't remember ever being concerned about that.

EM: I have to tell you something interesting. Rene married Derrick, who of course was from the black community. And she said to me, "You know, Mom, when I am with you and Dad and the rest of our family, I feel white, and when I'm with Derrick's family I feel black." And I said, "Well, good for you." Her identification is very strong, on her black side. I tell you, our kids love each other. Michelle and Rene are so close and Dan too. To me I could have borne them myself. Dan, too, is so appreciative, so very appreciative. Always, when he calls, he tells us that he loves us. And he's still single, so we send him a package off and on, and we have such a close relationship with him and the same with Rene. We had an anniversary this summer, and she invited a lot of people, and our children made it a big celebration. It was just wonderful.

RR: Have the two of you interacted with Rene's husband's family?

AM: Not on a regular basis but off and on. When we visit Derrick and Rene, sometimes her birth father will be there, so we know her biological father and his wife and their children.

AM: Her biological father is black or half black; he married a white person, and so the kids are biracial. We know Derrick's mom and have met their neighbors. But we are there so seldom that we don't have much of a chance to really get to know them well. We go to Michigan once a year, or sometimes twice, where they live.

RR: What have you learned from having such a wonderful group of kids and some bringing their genetic Dutch heritage with them and some also bringing their African American heritage?

EM: I would say we were not prejudiced to begin with, and I think that we have learned that the blending is wonderful and is very positive and that the love that our children feel for each other is very much of a blessing and that God guided us to do this. We are very thankful. I can look at each of our children and say, "Thank you, Lord, for your gift."

RR: What would you say about the adoption experience that surprised you the most?

AM: It was just very exciting. Our second, third, and fourth kids were one year apart. They were close, but having Rene while Annette was a year old, and then Michelle a year later, it was exciting to adopt the two, and it was kind of a challenge to keep up with those four kids. But they got along well. And there weren't any big surprises, really, not any more than in an all-birth family.

EM: There were some instances, though—for example, Rene was dark and obviously different, and I remember my husband's taking Annette and Rene to the store. And the store owner would fuss over Rene. Then Al would say, "Well, here's another one." Sometimes I think that happens. You can't avoid that. But you can deal with it.

AM: It reminds me of another situation. After adopting interracially, we had faculty members over at two different times. And both of those visitors said, "Well, what are you going to do when they grow up?" They were concerned about having these "different" kids. I said, "Well, when they grow up, we're going to do the same thing you're going to do with your kids." They weren't very happy about this interracial business. We were really surprised about that. We thought that, of course, everybody loves kids and, of course, you accept people for who they are. Coming from white Dutchmen, it didn't sit too well with me. I was surprised that they were actually that prejudiced.

RR: Do you think, given the way American society is, where there is so much division, racially speaking, where you have black communities over here, Hispanic communities over here, white communities over there, that your children were prepared to not only thrive in their family but to thrive in society?

AM: I don't think we ever really thought that through, that they would be thriving in society at large. We just expected the kids to grow up and to go out and live for the Lord and do what is right. But personally, we have no racial bias. We interact with Asian people and Hispanic people and even Dutchmen.

RR: Have your adult kids, any of them, said to you how the world is so different outside of Sioux Center, Iowa?

AM: Not really.

RR: So they've been able to do OK, then?

AM: Oh, yes. They are all doing fine.

EM: Rene could have also originated from India. A lot of people thought she was from India. And I think that kind of humored her. She is a very beautiful person, very outgoing and very bright, and I cannot think of any occasion where people would not hire her because of her racial background. I don't think she ever came across that at all, and at college they both were very well accepted, no problem.

RR: Do you think your son, Daniel, has been able to interact well in society?

AM: Yes. He has both black and white friends. Daniel is a writer for a big company. He is part of a soccer team and is a member of the Austin Singers; and he was a member of the board, and so he is mixing in at different levels of society in Texas.

RR: Looking back, what would you say is your happiest memory with Daniel?

AM: We could make a long list —it would be hard to say which is the best. One of the happiest moments was when the Lord gave him to us.

EM: And it is interesting to us that as a baby, right away, I felt so very close to him. I don't know—there was just something there. He was ours and the same with Rene. And I had difficulty with pregnancies, and so that made me doubly thankful for the others that God gave us. I was on bed rest for seven months with Annette, and I had difficulty with the first one, carrying the baby. And Michelle again, toward the end there were problems. So I think we're not taking children for granted, and we were very grateful that God gave us two in a very special way.

RR: What would be one of the saddest memories with Daniel or with any of your kids?

EM: One of the saddest was when the kids were giving Dan a hard time in that fight. He was not only hurt physically but he was emotionally hurt, and for me that was very sad because that wasn't necessary. We had no idea that this was going on. Afterward, the kids that were involved I think perhaps understood how bad it was. There also was one instance where we were at a basketball game where our youngest daughter was playing, and so our kids were all there. And somebody looked at Dan and said, "Well, I would never want my child to marry someone from another race." But she didn't realize that Dan was our son. At first I was going to give a retort, but I thought, "Lady, that's your problem." That's sad when you feel that way and when you have that fear. But otherwise, Dan has dated some of the girls, and there didn't seem to be any problem.

RR: Have you heard of the National Association of Black Social Workers?

AM: No.

RR: This is a group that in the early '70s went on record to say that white parents in the United States who are adopting black children or biracial children should not do that because it would take these black children away from their ethnic communities and it would allow them to grow up confused about who they were. Do you agree with that statement?

AM: That's not a very wise statement. I would say that the great majority of what we call black people really is a mix. There are very few really black people. So whether they are one notch removed from black or from white really is not important. Whether you are one-half or three-quarters or one-quarter or one-sixteenth or one-sixty-fourth white or black, it is all the same, isn't it?

RR: Do you think that it is important, just as the two of you embraced your Dutch heritage, that your black children can embrace their African American heritage?

AM: I think they are doing that.

RR: How were they able to do that?

AM: They never told us, but the kind of people they have become—marrying a black person and interacting with the families, mingling and fitting in. I think it was fairly natural.

EM: I worked at the Christian bookstore. So if I saw a CD with black singers that was very good, I would buy it for the children, and I bought a CD from a select group last year that I gave to Dan. He was so thrilled because it was a group that really revived all the black spirituals. And so for his birthday we sent him a Mahalia Jackson CD. I have sent Rene some books about African Americans that are wonderful. There is one where a black and a white girl learn to live together in the South after the war. It is a beautiful story, and it is so revealing that there is no difference.

RR: What would you say are the benefits of raising a family in a small town as opposed to an urban area or a more diverse suburban setting?

EM: It was the freedom where we lived. For example, one of our nephews came from Muskegon, Michigan, and he stayed with us for the summer. Dan and he are very close. They would hop on their bikes and go downtown, and they'd do all kinds of things. And when Matthew was back home, he cried and said he wanted to go back to Sioux Center, because he wasn't able to do all that where they lived. And I think our children had a freedom that we would take for granted.

EM: I would like to add that having an excellent Christian school, Christian high school, was wonderful for us as far as the children's upbringing. And having a college community, there were concerts, there were films, and there were a lot of things that were educational that we could take in because of the college.

AM: We also had the children take music lessons—violin and piano—all five of them. So it is part of their heritage now. They were on the swim team so they intermingled also with the public school kids, and that was great. And they did well. They did very well. They were active in sports all the way around. They had a lot of positive experiences. In fact, Dan plays the piano and he wants to go back to his violin. We did not shelter them. We did not protect them from other people. They mixed with all kinds of people throughout the years.

RR: Would you recommend [to] other families to adopt transracially?

AM: Sure, if they are not prejudiced. If they have reservations about people of other skin color, they probably shouldn't. But it was a terrific experience for us. It was a great gift. So if other families could do the same thing, and be blessed the way we have been blessed, then I think it would be great for them.

RIKK LARSEN

BOSTON, MASSACHUSETTS

APRIL 2005

Rikk Larsen is 58. He is the father of four biological children and six adopted children. Tage is African American, Jens is Native American, and the other four are from Vietnam, Cambodia, and El Salvador. At the time of their adoption Tage, Jens, Peik, and Siri were less than a year old, Kari was between 3 and 5 years old, and Christian was 7. The family lived in Cambridge, Massachusetts. Rikk Larsen was divorced from the mother of his children in 2002. He received his M.B.A. from the Harvard Business School and works as a family mediator. He reports no religious affiliation. He characterizes himself as upper middle class.

> *As an African American, being adopted into a white family with siblings from different cultures and ethnicities was really wonderful. The worlds that we were exposed to and the fact that these were our siblings and we loved one another was truly awesome. I loved my brother Peik, who was Vietnamese, and my sister Siri, who is my parents' biological daughter. Anika was white and was my sister and I loved her.*

> —TAGE LARSEN, 27, AUGUST 1997

INTERVIEW

RR: Describe please your family in the early 1970s.

RL: We were a product of our time. We were a liberal upper-class East Coast family, and I come from a family of five, and my wife had come from a family of three, and we were into antiwar and save the world and all the issues of the day. When we got married, we wanted to have kids right away. We were slightly infertile in that it took two or three years to get pregnant, which isn't necessarily that long, but my wife didn't want to wait, and I like kids so it didn't seem like an issue. So we very naively looked into adoption, and it seemed like at that time for every healthy white kid, there are ten families or whatever who want them. For healthy nonwhite kids there are ten kids for every family [or] whatever the proportion is. So we naively thought, well, why not adopt the black kid? and so we did it through an adoption agency in Hartford, Connecticut, where we were living at the time, just before we moved here. So that is how we got Tage. I was 22 when I got married, and I had no idea that by the time I was 30, I would have seven kids. I think the principal reason was that it was extremely easy to adopt before black social workers made it more difficult. And if you don't care about the race of the kids, it is easier to adopt. You can adopt kids from Cambodia and Vietnam, and my wife got involved in the adoption movement, and she helped start an adoption agency for Vietnamese kids. It was very easy to do, and they were lovable little things, and they listened to us, and—I mean this in a positive way—my wife was a professional savior type. She did everything, she pushed hard. My sense, from what I can tell, 99 percent, it was the wife who was the person who was the engine who drove getting the kids in large adoptive families.

RR: You raised your family in Cambridge, Massachusetts. Describe the community that you lived in.

RL: We had been living in Cambridge because I was at Harvard Business School. Cambridge is a wonderful community to be in, because it is very diverse ethnically and racially. We believed in the public school system. All of our kids went through the Cambridge public school system, and there are forty different nationalities at the school, so it's a university city, but it is very diverse, which was a very easy place to raise a large, diverse family.

And we were living in the city so the kids could get everywhere without having to drive so we didn't have to have a fleet of cars when they got to be teenagers. They could get everywhere without any problem.

RR: Was it a conscious decision for you to live in a diverse community?

RL: Yes, it was. And since we were already in the community—we loved Cambridge. I think that we would have moved to a place like that if we weren't there already.

RR: When you were adopting your six kids, from places all over the world, can you think back to the process that you went through when you adopted

Tage, when you adopted Christian from El Salvador, and some of your other children? What was that like?

RL: You had to do a home study for each kid you got, and I think that, I don't know whether it is true today, the process is intensely unhelpful for potential parents because adoption agencies pretend like they are not playing God, but they are. They are judging you, and I think [that], unless you are a psychopath, anybody can hold it together for the hour or two that they are with the social worker. It was ironic, especially when we got down to the sixth, and Pam, my wife at that point, was running an adoption agency, but we still had to go through the process. And I remember once, a social worker, a middle-aged woman, came out, a white woman, to interview us and in the middle of her list of questions was, "Does it bother you that some of your children are illegitimate?" And I have a silly sense of humor. I wanted to go, "You mean, they're illegitimate? I had NO idea!" A crazy set of questions like that—it was ridiculous.

I also think that they were concerned that we had too many kids at that point and how could we possibly provide for them? And I just wanted to say, "Don't tell me we can't do what we are already doing." In general I think that adoption agencies should say to people, you are already approved, and 90 percent of the people should be allowed to have kids—but have the process be helpful just in terms of the questions you ask. Which is, what are parenting issues, what are issues around adoption? Adopted kids do tend to have more issues during teen years than bio kids, and dealing with search [for biological parents] and all of those things that are specific to the process.

Help parents with those issues, instead of all of those silly things. But I have no idea if that is true now of adoption agencies, but I didn't find the process helpful at all. We had a group of families that were like us that we could communicate with and tell war stories to. That was more helpful than anything the adoption agency did, and when it got down to our last kid, the one from El Salvador, it turned out that not only was he not 4, which we had said, but the adoption agency had hired a bandito lawyer down there to find a kid. We were also comfortable with postpolio because one of our sons from Vietnam had polio, so they found this postpolio kid. The first picture we got of him was him on a tricycle, which would imply that he could actually ride the tricycle. But his legs are fully—he could finally walk with braces, but he was severely handicapped. That part didn't bother us at all, but what we didn't know was that he had been sexually abused before he came, and so not only was he three years older, he had been told by the lawyer to put up four fingers when he got here, otherwise we'd send him back. It was a nightmare because for four years he was fine, and then, when he was biologically 11, we thought he was 8, he started sneaking around at night into the girls' rooms, and lots of weird sexual stuff that we had no idea where it was coming from, and through a lot of therapy we finally found out what had gone on back in El Salvador. There was an adoption agency that hadn't done its job. And I think that happens a lot. The issue of dealing with older adoptees is a huge one, and I'm all for it, but I think parents have to be prepared for what are some of the issues that have happened prior to the adoption and start therapy right away.

RR: Adopting transracially, domestically, is a challenge enough, according to many parents who have done it, and those who are observing it. Both you and your former wife, you made the decision to adopt transracially domestically and internationally, and you made the decision to adopt older kids, physically challenged kids. What was it about the two of you that you believe allowed you to do that?

RL: I think we were extremely naive, and we were successful with the kids, we were very successful with our kids when they were little. It was fun, and I was a fully engaged father. I had a business where I could do the carpooling, and I liked to cook, and I liked all that stuff. And we, and this is hopefully true of families that have a lot of kids, tended to take more chances in terms of older, more difficult children, and then what we found is that our family, families in general, are very fragile, and when you have a kid where love does not conquer all, where normal behavioral—parenting behavior—rewarding good behavior did not work with a person who doesn't love themselves, it is extremely difficult. And it damn near destroyed our family, and probably one of the reasons we are divorced now is partly because of that experience. So I think really it was easy and it was fun and we didn't—even when Christian first came, when he was in his grace period—it was simple. And we naively thought that if we spent as much time and energy as we had on the kids, that we wouldn't have issues in teenager-hood, which was very stupid…. [Up] until my father died in 1982, [it was] really simple. We took all nine of them at that point to Norway [before their difficult teenage years]—both my wife and I remembered trips when we were teenagers with our parents, and we hated being there. And we knew we didn't want to take all those kids on a trip [they would hate], so we did it with Tage, who was 12…. It was a really wonderful summer…. After that, it slowly started with the issues of teenager-hood … impinging on us. So it was simple. It was an easy progression.

RR: In *In Their Own Voices* Tage talks about your influence on him professionally and also as a father, but he attributes a lot of his excitement and focus on his classical music profession to you.

RL: I know that and I love it.

RR: My question is how did you introduce him to classical music and also introduce him to the passion that you have toward that type of music?

RL: I think I have sort of a normal interest in classical music. I always played music at home, and I played classical tapes and all kinds of music. But I don't think I am necessarily different than a lot of people. I am glad Tage is giving me all of this credit, but I think what was amazing to me—I remembered being forced to play the piano when I was kid and swore I was never going to force my kids to do that, and he came home with this trumpet when he was 10 or whatever, fourth or fifth grade, and he wanted to play, and I kind of rolled my eyes and said sure, go ahead. I was supportive, but I didn't have expectations that it would take off.

I remember when he was punished for doing something, whatever it was, and I sent him to his room, and he ran up to his room, and he slammed the door, and he started playing his trumpet—that was his release. And that was when I knew, this kid loves the instrument, in a very different way. That was when I first got the hint that he had this special ability.

RR: How did you nurture his talent?

RL: He luckily had a very good music program in his school system, and there were two excellent teachers there who saw his talent and helped him. Then we got him into private lessons and the Boston Youth Symphony and summer camps for musicians. He was a real hard teenager, so every chance we could get to get him out of the house was great. We supported his passion. It was wonderful when he went off to the camp in Maine. He is such a gentle person now, but back then he was a tough teenager, in a normal range of teenager-hood, but it wasn't easy.

RR: What was the hard part?

RL: My belief is—it is a bell-shaped curve—but adopted teenagers have issues that bio kids don't have, in terms of dealing with their sense of parental loss, and everything was our fault. I can't remember specific issues, but he was not an easy teenager. None of the boys were [easy]; the girls were all pretty good. It was a constant struggle with independence and going out and staying out and all that kind of stuff. It's normal, but it is very hard on the parents.

RR: Tage talks about how he was close to his siblings, and pretty much he didn't identify with the ones that were adopted over the ones that were biological—to him they were all his siblings. And he stated that he played with the ones that were available. Did you see differences in your family between the biological kids and the adoptive kids, as far as what they were going through?

RL: I think that from the kids' perspective, it was actually—when they were young—it was cooler to be adopted than be bio because adopted kids had both an adoption day and a birthday, which we celebrated, whereas the bio kids just had a birthday, and the bio kids didn't think that was fair, so little things like that. We also did a thing where we had nights to stay up where one kid would stay up an extra hour, and everybody else had to go to bed. It was a different kid every night. So that was giving the kids individuality. I think the connections they made in terms of playing and who they were close to was really personality based as opposed to how they came in the door. There was always how the outside world treated us. We'd be standing there, and people would say, "Oh, I could take that one," in front of the kids.

And I remember another thing, with our kids there was none of this "coddling" or negotiations…. We could take our kids even when they were little out to a restaurant, and they'd behave perfectly just because they knew they had to. But we would get stared at for all the obvious reasons when we went into restaurants. The kids didn't like that. We had our lawyer, who was a black man, and he said, "You know what I do when people stare at me when I go anyplace, is I go up to them when they are staring at me and I say, 'Hi, how are you doing?'" So we tried that once when we went someplace and found people staring at us. The kids all went over and started shaking hands with people who were staring at us. Boy, did that stop that! It was a fun thing. In the house it was so normal to have multicolor, different kids—it was wonderful. I will always be a racist and a sexist, but I think my kids have had the opportunity to truly be comfortable in a fundamental way with cultural and racial differences. For them it is no biggie.

RR: How did you talk about cultural and racial diversity in your family?

RL: It was just always there. I think [that] if you can remember when you were told you were adopted, it was done wrong. For us adoption was just in the air. In our family we celebrated Kwanzaa and Martin Luther King Jr. Day, and so it was always a messy house, and a community of a lot of differences, and our kids had friends who were different, so it was just there.

RR: You have friends from all different ethnic backgrounds. How did you develop those friendships?

RL: It just happened. If you live in the community with different people, you just do. I think it is personality based—like living in New York City, when you have a diverse community, it is easy to find people, unless you are trying not to, which we never were.

RR: It was natural for you?

RL: Yes. It was very easy.

RR: You had an understanding within your own family that you were a family and it was normal. But the outside world looked at your [family] differently. I know at one of the schools that Tage went to, I think it was the first school that he went to, he talked about how that school didn't really want him there because he was black. Do you recall that?

RL: He was there for kindergarten. And we took him out after that. It is interesting that he says that. They wanted him because he was black, and it was pressure and we didn't like that. I don't know if that is what he is talking about. That is interesting that he said that. For instance, he was in a play group with other adopted black kids right from the beginning—again, partly because it was nice to be able to let your hair down, with other large, multiracial families who were our closest friends at the time, and they had lots of kids who were different colors. So we got together often. We were in an adoption movement so our kids were exposed, probably more than they wanted to be, to kids who looked like them. I remember one of our kids visited a large Catholic family down the street and came back and said, "You know, Mom, it's weird, the Fitzgeralds—they all look alike!" To him it was odd that they all looked the same. I guess it is all in your perspective.

RR: How did you talk to your kids about how to respond if people called them *nigger* or other derogatory names?

RL: We did talk about it. I don't think we had any specific plan, particularly, except to explain why people were doing that, and that it was their problem. And I know it's happened to all the kids. We both at the time, my wife and I, we subscribed to the *New York Times* and the *Boston Globe*, and we listened to the news, and we would talk as a family about what was going on in the world. It came up like all issues did.

We viewed it as a sad part of our world and at a microlevel our kids' school managed those same issues too. Our kids were in an elementary school with a black principal, and issues would come up in school, and they would be dealing with similar issues that we discussed on a national level at home. The first-grade teacher, our good friend, was black, and so I think all those issues came up everywhere anyway. We had friends who adopted black kids and lived out in very white communities in suburban

Boston, and I think it was a little different there for their kids because they were so isolated. They were the only black kids out there. Yes, I think the name calling obviously happened to our kids, but I think because they were secure in their family and were loved that it didn't bother them as much as it would, I think, if you are not secure in your family. I think you can't deal with the issue of whether it is better for kids to be in no home versus a white home. The answer is anybody is better off in a loving home. I had a friend, a black friend, who said, "You know your kids are so lucky because they have a white man who will die for them—how many people can say that?" We were imperfect, and our kids struggled with these issues at times being called niggers, but the great thing is that if you are secure in your own personhood, you can deal with it much better than if you are not.

RR: How does a white man get to a point where he is OK to adopt children, specifically, a black male, that are in the minority group and raise them to succeed and be OK with it?

RL: Part of my own awareness through the process of adopting and raising kids was to come to grips with my own racism. I grew up in a very wealthy New York family. The only black person I ever saw growing up was our cleaning lady. I went to an elementary school where I don't remember any black faces. I went to a boarding school, Choate, in Connecticut, where we had one black kid in the '60s, and then I went to Williams College, which didn't have many minorities. So I was raised in a very, very white world and full of liberal Democrats. But I had virtually no exposure to minorities.

And when I very naively started thinking of adopting in '70, I had no problem thinking of adopting a black kid—sure, why not adopt a black kid? I was stunned, when I went and told my parents that I was doing this, at their extreme negative reaction. I said, "We're liberal Democrats, I can't understand your feelings about this." And then when my wife and I went to racial awareness weekends, and I started realizing, you know, I am a racist, it's part of me and I have to accept that I am, and I'm also a sexist being a white male, and that's the way it is. I will be recovering for the rest of my life, essentially—so I've accepted that, and I've told my kids that. I may not handle issue "X" perfectly or properly, but my attitude around myself and my kids, again, I go back to if you give your kids love and good self-esteem, and they know they got a "white man who'll die for them," you can make up for a lot of errors in what you do. And I think the fact that Tage talks positively about me now, when we had a really, really tough teenager-hood with him, speaks to a normal arch of a relationship.

For me, people say, oh, what a wonderful thing you did, adopting all these kids. For me it has been an amazing self-learning and growth process and hopefully made me a better person. It has been an incredible experience. I know I can never feel and understand what it is like to be a minority, but I think I've got some little sense of it. As I look at my kids, now adults, and the stuff that they do well and handle well, it is pretty interesting. Tage is the first black that the Chicago Symphony ever hired full time. He's the only one. He was actually asked a couple years ago to apply for a seat at the New York Philharmonic, because they were instituting an accelerated program for minorities. And he refused. He said he didn't want to do that because he said he wanted to get in as a musician, not because he happened to be black. And I said, "Tage, Tage, take it! Go ahead, do it!" I was really impressed. So as he deals with being a black man in America, I think there is some wonderful naïveté, I think it is also hard because I think he culturally doesn't feel — I mean, he comes from quite a white world — I think there is probably a discomfort at times with his reality. But ultimately he is able to deal with his blackness.

I look at my son Peik, who had a black serviceman father and Vietnamese mother, he looks black by our cultural standards. Professionally he is head of ground operations for Jet Blue in Boston. He's actually my favorite child now because parents fly for free. So I love him best. [Laugh] Talk about a tough job. He's dealing with disgruntled people all the time and dealing with the broad range of people not often on their best behavior, and he is wonderful at it. I think part of that is because he grew up in a family with lots of issues going on, and he's comfortable with his own skin and is able to deal with stuff. It doesn't mean that it is always easy or isn't a struggle, or that Peik or the rest of our kids haven't had to deal with tough issues, but ultimately it is that they really do stick together. I have five daughters who all live in New York, and they all had their spats and stuff, but they get together. The boys don't have the same sense of camaraderie that the girls do, but they do get together as a group. You can't force that kind of desire to be a family and continue to party together and vacation together, which they do.

RR: You started by saying that when you and your former wife, Pam, initially adopted in the '70s, you had a naïveté. Now it's about thirty years later, and you are still with your children. What is the glue that holds you together? You could conveniently say, whew, I'm done, I'm going to go back into my world.

RL: I think for both of us, even though she and I don't have a relationship, my ex-wife and I, but our kids — I would say the proudest thing we have done in our lives is to create this family. And for me, I really enjoy getting together with them. Yesterday I drove to New York for my granddaughter's first birthday party, and four of my daughters were there. It was nice to see everybody. It is work but it is good work. Their ages range from 19 to 34, and life doesn't always go perfectly. There are issues all the time, but I think it is a priority for me, and I think it is priority for my [ex-]wife, to continue to try and have a good relationship with the kids as best as we can. I enjoy it.

RR: Since you may get married again, do you think it will be a requirement for you that your future wife will be as dedicated to your children as you are, and is that important?

RL: The reality is we've, my fiancé and I, been together eight years now and just decided to get married several months ago. She has one son who lives in LA who is 30. One of the reasons for the delay was, first of all, it was important to me that, if and when I got married again, that my kids be supportive, and that took six years for all of the kids to get to the point where they accepted her. And I was separated a year when I met her, so she had nothing to do with my divorce. Although as a symbol of the permanence of it, she is the lightning rod. That was really important for me, that if I got married again that my kids would be happy to be there at that event.

Ironically it was the biological kids who had the hardest time with our divorce and accepting my ex-wife's boyfriend, and my relationship. I attribute that to the fact that I think adoptive kids have had to deal with parental loss and defining themselves in a nontraditional family, whereas biological kids sort of accepted their nuclear family kind of thing as a birthright, which is kind of fun, doing that. So Anika, the oldest, was 30 and was the toughest. She wasn't going to accept Julie until hell froze over, and finally hell froze over last year. It's a normal process, but for me that was what was important. Julie has one brother who was killed by a drunk driver thirty years ago, so she's an "only child." Her mother is still alive, wonderful woman, and [Julie] has one son. I think part of my attractiveness was that I had this large family, which she likes. I don't think I'd be with someone who wasn't committed to being part of the family or being committed to my kids—wanted to be part of it. That has worked out, I think.

RR: Can you pinpoint when you saw yourself changing as a parent for the better because of this interracial adoption experience? Was there an event that just made it click for you?

RL: I wish I had some specific "eureka" moments. I had grown up in a family with a very distant father. I had no memory of my father ever going in the kitchen. As discipline he spanked me. And I was parenting a lot of ways like my parents did, and I think I slowly learned that that was not right. We studied parenting skills and went to conferences. I think that as I grew older, and the whole concept of accepting individual differences, that I realized part of my internal prejudice was that while I could certainly spout all this verbiage about celebrating individual differences, what I really imagined in the beginning was kind of us or me receiving a Nobel Prize—that's the kind of differences I wanted my kids to have. But when they truly were different, and different in ways that I didn't sanction, or I didn't like, that was a big challenge for me to be able to accept that.

It was a painful slow process in dealing with Christian, who—one of the toughest moments in my life was when his deviant sexual behaviors were coming out and finding out that my daughters barred their doors at night because he would sneak into their rooms. And I didn't even know. I couldn't protect my own daughters in our house. That was a really tough process. It was like, here is a competent person who is successful at everything, both of us, at all we've done all our lives, and we were not able to parent this kid. I learned love does not conquer all, and that there are people with so much damage that you can't help them. And that was a big issue for me. Part of the way people treated us as a family was to put us on this pedestal, this wonderful Larsen family, and it was a little bit intoxicating. It was about me coming down to the point of realizing that I had limits as a man and as a father, and certainly that this kid in the wheelchair had the ability and the power to truly almost ruin our family. It was a humbling experience. So as I look at my kids today, I'm just proud that we survived it. We all have. It's been an amazing growth process.

RR: Tage, in the past few years, has come in contact with his biological mother, and he talks about that in the book. How do you feel about that?

RL: That's something where adoption agencies should do some real serious early intervention with parents who are going to adopt. I feel that if you can't be comfortable with the idea of search, and your kids' having biological parents who they are connected with, you have some issues to deal with. I have ten kids and I can love them all, why can't my kids have more than two parents and love them? It is not a zero-sum game. Traditionally, if adopted kids have had a reasonable upbringing, they view their adoptive parents as their emotional parents and their bio parents, whatever their relationship is, as that. And I am not threatened at all at the concept, and we have encouraged all of our kids to do searches if they could.

The irony is actually that the two, Tage and Jens, who had the ability to actually find their bio parents, were the least interested. It is interesting that both Jens's and Tage's mothers were the ones who did the work to make it happen. Actually, Tage came home sometime when he was 21 or 22, and he said, "I want to go find my mother." He drove down to West Hartford, where the agency was, and he came back three or four hours later, and he was grumpy and he said, "Well, it's going to cost me $200, and I've got to do this research," and we realized that what he had done is he had driven down there, and it was like he expected to walk in to this receptionist and say, "Hi, I'm Tage Larsen and I want to find my mother." And she would say, OK, and pull out a drawer and go through her little files, and say here it is! The idea that records might not be in that building or that it might take some research—it was a little too much work, and emotional issues were raised. It is all very normal.

When he did look for his records, they couldn't find them, and it turned out that his file had been—it was actually in Jens's file, probably because when we adopted Jens the social worker had probably put them together, and they had gotten filed away. At that time it wasn't that easy to do searches. I feel very strongly that a part of your process of... adopting is to deal with that issue when you are starting to adopt. Your comfort level—it is not healthy to pretend kind of that you are not adopting. When you have kids who look very different physically from you, you are forced to deal with the issue of what is "ownership" of kids, and parenting and roles, pretty early on.

RR: You are familiar with the stance that the National Association of Black Social Workers took in the early 1970s. And that stance back then was clearly that this type of adoption, transracial adoption, specifically, dealing with black children in white homes, is not really a successful thing. It can destroy the child, and it certainly can strip that child from his or her black community. What is your view on that?

RL: Yes. First of all, a positive thing was that certainly there were not enough efforts being made to find black families for black kids. In a perfect world, obviously, I think black kids should have the opportunity to be adopted by black families and that that helps spur more outreach by mostly white agencies to find black families. I actually believe that if you are in a loving home, it doesn't really matter that the color of parents is different. I thought it was ironic, because here they were, taking this very strong stand with no research of kids who had grown up in white families to justify their stance. I guess what's happened now is that probably the research results are that it's perfectly OK, and, yes, there are issues, but it is not like it can be proven that black kids left alone in institutions are better off than ones in white homes. Black people should be allowed to adopt white babies, and God knows there are an awful lot of southern white folks who were truly raised by black women and turned out to be fine. I understand their position, but I think it is harmful [if] any kid…is denied a home and an opportunity to have loving parents because of race. In order to be culturally comfortable, you have got to love yourself.

RR: Did their position impact you as a family?

RL: We had adopted our two black American kids before their statement made an impact, and then we had started adopting internationally, so it did not impact our family. Pam got involved as an adoption agency executive and spoke out against their position, but it didn't affect us.

RR: Would you recommend transracial adoption to other families who do not live in an ethnically diverse community?

RL: Yes, I absolutely would recommend it, but, again, I think people should be aware of what their motives are and who they are as people. And that going to racial consultations, understanding all the issues around different cultures, it is harder to do in an all-white community. The key is arming families for the battles ahead, as opposed to judging them as potential parents. That is where the focus should be.

RR: Motives—what are good and what are bad motives?

RL: You can be a good parent with bad motives. People have to be clear about the motives. There is nothing wrong with wanting to have a kid who looks like you. If that is your motive, who am I to say, if it is very important for you? If you are truly uncomfortable with race, then you probably shouldn't transracially adopt. But it should be a decision *you* are making, as opposed to an adoption agency's decision. I know that people are not all the same in that area. There are a lot of people who could be educated and grow to accept and understand what their prejudices are and want to change them a bit in order to make different decisions about adoption and that should be the educational process that happens.

RR: What advice would you give to parents who are looking to adopt transracially?

RL: Be extremely careful when you are adopting older kids, which is not to say don't. But looking at our family—Kari was 3 to 5 years old and is a wonderful person, and somehow she got the emotional and prenatal support that she needed as a kid to become a wonderful parent. You think someone spending that much time in an orphanage would be damaged, and she's not. And then you look at Christian, and he was truly damaged, and he was never in an orphanage. So I think older adoptee issues, kids from Romania, Russia, or China or wherever, you have to be very careful about finding out what the nature and deprivations are of the kid. I think it is the best thing I have ever done in my life, and it made me a better person so I highly recommend it for people. Just educate yourself. The adoption agency will just take your money and help you get your kid; they're not going to be very helpful.

CHARLES AND PAM ADAMS

SIOUX CENTER, IOWA
FEBRUARY 2004

Charles Adams is 57, and Pam is 55. They have two biological children, Charles and Michael, and one adopted child, David. David was 3 months old when he was adopted. The children were reared in Sioux Center, Iowa, briefly in Connecticut, and in Wanaque, New Jersey. The Adamses are members of the Christian Reformed Church. Both Charles and Pam have Ph.D.'s and are professors at Dordt College in Iowa. They describe their economic status as middle class.

> *Growing up I did not feel I could be a black voice living in a white community. I more or less was a showpiece in the white community. If somebody asked me about black issues I would speak my mind, but I didn't feel that I was qualified to speak as a representative of black people.*
>
> —DAVID T. ADAMS, 27, SEPTEMBER 1997

INTERVIEW

RR: How did you plan for your family?

CA: We planned to have a baby as soon as I was working full time. We got married the summer before my senior year in college. Pam was working, she didn't have her degree yet, so she was working for a chemical company in a low-paying job. Since I was going to graduate from college in a year, we planned that the first child would be born sometime after I graduated and started working and having a regular income. It turned out

I started working in June of 1968, and Chuck was born a few months later in October. Thankfully, it worked out pretty well.

RR: What motivated you to adopt your son David?

PA: We became aware that there were children that didn't have homes, hard-to-adopt kids for various reasons. We were also very much influenced by Charlie's mother, who was a foster mother with Bethany Christian Services. I believe she became a foster mother either right before or right after we were married. I remember when we would go to visit her, there were babies at the house, and some of them were of different races. Because of this experience it didn't seem so unusual for us to adopt a child from another race, especially knowing that there were a lot of children in need of homes. Remember, at that time it was in the late 1960s, before abortion was legal, so there were more kids that were available in the foster care system. Another factor in our decision to adopt was that the minister in the church that we went to in Connecticut adopted a son—his son was black/biracial. Our initial plans had been to adopt more children. We didn't, partly because of financial circumstances. My husband was a Christian school teacher.

RR: Did race play a part in your decision as to what child racially or ethnically you adopted and how you were going to raise that child?

PA: I think the fact that David was of a different race, he was a hard-to-place child, particularly because he was biracial. I knew that there were hard-to-place children in need of adoption. We were very young. The idea of adopting a child with a lot of physical needs was overwhelming for us at the time.

RR: How old were you when you adopted David?

PA: Twenty-one.

RR: You moved from Connecticut to Sioux Center, Iowa, is that correct?

PA: We lived in New Jersey after Connecticut. When we first married, we lived in New Jersey for a year, then we were in Connecticut for only three years, and that is actually where we had all of our children, in those three years. First, Chuck was born, then David was adopted, and then Michael was born in three years. And then we moved to northern New Jersey, and that is where my husband started his teaching career. We were there for eight years.

RR: David was primarily raised in Iowa.

PA: Yes. When he was 9 years old, we moved to Sioux Center, Iowa.

RR: Describe Sioux Center for me as far as the demographics.

CA: It was about five thousand people then (now it is about sixty-five hundred). It's rural, located halfway between Sioux City, Iowa, and Sioux Falls, South Dakota. It's changed significantly over the past twenty-five years. When we arrived in Sioux Center, the population was made up of probably 90 percent of Dutch Reformed and Christian Reformed people. Because Dordt College was here, there were some interesting people. For example, one of my colleagues, Al Mennega, whom you also interviewed for *In Their Own Voices*, had a biracial son the same age as David, so those guys became friends.

RR: Would you say that raising your children in Sioux Center was helpful because of the college nearby, as far as introducing them to a variety of different people?

PA: I think having the college in Sioux Center made people a bit more open minded, and I never felt that the community in general was anything but supportive and interested in our family.

CA: There is a residual racism that existed here, and I believe it still does, although it is less than it was twenty-five years ago. Still, Sioux Center was a pretty nice place to raise kids.

RR: What were some of the things that made it a nice place?

CA: The most important thing was that it was a Christian community. Basically, when you've got 90 percent of your population going to two similar churches, and they get along pretty well—people cared for other people, there wasn't competition, there wasn't a lot of keeping up with the Joneses—that makes for a nice place to live.

RR: Did you as a family deal with any negative attitudes because your family was ethnically diverse?

PA: I don't remember anything.

CA: We weren't the only ones.

RR: Did you find, because you did live in a primarily Caucasian community, that you needed to incorporate things from other cultures for your family?

PA: Well, we tried. But, of course, you only know your own culture. I would say even today that the most important part of our culture is being a Christian, and it is not necessarily an ethnic thing.

CA: We were influenced, of course, by the fact that we grew up in the time of the civil rights movement. We went to high school and then to college at that time. And we naturally wanted our kids to have an understanding of the movement, not just David but everyone. There was always an attempt on our part to radicalize our kids. That was really the way to bring them up. Not to conform to the culture around us in any way, that is to say, there are all sorts of different influences in your culture, liberal influences, conservative influences, and our attempt was to try to live a distinctive Christian lifestyle that was concerned with love and justice, not only on a personal scale but also on a corporate scale.

RR: I was raised Christian Reformed, too, and we talked a lot in our family and in our church about loving our neighbors as ourselves. That is a wonderful value I learned, but I found sometimes that, when your neighbors were different than you, it was a little bit more challenging. Did you find that your religious thoughts, perspectives, grew because you adopted David?

PA: I think for me so much of that came together at the same time. All of this happened when I was college age, even though I wasn't in college then. I was introduced to the Reformed faith, and I also read a lot of black literature. It all came together and I think those factors all reinforced each other.

RR: Do you think, as you raised all three of your kids, that you and your husband grew as individuals because of the dynamics of your family?

PA: Sure.

CA: If we hadn't adopted David, for example, our interest in issues of justice, particularly racial justice, probably would not have developed as it has. It is so easy to forget all these things that you are enthusiastic about in your youth. But when you embrace them in such a way that they are going to be with you the rest of your life, you don't forget about them.

RR: Looking back on when you raised your kids: Are there events that are poignant in your mind now that illustrate how you addressed issues about race?

CA: Yes, in a way. Because David was part of our family, we were more aware, more sensitive, to racial issues, on a larger scale and certainly more aware of what was going on a smaller scale. The little bit of discrimination that David might have experienced, and it was very small, we took that as an opportunity to talk about the issues; and I think we raised our kids to grow up with a strong sense of biblical justice and social justice to combat prejudice.

RR: As your children were growing up, specifically David, what were your expectations about the quality of the relationship you would have with him?

PA: It was just like it was with the other kids. We never felt any different. We were certainly reminded at times that our child was adopted, but for the most part we didn't think about it. We treat David just like we do the other kids, so we expect the relationship would be the same.

RR: Were there differences in interests? I know that, like with my family, my brother and I are very close, but I have some strengths that he doesn't have and vice versa or things that he might be interested in, and I'm not. Did you see differences and how did you accommodate?

CA: We had three very different kids. They were very different all in their own ways.

PA: Even today as adults, they are three very different kids—adults. But, you know, I had my children and I went back to school, and I became a classroom teacher. I think that having three different kids and having an adopted kid made me much more sensitive as a teacher as well. Realizing that kids are unique and different and they're not clones of their parents.

RR: What is your relationship with David?

CA: Good. The only problem with our relationship is that David and his family are out on the West Coast, in Washington. And because their youngest son has a medical disability, they really can't travel, so we go out there. So that limits the amount of time we share with him and his family. We have another son who is in Wisconsin, and we see him and his family a little bit more. And the one up in Sioux Falls is only fifty miles away.

PA: Yes, we see them a lot.

CA: So we would like it to be a little bit more even, but it's a problem of geography.

RR: What helped you to stay engaged as your children grew and went their own separate ways?

CA: There is no question that the most fundamental force that held us together is the fact that all of us are committed Christians. That's the basis of everything, and that has really been gratifying when there have been problems here or there with any of our three sons and their families—like sickness and health concerns. Our faith in God and commitment to each other seem to be still the rock that holds our family together. We pray that it will continue that way, and we have been blessed so far.

PA: Charlie, you didn't mention the most important part, though, the grandchildren.

CA: In talking about David's kids, one of the things that I think we are most pleased with is the way in which David has been able to function—he was a little wild as a kid—and now is a wonderful father. All of his kids have been brought up with a sense of secure love and home. Of course there are a few things that might be excessive, like his children playing too many video games and that sort of stuff, from our point of view. Yet our relationship with David's family has really been a strength. His kids are the oldest, and we have really had some fantastic times with those kids, even though we haven't seen them quite as much as we've seen, maybe, some of the other grandkids. But when we've been out there it's really been—still the best times of all, if I had to pick them all out, were . times with those kids. I can remember a weekend that we spent tromping around Point Roberts, a crazy place that comes down out of Canada, yet it is still part of the United States, and you have to go through Canada to get to it, which was quite an experience for all of us.

RR: With all the thought and preparation that went into not only adopting your son but also raising your son, what would you say is the paramount event or point in that experience?

PA: The day both Luke, our oldest grandson, was baptized in the church and David made his profession of faith was particularly poignant to me. It was an intense feeling because Luke was our first grandchild, and David was quite a young father. And I'm a real teary-type person. I just bawled and I bawl now just thinking about it.

RR: What was one of the saddest moments?

PA: When he came to us and said they were going to have a baby, and they weren't married yet.

RR: How did you work through that?

CA: I was debating whether to answer your former question—what was the best and most important point—with that answer, because David came to my office and it was an extremely emotional time, but we both knew, I think, because we have a grounding together in Christ, that we couldn't be phony with each other. And that there was a real need here, regardless of what happened in the past. I said to David that we were going to help him out and that we were going to work through it. Because I believe he knew the seriousness of the situation, which I could tell by his face as he sat there in my office. I sensed that he knew too that he was in a helpless situation in a way. At that moment I felt very much, maybe more, love for him than I can imagine any other time. I felt that here was the opportunity to be who I am called to be—a father in that situation. It wasn't a comfortable thing, either. So in one sense it was very positive but also, I don't know how to describe it—not really sad, disappointing, yes, maybe that. It was a combination of things—but it was very pivotal.

RR: Can you think of another pivotal point?

PA: We never experienced any other crisis to that level when they were kids.

RR: Growing up, I enjoyed the times with my family when we went on picnics together and went camping. Were there activities as a family that you enjoyed together?

CA: Pam and I invested a lot of our time in the academic arena. You could say we were workaholics. So the few times we did vacation as a family were special. [On] one occasion our family enjoyed time together at a lake up in Minnesota. Another highlight was time we spent getting to know our extended family. We vacationed with my brothers and parents in Wisconsin, also at a lake. When Pam couldn't go on one trip, the kids and I went with a single colleague of mine and a boy David's age, for whom my colleague was serving as a Big Brother. It was good that David had someone his same age. But, yes, those kind of events, where they got to know their cousins and uncles and aunts, were really formative. My brother Bud, for instance, is a different kind of guy. The rest of us in my family all have college degrees, and Bud didn't go to college. He has a wonderful family, and he's just been a wonderful father with his three daughters and his son. He also is a very caring guy and would communicate with Dave quite a bit too. I think David and the rest of our kids felt a sense of belonging from the rest of our larger family.

PA: Our kids also have a good relationship with their grandparents.

RR: Many people may not have your experiences as far as raising your family in the location that you did and with your values. Do you have any words of wisdom to [pass along to] young parents who've just adopted biracial, African American, Latino children [and] who are a little apprehensive at this point?

CA: My words of advice are just to be yourself, and don't let your situation be dictated to by the culture.

RR: Can you explain that a little bit more?

CA: There have been a lot of changes in our culture over the past thirty-five years, from the time we adopted David, for example, which was just shortly after the civil rights movement. Adoptions were very, very different back then. They were private. We never had any contact with the biological parents or anything like that. That's changed a lot. There's been an enormous change with respect to the expectations of racial groups, which to me is a form of racism—when you expect that, because of the color of a person's skin, they've got to be raised a certain way. Our culture, because of its narcissism, its egocentricity, which functions on both an individual and a communal scale (and that is racism, whether it be white racism, black racism, or whatever), tries to tell people that they have to live a certain way or be a certain way. So my advice is be yourself. Don't listen to any of that stuff out there. Your responsibility is to raise your family before the face of the Lord, in love and security, and in resistance of the culture. You have to resist.

PA: Well, it's right to at least try to do that. I'm sure we didn't do everything right for any of our children. You try to be the best parents you can possibly be, but that's always flawed. But I wonder if we had stressed more the fact that David was racially different if that would have been good or bad. I think it would have been bad.

RR: Why so?

PA: Because he felt very secure, and we did try to teach him about African American heritage, because it was something I was interested in. But I think if we had tried to make it such a strong point, constantly hitting him over the head with it, I don't know. Little children are sort of unaware of that kind of thing. It's just who they are, and if they are loved by their parents, they don't even notice differences until they get a little bit older, and by that time, hopefully, they are fairly secure and they can deal with those differences. I have a friend who has two biological children and two adopted Asian children. She's asked her little boy, who is Asian, do you look more like your sister, Zoe, who is Asian, or do you look more like your brothers (who are white)? He identifies with the boys. He doesn't see the racial part at all. He's a boy like his brothers, not a girl like his sister. And I think if she'd tried to push him, at this very young age, with the fact that he is Asian and different than his brothers, I don't think that would be all that healthy.

RR: When you adopted David, were you aware of the discussion happening on the national stage against transracial adoptions, led by the National Association of Black Social Workers?

PA: No, we weren't. I think we became aware of this quite a few years later.

RR: And what were your thoughts on their stance?

CA: I think it is an example of racism.

PA: I don't fully agree with their perspective. I do, however, sometimes tread a little softly because of it. We adopted David for certain reasons, and consequently some people have difficulty with that. They're allowed to have their opinions too. We did it, though, without thinking so much that black people would have difficulty with us adopting a black child.

RR: Did it affect you one way or the other, the fact that some people in the African American community, or other people, may have had a problem with your adopting transracially?

PA: Well, of course it affects us. We don't want to do something that's going to hurt anybody, and if it is hurtful to some people, then obviously it affects us. We may not think they are right—but you have to be careful.

CA: Yeah, but you must be the light too.

PA: True. However, the danger is if you think of yourself as this "white savior"—going out rescuing all these little black kids. We didn't do it that way. For us it was a matter of kids needing homes. But I can understand the NABSW's position to some degree.

CA: In a hundred years from now there's not going to be any black, white, because we will have sufficiently intermarried, and it is not going to be an issue anymore. It is going to be an historical occurrence.

PA: Still, I think you need to be sensitive to one's cultural identity. White people have adopted Native American kids, and that has somewhat taken away from Native American culture because there are relatively few Native Americans left. If they, the children, are taken away from their cultural community, their culture is decimated to some degree, and so is the community.

RR: And what is your view on the value of a culture?

PA: I think that people have a right to have a culture, but at the same time the individual is very important too. And if a child could be placed either in a foster home or in a good Christian home, regardless of one's culture, I would certainly opt for the good Christian home.

CA: Cultures are not equal. You can really go in the wrong direction with this, by norms. There are norms for how you relate to your kids, you love your kids, right? So if you have a culture that destroys their female children at birth, there's a problem with that culture. It is an antinormative culture, at least in that sense. And if there are other kinds of deeply ingrained antinormative values in a given culture, then you can begin to look at a culture as being more fragmented than another culture.

RR: What is the balance?

CA: There are issues for both the individual and for the community. I think individuals need to be given opportunities to grow and blossom, and so do communities. That could mean cultural communities that need to grow away from certain ways of doing things because they are antinormative, like killing their baby girls. And grow in other ways that are positive and unique for that community. You've got to find that balance.

RR: And you believe that your family had that opportunity to blossom?

CA: Yes, by the grace of God. I am not suggesting that our family somehow had everything right.

RR: Given the way you raised your family, would you recommend transracial adoption to other families?

PA: Yes, and I have. There are quite a few professors at Dordt who are adopting transracially right now. It's kind of popular.

RR: Do you know why they have chosen to adopt transracially? Is it for the same reasons you adopted David some thirty years ago?

PA: They have biological children, too, and they just want the children to have a good Christian home. I would say it is the identical reason we did.

DAVID AND LOLA HIMROD

EVANSTON, ILLINOIS

FEBRUARY 2004

David Himrod is 66, and Lola is 61. They have no biological children and one adopted child, Seth. Seth was 4½ months old at the time of his adoption. Their home is in Evanston, Illinois, and they are Episcopalian. David Himrod has a Ph.D. and is a retired reference librarian. Lola Himrod's Ph.D. is in clinical social work, and she is a part-time school social worker. They describe their economic status as upper middle class.

My experiences growing up with my family have helped me not only socially but also in my career choices. I'm able to deal with people in a variety of cultures. I can talk with rich white Americans, I can talk with rich black Americans. I can talk with middle class whites and blacks, and I can talk with poor people.

—SETH D. HIMROD, 27, MAY 1998

INTERVIEW

RR: You adopted your only child, son Seth. Can you tell me about the events leading up to that step?

LH: It was in the fall of 1970 and the winter of 1971. I was working as a social worker for a county agency in Los Angeles at the time. My husband and I became interested in adopting a child. In order to begin the process we needed to go to an agency other than my own. The rule was you could not adopt through your own agency, so we went to a private agency in the area, a well-respected one. One of the questions they asked us was what kind of child are you interested in? We said we were interested in either a boy or a girl but had more experience with girls and that we did not care about the child's race. We did feel at the time that we probably would not be real good with a child with serious health problems. Because I was aware of the statistics and demographics of children in the child welfare system, especially in California, I knew it was more likely that we would get a child that was a boy of a different race than ours.

LH: Another factor was that Dave was finishing his doctorate and was looking for a teaching position. At some point in the adoption process he was offered a job at Northwestern University in Illinois, which was promising, but we knew that meant we were going to leave Los Angeles in the near future. Given our time frame, it became even more certain that the agency was going to find a mixed-race child for us.

DH: Well, one correction: after a long discussion Lola said to me, "I think we should get a boy so you could have a son."

LH: I did?

DH: Yes. And then the agency had to go outside of California to locate a boy.

LH: To put this in context, in Southern California then, the county agencies were doing what, at that time, were experiments in different kinds of adoptions. They were letting single parents adopt and created programs to encourage and push adoptions in the black community. So that really had reduced the number of *infant* children awaiting adoption in Los Angeles, leaving increased percentages of older children in the system. We specified that we wanted an infant. The agency we were working with had formed a compact with other independent agencies from states that had similar adoption laws to place children with special needs. That increased our access (and other families', too) to children awaiting adoption with our specifications. At the end of the process we were blessed to have a baby boy who was biracial. Our son, Seth, was what I would call a "primo" baby. Had he been born in Southern California, Seth would not have been 4 1/2 months old by the time he was placed for adoption. He would have been placed as soon as he was relinquished.

RR: Why did you choose to adopt?

LH: We needed to adopt. We had been told we would not likely have children of our own.

RR: Did you want to have a white child?

DH: Not necessarily.

LH: It might have been naive of us, but we really didn't feel that the child's race would make much difference to us.

RR: What was your background prior to your adopting Seth?

DH: We had been involved in inner-city churches in Los Angeles throughout the '60s, and I eventually became the minister of one of them. The year before we got Seth, we lived in a mixed-racial area, with younger African American couples and older white women who were widowed.

LH: At the inner-city church where we previously had been involved, we had made friends of a variety of races, with African Americans and people of color from various countries, and we were comfortable with that. In the 1960s there certainly had been a lot of civil rights activity, especially at the national level. While we had not marched in the South or registered voters or anything along those lines—we had been involved in our own way through the people we had participated with in Southern California.

DH: We helped open up neighborhoods to minorities disenfranchised by major redlining in California, along with participating in other civil rights activities on a local level. Yes, we hadn't marched in the South, but we had been active in our community in Southern California.

RR: Against that backdrop, how did the story begin with the new addition to your family?

LH: Seth was flown to California from Texas, where he was born, and we brought him home. Seth was an attractive child. He was half African American and half Anglo. About six weeks later we moved to Evanston, Illinois, where we still live.

DH: We were very lucky back then, because the apartment that we got through friends was in a neighborhood that was racially mixed. In fact, this particular neighborhood has always had an ethnic mix.

LH: Interestingly, that apartment is in the same general neighborhood as our present house that we have lived in for about twenty years. Someone back in the early 1970s did a survey that said the school population in our community was made up of 30 percent Anglo, 30 percent Mexican, and 30 percent black, or African American. I think it has changed somewhat since then, but it has maintained a lot of the mixture. Evanston is a suburb of Chicago; it is made up of about eighty thousand people. It's a very urban suburb, and it has Northwestern University. Northwestern is one of the major employers, so there are a lot of highly educated university types in this community. It also has a lot of old money. I think it has less old money now than it did when we moved here. The City of Evanston has sections where people have a very high income; it also has a section that was primarily, if not exclusively, African American; that was originally where the servants that came to Evanston lived. And of course the black population has changed a lot, and in Evanston now there are Caribbean blacks and others have moved in. But it is a city, I would say, probably in some ways an ideal city, to come to with a child like Seth.

RR: When you were raising Seth, do you recall any moments in that process where you were stretched?

LH: I remember early on when Seth needed a haircut, trying to decide where to go to get a haircut in this town. At that time in the early '70s the barbershops were not mixed. You had to either go into the black community to do black hair, or you went downtown; they didn't do black hair downtown. Actually I think that is how I got started cutting his hair myself. I was too shy to pursue any other alternative then. However, one time I did take Seth and his friend Jimmie to a black barber shop to get their hair cut. I found that experience to be somewhat uncomfortable for me, partly because I didn't have any friends close enough when Seth was little that were African Americans to say to one of them, take me with you! Sadly, we had lost our black friends when we moved to Evanston, and it took us a while to make new friends that were African American. I know we were also stretched by simply seeing how people saw us as a family. Seth was very light skinned when he was little, and I noticed that when white people saw him, they perceived him as just a cute baby. But African Americans always seemed to know that he was *African American*. And sometimes I felt like I was getting strange looks from them. Another challenge we faced was that when we enrolled Seth in school, we were asked to register our child by race. What do you do? And of course that is a whole issue in Evanston right now, again. And No Child Left Behind has made that a big issue in some ways. What do you put down? Do you go along with society's version of this?

I think the biggest difficulty—the racial impact—that we were aware of when he was young was when we took him on a visit to Texas when he was 3. We had some friends who had moved from Evanston down there, and we went to visit them and the adoption agency that we got Seth from. Immediately, we were very aware of the many stares that were directed toward us. Nobody directly approached us, but we were aware that the climate was different in Texas than it was in Evanston. For example, we had never traveled in the South with Seth when he was young, because we weren't sure that the climate had changed enough to be open to white parents raising a black child.

RR: Given the obstacles you faced as a blended family in your community, where did you go for help?

DH: Lo joined a play group when Seth was little. It was composed of other white families who had adopted mixed-race children; that was a help. We discovered that we could share resources with each other.

LH: I think about what else would have been helpful when he was little. I guess I would have liked, for my own sake, to have had some more African American friends, and I probably could have pursued that further. At the time I was a stay-at-home mom. The church we went to was affiliated with the university, and I am not quite sure how I could have found African Americans. I don't think Seth was harmed in any way. I think when he went to school, it helped being in this neighborhood, and it was very important to us that he go to the local neighborhood school, where he and we could have contact with teachers and other families. There were even a few families in those days that were mixed families. So we felt it was very important for that type of family to be as natural as possible for him. Seth tells us how little emphasis we put on his racial background—how he didn't really learn about black history until he went to high school and took a class. I think in a way that surprised us because we had tried to make him aware of his culture.

RR: How so?

DH: We read him storybooks about his ethnic heritage.

LH: Yes, maybe instead of making him aware of his heritage, though, reading these books made him feel more that it was OK to be him[self] as an individual. Today I think that there is still relatively little emphasis on African American history in our schools, but there is a lot more than there used to be.

DH: Our grandson is learning more in school about African American history.

LH: And certainly I have attended Martin Luther King Jr. Day celebrations at my grandson's school, which is the same elementary school that Seth attended. I think that in Seth's early years we just tried to be aware and keep him around as many varieties of people and to make him feel that his color and background et cetera were as mainstream as possible, and that it was all right for him to be him.

RR: What were the values you wanted Seth to embrace?

LH: We wanted Seth to be honest. We wanted him to be kind; we wanted him to be happy. We wanted him to be caring. We wanted him to try hard in life—he certainly picked that up, even more than we intended.

DH: We also wanted him to have a sense of justice and injustice but not be angry about it, I think. Be aware of it, and work toward justice.

RR: In Seth's interview he does talk about his strong relationship with both of you. Specifically, he mentions that he felt comfortable to talk with you, David, about what he was experiencing in society as a young black man [racial profiling]. What did you two do to make him to feel comfortable to share his inner struggles?

DH: My relationship with our son was more difficult in some years, say, in middle school, than it was later on. I would attribute our relationship now in part to my being a good listener.

RR: What has allowed you to be and remain committed to Seth?

LH: We really love him. Also, family and connectedness are very important to us. Just as important is our understanding about adoption—that it's like a contract: it needs to be renewed over and over again.

RR: Can you explain that?

LH: Seth never openly processed (to our knowledge) what it really meant for him to be adopted. He knew early on that he was adopted. We had pictures of him as a baby; we told him the story about when we adopted him. Even when he looked at the pictures in his book of our family, it was clear that we had adopted him. Yet there would be times in which, particularly when he would do something that he thought was maybe against our values or that we would be unhappy with, that I think he may have questioned his adoption. On one occasion that I can remember, he basically offered that if we were too disappointed in him, he didn't have to be our son any longer. That was the most overt expression of it. And it was important to tell him that these things happened in families, and of course we were upset, but we would all work through it together. I've seen adopted kids do this before, where it is real important for them to figure out who they are in their family. Maybe they look different, maybe they feel different, and maybe they feel they've disappointed their parents. They need to know that you still want them to be your child. I don't know if this happens in biological families. I know it happens in adopted families. We wanted to affirm that Seth was our son and an important part of our family.

RR: And now that Seth is a grown man and married with children, would you say that your expectations are consistent with who he is as a person?

LH: Let me say one thing further about the previous question. Just as the child needs to know that you love them still, that you want them, that they are part of the family, that also is true for the adoptive parents—particularly as their child becomes a teenager and a young adult, you need to know that they really care for you as their parents, that they have as much love for you and want as much closeness to you as you feel for them. I remember that when I felt that, when I felt confident that Seth did love me, that I was important to him, that I was his mom, regardless of his relationship with whoever, it really solidified things for me. Now Seth has his own life, his own family. He still lives geographically close to us, and we see him a fair amount. But it is not at all the same as it was when he was a little kid.

DH: But we still have the washing machine!

LH: I wonder, sometimes, if we didn't have a washing machine, how often we would see him. Currently Seth and his family live in an apartment, and they can't use the washers in the apartment, so Seth uses our washer. In addition to those visits, we do see him other times. Certainly if we call and ask him for help on a project, he's quite willing. And we go to the same church. He and our grandson, Tim, come to our church, and Seth's wife, Lisa, and the girls go to her church. So we see him there. We make a point, even if we don't have occasion to get together, we try to see the grandchildren at least once a week. So we have a connection. He's in his early thirties—he's young enough so that we're still kind of getting used to this, what is an adult child-parent relationship supposed to be?

DH: And every once in a while I say, "He's really growing up," somewhat in amazement and also in admiration.

DH: And I think the fact that he had Timothy when he was so young (and was a single father for a period) kept him closer to us longer, in the sense that he needed more from us longer. And so he's finally growing up.

RR: He married an African American woman?

LH: Yes.

RR: And, as you mentioned, you now have grandchildren. With an added layer to your family circle, has that impacted your comfort zone in any way?

LH: For me in some ways it has had more impact than when Seth was little. Many times, when I take the girls out in a stroller for a walk in the neighborhood, we see other children, and they are very curious about the color difference between me and my grandchildren. And I would explain to them, these are my granddaughters (this was before the girls could talk). And they'd look quite puzzled. "You're their grandmother?" they would ask. It gives me a little bit more insight into what it must be like for African Americans in majority settings. I wouldn't say this experience has brought us closer to the African American community, for instance, we don't have a whole lot of contact with Lisa's family, but it has certainly given us a different viewpoint, a window. I can only say that I am sure the adventure will continue.

DH: To give you some background, Lisa's family is a large extended family in Evanston. And because it is so large, it tends to be kind of ingrown, because everyone they know and get together with seems to be part of the family. I, more than Lo, have been to several Fourth of July barbeques and various activities like this with Lisa's family.

RR: How does that make you feel?

DH: I'm getting used to it. But it is always a little different—Lisa's family is very welcoming and everything—

LH: We're the token whites.

RR: Tell me about your most exciting moment with Seth?

LH: It was probably welcoming him back from the Gulf War.

DH: My favorite picture is one that was taken when he came through the gate of Chicago's O'Hare airport.

RR: This was in 1991?

LH: Yes—about March. He'd been suddenly called up back from a leave in August and very shortly was over in Saudi Arabia and was there until March of 1991.

DH: And then in Iraq.

RR: What was one of the most challenging moments you experienced as a family?

DH: When we suddenly learned about our grandson, Tim. Tim was 3 months old before Seth learned about him. I learned that Seth had a son about a week after he did. And he apparently learned about it the night of his prom, when Tim's biological mother told Seth that Tim was his son. When Seth saw Tim, there was no doubt in his mind that he was the father, because Tim looks very much like Seth. A few days later, then, Seth told me he had a son. It took me about a day to react to the news. In those days, when we would have quarrels or were upset with each other, Seth usually went into a silent phase and didn't speak for a week, and then we would slowly come back together after that week. That is what happened in this situation.

LH: A big part of our concern was for our son's future, knowing that having a baby would affect him the rest of his life, which it does. Inwardly, I struggled. I questioned myself as to whether, had I been a good enough parent, this wouldn't have happened. Once we got to know our grandson, and then later when Tim came to live with Seth, we became very involved with his life for several years. Now that Seth is married, we are still involved but in a different way. We love Tim, and he is a wonderful child, and we are very happy that he is in the family. Given the circumstances, we wished it had been different, but we're so glad to have Tim.

RR: What is Seth doing now?

LH: Seth is working as a sanitation worker for the City of Evanston. He had been working in financial services but changes in the economy and various other factors—like affording health care insurance for a growing family—made him change his career direction.

RR: Do you believe you have successfully prepared your son with the foundation to make it in this society, to thrive in this society?

LH: I think so. Given that all parents make mistakes, one of the things that I feel good about, from what Seth says, is that he is able to walk the line between races. For one example, Seth shared with us that some of the men he met in the army were black soldiers who were very angry at whites, and he was able to say to them that not all white people are the monsters you think they are or that your experience has suggested. (Seth certainly didn't deny that these soldiers confronted racist behavior from some whites.) He said he knew, because he grew up with us, that not all whites are the same. And certainly as a black man he has had his own experiences with white society, and yet I have this sense that he is very comfortable going between both societies, which I think is one of the benefits of black or biracial children adopted into white families. I know that biracial children are black, but one of the benefits that they have in this society is that they can walk, hopefully, between both cultures.

RR: By adopting Seth do you think that you gained more of an insight into race issues in this society?

DH: Oh, yes. Seth used to say when he was in high school, there were four types of groups: the black kids who only interacted with other black kids, black kids who knew and had some friends in the white community, white kids who had a few friends who were black, and white kids who never associated with black kids. And he found himself in the middle of those four groups, right in the middle. And that's the way he would describe himself.

RR: And how have you grown through this process at this point?

LH: Now we know a little more about the reality of being a black person even in today's society. And I think that we've been challenged to see things from a different perspective. In a way I've been able to see a little bit more about the *variety* of African American people because I've been a little closer to the community. I think also, however, in some ways it is a lonely position to be in. Personally, I have known families of transracial adoption who really have made a strong point to go out and develop solid friendships with African Americans; and we didn't do that. We have some friends that are of other races, but when I am not with my family, people don't know that my family is of color, or the people in my family are African American, and it's really a strange feeling for me. It is lonely sometimes, because unless they care to know something about me, black people or people of color may assume that I am like all the other whites. That probably has been a growth experience too.

RR: Do you think that it does make a difference raising a child in a place like Evanston, where you do see people from different ethnic and economic backgrounds as opposed to a rural community, where there are not people of color or people that are different than you racially or even religiously?

DH: I would say yes. We are lucky that we live in Evanston. Just as an example of the contrast, years ago when Seth was young, and then later when he had Timothy, we went to a family camp up in the middle of Wisconsin in an all-white and rural area. When we went to town, we were quite a mixture ethnically, because there was our family and another very good friend of Seth's who was Caribbean and dark skinned, and then there was a mixed racial Japanese American family vacationing with us too. So we had a mixture of African American, white, Japanese, Japanese American. The local people would take a look at us going down the street and stare.

RR: In your opinion is it a positive influence for the transracially placed child and the family to live in a community that is diverse or is it OK to be raised in a rural area and predominately white area?

LH: I think for the child to feel that there are other people like him/her is important. My understanding is that, especially for adopted kids, that it is an issue that there is nobody else in their family that looks like them or in their community; they at times feel alone. It is one of the reasons why it is important for there to be people of different races and occupations, and gender, on television, so that our transracially adopted children will know what is possible.

In reading your book about the stories of young adults, I really felt that some young adults had their only contact with African Americans later, when they were older and their contacts were with a certain type of African Americans; and they seemed to assume that that was what it meant to be an African American. And there is much more variety in the African American community than that. I really felt that they were somewhat hampered by feeling they had to identify with that particular group, at least initially. I don't think it is impossible to raise a black child in a predominately white area. I still believe that the most important thing for children is to grow up knowing that they are loved and cared for and valued and worthwhile. I think that it is better for them to be adopted by whites than to not be adopted—you know, children can't sit on a shelf while we sort out all of society's problems. If there aren't other choices for them long term, then, yes, place these children with families who will love them and care for them.

Back in the early '70s, shortly after we adopted Seth, the black social workers came out with a position paper that was against transracial adoptions. I think I understood some of where they were coming from that had value. But one of my problems with their position was that children are not commodities in our societies' struggles, and they can't wait until we get it all sorted out. So I think that for people who are in a position where they don't live in a mixed community, that if there is a child who needs a home, it needs a home regardless of race.

RR: Do you think that the view of the National Association of Black Social Workers then affected you as you were raising Seth?

DH: Not really, except as Lo just indicated, we reacted to it.

LH: In a funny sense, if we had not lived in a multicultural place like Evanston, I think it would have affected Seth, because I believe their position slowed the number of transracial adoptions, providing fewer images of blended families. And I think that that may have affected some other children in these placements living in more rural areas. But other than having strong opinions about their position, it did not affect us. Also I felt in Seth's case that since he was biracial, if he had been raised by his birth mother, he would have been with a white family. His biological family was asking whoever was placing him for adoption to make a choice for him of which parents he would be with, black or white.

RR: Where do you Lola, as a social work professional, see adoption going in the future—or where do you want it to go?

LH: One of the things I am struck by is the number of people who do not adopt through agencies these days. In Southern California, when I was a social worker in adoption, there were some independent adoptions but most were through agencies. I think that was less so in the Midwest, where we now live, but it also may have been true here. The agencies that now place kids for adoptions, unless they are set up for specifically international adoptions, seem to really see themselves more as facilitating, getting parents and kids together, not as placing children for adoption. I think they may be missing a step in helping potential parents think about the variety of children that they could adopt. I think it is easier for Americans to adopt Asian children or European children or even Latin American children than it is for them to adopt African Americans domestically.

RR: Why?

LH: I think that the others look more like us and are more accepted in white communities. There are some agencies that are doing a wonderful job promoting the adoption of black kids like the Cradle here in Evanston, and I know there are some other agencies also that either urge or require their applicants who might be interested in transracial adoption to go through an educational process to help them think through some of the issues that may surface with this type of adoption. I think that is terrific. One of my concerns about adoption is that people aren't being encouraged to explore what is possible. And I think that our social climate now—you asked what was the social climate in the early '70s—and I think right now, I mean, I am sure we were affected in some way by the fact that we were young and relatively activist and were part of a movement for equality. We had gotten to know a variety of people through that that we could identify with in many ways. I don't know how people today form those identifications with African Americans. I hope it is possible, but I think that would perhaps hinder the numbers of transracial adoption placements. I do think there has been some improvement in the efforts to find families in the black community, middle-class African Americans, but I still know that there are a lot of kids waiting for adoption, and many of them are the older ones and harder to place, and I think they take more special parenting.

RR: For parents who are looking to adopt, what would your advice be as they go through the process?

LH: My advice is to stretch yourself, get to know yourself and your motivations for adopting, and learn as much as you can about your child and his/her culture. Adopting a child is not just about us and making us feel good. We wanted a child because we couldn't give birth to children, and if people are in that position, yes, I think they should explore adoption because in a real way children are still children. They are in some sense just like your biological children, and in other senses they are not. Even adopted children who are the same race as their parents will have different temperaments, different histories, and some will have learning disabilities. In our case neither Dave nor I have learning disabilities so working with Seth in that area was a whole new challenge for us. You can't count on any adopted child to become like you. And I don't think you can count on your biological children to be just like you. And that is a challenge, and I think if you are going to take on a challenge, you might as well consider all types of children.

DH: On this last point I think it is neat that both Seth and Lo have gone down to talk to classes about their experiences.

LH: One of the ways that I think about adoption is that all of us have things in our lives to deal with, and a mixed-race or a child of another race from the majority of their community—that's certainly one of the things they have to deal with. Being adopted is another thing that they have to deal with. In Seth's case he had a learning disability. I think that was the most challenging obstacle, because that was what I think affected his self-esteem the most. So it makes me feel that whatever challenges the child the most, that's where it is the hardest for them. If Seth hadn't had a learning disability, his whole life would have been different. And I suppose being adopted and being African American affected it further. Maybe if he had a learning disability and hadn't had those two other factors, the learning disability might not have affected him as much. It is all a dynamic mix. I think his identity is as somebody who is kind of in the middle, his identity has to be as somebody who is never quite like everybody else, he is always a little different. I think he has made that an advantage rather than a disadvantage.

When we first adopted Seth, we were featured in a news article. One of the adoption agencies in our area was promoting transracial adoption placements, and I think because I had been a social worker and because of our story, they asked if they could do a news feature on us. So this cameraman came with this African American interviewer to our home. One of the first questions she asked me was, "Why did you adopt a transracial child?" I said something to the effect that we decided that it didn't matter—it didn't matter that our child looked differently than us. And I have cringed since then, realizing that I am sure that many black people seeing this on TV rolled their eyes at that, thinking that I had no idea of what we were getting into. But in some ways I think it was a good motivation. I wasn't doing it because of a social movement. I was adopting him because I wanted a child, and it truly didn't matter to me that he was of a different color or background. And in some ways it is true that I wasn't well qualified to give him his heritage, but I was well qualified to love him and care about him as a person. I think that, with all good intentions, if you were doing this as part of a cause that you believed in, then you were set up to be disappointed.

DH: I would second that, with the qualification that we wouldn't even have thought of transracial adoption if we hadn't been somewhat active in the civil rights movement in churches.

KEN AND JEAN

KENTWOOD, MICHIGAN
JANUARY 2005

Ken is 64 and Jean is 63. They have no biological children and have adopted twins, Ned and Tonya, who were 6 weeks old when they were adopted. The children were reared in Grand Rapids, Michigan. Jean and Ken are members of the Christian Reformed Church. Ken has a B.A. in education and a master's in communication arts and sciences and was a high school teacher; he also spent half his career teaching in the prison system. Jean has a B.A. and did graduate work in education; she taught elementary and middle school. She now works with refugees. They describe their economic status as middle class.

> *In my workplace I can associate and fit in to a degree, but it only goes so far ...*
> *I still feel too black for my coworkers and yet with some of my students I'm too*
> *white. They say: "He talks too white, he's a sellout." I guess I have a lifelong*
> *challenge of trying to figure out where I fit in, who I am, and how I can find*
> *happiness in my particular life circumstances.*

—NED, 29, JUNE 1997

INTERVIEW

RR: Going back to 1968, when you were looking to start your family, you adopted twins. Why did you choose to adopt, and what was that process like for you?

K: We chose to adopt because we could not have our own children. The process amounted to almost nothing. We contacted an adoption agency and had an informal interview with them in November, and then we actually had our first official interview on January 25, the day the twins were born. And on that day they asked us if we would take the twins.

RR: And what was your response to that?

J: Not just one child but twins! OK.

RR: You adopted biracial children in 1968. Where did you live?

K: We lived in Grand Rapids, Michigan, on the southeast side. Our neighborhood was multicultural. Both the elementary school that I went to and the high school, South High, were the most racially mixed schools in Grand Rapids at that time.

RR: The reality of adopting black children didn't seem to be overwhelming for the two of you?

J: No, although I had no experience with other races to speak of.

K: We didn't go in asking to adopt biracial children; they asked us when we applied, and they asked us if we would give it some thought.

RR: Did the agency you went through prepare you for adopting transracially?

J: No, we had no preparation.

K: There were other parents that were doing the same thing, and for a couple years after we adopted, we were hooked up with them—support groups.

RR: Were both of your families supportive of your adopting transracially?

K: As far as I know, my family was supportive.

J: Your family was supportive, but my family had a lot of questions about it and wondered why. This was expressed especially when we moved from Rockford, which was rural and an all-white city, into the inner city to give our kids life experiences and identity within the black community.

K: We had planned on living in that part of town anyway. We were living in Rockford, because I had gotten a job there, but we were going to buy a house in a neighborhood in the city, and that's what we did.

RR: Looking at just the experience of raising your kids early on, what was that like for you? Did race enter into the picture? Did you have to confront anything different because your kids were different ethnically?

J: For one thing, when we went places, we'd be stared at a lot by white people. The black people in our neighborhood didn't seem to have a problem with it.

K: In fact, they tried to make sense of it. They thought I was black, which I thought was weird.

J: We had a white neighbor who accused me of having an affair with a black man—and that was where these babies came from. She thought I should put a sign on their backs when they were outside saying that they were adopted.

RR: How did you teach your kids to deal with the times when there was this awkwardness going on?

J: I thought we were quite open about it, although they were too young at that time. I have talked with them about it since. And knowing the people involved, they can understand why that happened.

RR: How did you process this?

J: It was very difficult. At the same time I had close relatives and some friends asking me why we did this. Some were afraid to come into our neighborhood.

RR: When you adopted your two kids, were there factors that came into play during that time, where you said, maybe I wasn't prepared or I need to get more prepared?

J: I felt that we needed more education, and that's why we joined the support group. And then, when our kids were ready for preschool, we put them in a ... setting ... where we could tell if they were having a proper upbringing as far as their racial identity went.

RR: What were the values that were most important to you as a family?

J: It was important to us that we learn to accept everyone regardless of race, ethnicity, or disability.

K: We were pretty strong on social justice issues. I taught in a prison and was very sensitive to what was going on there; people tended to segregate by race, and that is how they came out of the prison system, racially segregated.

J: Because of my husband's experience and having biracial children, I made it a point of studying what causes racism, what causes prejudice, and what causes stereotyping, and became real aware of that. I did a lot of reading on it and for that reason became much more accepting of others myself through the process.

   It seems like the adoption of our two children forced me into supporting them as much as possible by gaining more knowledge on the black race and their history and their impact on society, and the good things that have happened because of them.

K: Our kids helped me with my work as a teacher. I became even more interested in black authors and so on. I introduced black writers to my class in Rockford, which was all white at that time. So that was good for me and for the students.

RR: What was it like being raised in [your] home? Did your kids feel comfortable that they could talk to you about what was going on in their lives?

J: Yes. I think they could. In our home we also had foster children. We had two foster children who were African American, not biracial, for a long time. And they were part of our house too. So we were quite an integrated situation. The part that really hurt was when they would go places, such as to camp, and they were called nigger. These things were really painful to me. And they would tell us about those incidents.

RR: How would you handle that as a family?

J: We would talk about it and try to reassure them that they were better than that and didn't have to accept that term or that label.

RR: What was your relationship with your son and daughter as they were growing up? Did you feel comfortable interacting with them and talking about difficult issues? Did they have a good rapport with you?

K: I thought it was good.

RR: What were some of the fun things you did as a family?

K: I remember one time the four of us [were] in a restaurant, and some guy from another spot in the restaurant came over and looked at us and said something like, "I just think you are a beautiful family."

J: And one of the most fun experiences that the kids remember is taking the train to San Diego. They were 6 years old. They were so cute and they met people well. They had a nice presence about them, and so people just took care of them—everybody on the train took care of them.

K: It was like a community—that one car. I don't know if you have ever traveled across country, but I remember at one point more tickets were sold than there were seats. One guy came in and he had Ned's seat—Ned and Tonya were running around the train, and someone told this guy that he couldn't sit there because that's a little boy's seat.

RR: Was it important to you that in your home you had pictures of your children and also things that reflected part of their heritage?

J: We had pictures of them. But we didn't do a lot with African American artifacts. I never even thought of it at the time, which is not how I feel now.

RR: What was Ned's view of that?

J: He thought we should have, I guess. That's what he said in the book.

K: He thought we were pretty Dutch. At first it didn't seem to be a big thing, but as he got older, he needed something that he could identify with. He makes a criticism of me in the book. At some points in his life I would ask him how we're doing in terms of is he learning enough about his culture. He felt that was too much to put on a little kid, and looking back I would agree with that. Even though we lived in a black and white neighborhood, he was also critical in the book that our neighbors were our acquaintances, but our good friends were people from church and other friends and relatives. In fact, it might have been a good thing to at least have tried a more integrated church.

J: But we were starting a church—

K: We were hoping there would be some integration, but it never quite happened—so in retrospect we think of things we should have done.

RR: What are some things that you think back on that you did [that] were
effective for both Ned and Tonya?

J: I don't know what I did, specifically.

K: Being straight with them. If we thought they should know something, we
tried to be up-front about the whole thing.

J: In middle school we started talking more about racial issues, because so
many things came up. For instance, the person then who was doing the
plays would traditionally put the black students into the maid roles, and
I remember raising a stink about that. Also, I remember talking to the
other teachers, trying to get them interested in the fact that black boys,
especially, are so stereotyped that by fourth grade they are turned off
from learning. And I remember giving a devotion way back on that at the
school, and everybody thought I was dead wrong, except the art teacher, who was black. She said she learned more from me than she ever
learned from anybody else because they never taught anything about
black people in the school before. And when I talked to Ned about it,
he said from that time on, it was really true, they didn't expect anything
of him. That made me so angry because Tonya and he both have such
good minds.

RR: From your perspective as white parents, as Christian individuals, how
were you able to effectively work with Ned in particular in that area, as
far as helping him feel competent as a black male?

J: I just built them up all the time. I didn't feel I grew up that way because
I was sometimes compared to other people. I wasn't going to do that to
my own children. So maybe that was part of it too. I really tried to help
make them feel they both had self-worth.

RR: How, specifically, did you do that?

J: One time, in fourth grade, Ned was creating problems in school. Mostly
because he was bored out of his mind—they were both reading the same
book they had already read in third grade. So they decided he had to be
tested. And the person that we chose to have him tested, tested him, and
he started out with the Rorschach test, which begins with a black page
with nothing on it. At the end of the test this psychiatrist said he has
never heard such a creative explanation of what was in that picture than
Ned's. He [the psychiatrist] just told the teacher that it is your problem,
not [Ned's]. He was a little stinker in school, but both of them were
always kids who looked out for the underdog. And I think that because
of those situations, they chose to sit next to the kids who were the under-

dogs in the classroom, whether they were white or black, it didn't make any difference. And they still are that way today. I think it came partly from us.

RR: From the mind-set of raising black children, did you have to do things differently from what you would do—was race not really a huge factor when it came to how you raised them?

K: No. Where race and culture became a factor was when they went to school, and particularly in the white community. When Ned and Tonya would talk, others didn't expect—and the black kids too—them to talk the way they did. They knew English well and didn't have accents. It was like, "Who are you?" That's when the problems started. It didn't really start in our home.

RR: How did you, from your lenses, see a way to address this with your kids? You talked about just giving them more and more self-worth and boosting them up. Is that how you see it too, Ken?

K: I am very much of an idea person. So when I dealt with them, I dealt with ideas. I would ask them questions and get them to think. I would tell them there are no limits. You are the ones that are going to set limits for yourself, but you can do whatever you want to do.

J: And some of the teachers.

K: We had some bad experiences with some of the teachers.

RR: Going into the high school arena, did you see things change? Did you see your children become more competent? Were there different issues? What happened?

J: I saw Tonya become less competent, and Ned had a way about him that he was very accepting of everybody, and they accepted him just because of his manner, his "bubbliness." Whereas I think Tonya was more serious. We offered them the opportunity, at different times, to go to a public school, because Tonya especially had black friends who went to Creston. I said if you want to go with them to Creston, you go ahead, but she had a hard time making that switch. Ned got himself so involved in sports and the kinds of things that were accepted by everybody, and being good at it, that he didn't seem to appear to have too much trouble.

K: And he was homecoming king. A friend on the staff of his high school said that he was sort of campaigning for that—naturally, not intentionally but unintentionally just because of his personality, but I think because of his race—it was fine in [middle school at] Oakdale, but it was a problem at Christian High. He even said something in the book, that being homecoming king was really a big deal but then afterward, in retrospect, it's like it didn't make any sense.

RR: In high school he seemed to be doing quite well. His self-esteem was there.

J: Yes.

K: Both communities of kids, white and black, didn't expect him to act the way that he did. The black kids especially wanted to know what was he trying to prove? Are you trying to say you are better than we are?

J: I taught several of those kids, and some were very streetwise, and at that point he didn't want to get into that. He couldn't relate to that.

K: The junior high and elementary school was a pretty good experience.

J: In middle school it began where the white kids were leaving the black kids out of parties. They had overnights, and gradually the black kids or the biracial kids would be left out of those. I saw that in teaching. In all my twenty years at Oakdale, the black kids and the white kids stayed in their own racial groups. It was not, in my opinion, a real integrated situation.

RR: During this time, let's say high school through college, did your children have mentors, were there people in the black community that they could connect with?

J: Randy, who teaches now at Calvin College, was involved in their lives, especially Ned's.

K: He was a minister at that time.

J: There was my mentor, David, who was a social worker at Oakdale. He really encouraged me to take some drastic steps there as far as my teaching's being racially and ethnically inclusive. I really changed my whole method of teaching. And also there was Jim, who was African American. He taught at Calvin, and I took classes from him while I was teaching. My principal at the time also strongly supported this and encouraged me to study the Bible from the African perspective. I did and taught Bible in that way. It was very exciting.

RR: When you're looking at the entire adoption experience, ups and downs, what can you draw from that? Let me phrase it this way. What did you as a family hold on to during challenging times that impacted particularly your children, to get you through?

J: I held on to my faith and relied on the church. I also received more support from my family. By that time they were real accepting, and Ned and Tonya were well integrated into the family.

K: I would agree. I would also say I think all the way through, we have been a really strong family. We've been there for each other no matter what the problems have been. All four of us have had problems and there was support. We realized there was a problem, we realized it a little too late, but we made it through.

RR: What I think is so remarkable is that you are still so connected as a family. Number one: What has allowed you to stay so committed to your family when either one of you could have said, I'm done?

J: The love for them is so deep that there has never been in my mind any difference between their being adopted or being my biological children. That has never—it has never even entered my mind. They are my children. I have to be there for them. This is my mandate, and even to this day I can get so angry with Ned sometimes—with his flippantness, but you know I would give my life for him and Tonya, no matter what they did. It is just such an unconditional love we share.

K: On the part of everybody.

J: It is that way all the way around. I just bought a pillow for Tonya today. It says, "To my daughter who is my best friend." She comes here every noon for lunch. She works nearby—we have such a tight relationship.

K: Next weekend Ned and I are going to go to Chicago.

RR: Tell me about Ned's family.

K: Ned married Sharon, who is African American. They adopted their first two children and recently had a daughter.

RR: What is the relationship like with your grandkids?

J: They would love to live here.

RR: I'm sure—I'm sure they would.

J: They are here a lot. Gabriel told Sharon a few weeks ago that he wished that his skin was lighter—he is the darkest one in the family. There's just not a problem. I just love those kids.

K: They just run in here and hug us and stay overnight a lot. It is always special.

RR: And what with all the preparation that you went into in this process, and all the work that you did to nurture your family, what would you say is the highest experience you've had with both Ned and Tonya?

J: They've written me letters on my birthday and have done things for me that have sent me into tears. It's expressions of their love. I don't know that there's an incident as such. However, last spring we, along with Ned, Sharon, the boys, and our granddaughter, Joy, traveled together in a car to Disney World for a week. It went so well. It was just a perfect trip. Nobody can believe that we did that.

RR: That is amazing—in a car with the whole family.

K: Three days driving.

RR: My family went in a Winnebago across country, and I am very close to my brother and love him dearly, deeply, in fact, but it was drama. That's amazing. Would you do that again, would you transracially adopt?

K: If we were much younger—you're not talking about this stage in our lives?

RR: Knowing what you know now, would you have done it in 1968?

J: Absolutely.

K: Yes, yes!

RR: Tell me why.

J: For me it has increased my horizons; meeting people of different races, ethnic backgrounds, that's life! It's not this little clique of white people that is the world. I feel like I have been exposed to the world because of it.

K: I would definitely do it again. These are my kids. I can't imagine life without them. I've always been happy that I didn't have to deal with somebody who looked and acted exactly like me. Sometimes the son is a spitting image of the father, and I'm not sure I'd want to be reminded of that all the time. I am also proof, my relationship is proof, that the father doesn't have to initiate all the learning—Ned learned things on his own. I'm not mechanical at all, I'd rather read a book than anything else. But Ned has such a good mind that he just figures things out. He didn't need me to show him how to use a hammer, and all that—which is what a lot of fathers brag about. I think what we have in common is ideas and wanting to talk things through. I feel like he is my best friend.

J: Tonya is so much like me—a perfectionist, organized, creative.

K: Being biologically related to somebody has its limitations in that you kind of see yourself, and that is not always pleasant. I think it was really good to have raised people, kids, who were just entirely different from us.

RR: Did the position taken by the National Association of Black Social Workers affect your decision to adopt additional nonwhite children?

J: Interestingly, I called the adoption agency we went through when Ned and Tonya were about 3, and that's when that came out, and I think they had stopped interracial adoptions for a while, and they wouldn't let us reapply.

K: Is that when we started fostering?

J: Yes.

RR: So when you adopted them, Ned and Tonya, you were aware of this stance.

K: No. That didn't happen until after—this was in 1971—

J: So it was when they were about 3, and we asked about adopting additional kids. They weren't real excited about it, and that's when we heard about their position.

RR: Do you think the position taken by the NABSW influenced your children's feelings about having been adopted into a white family?

J: No.

K: They didn't know about their position then.

J: They probably knew about it later on.

RR: Do you think—

J: We talked with our kids later on about whether or not it was a good thing. But they have always reassured us that they were glad we raised them.

K: I am not unhappy that they [NABSW] came up with that statement. I do think there is some truth in it.

RR: Would you recommend transracial adoption to other families?

J: I would, but I think for one thing you have to live in an integrated neighborhood.

RR: Why is that important?

J: Their children need to identify with other people like them.

K: This comes out in your book time and time again, where the adult adoptees mentioned in relation to your question, "I don't look like the rest of the kids." This was their view because they lived in predominately white environments.

J: I agree with that now, and we didn't so much then. For instance, if you are in a church, you should want it to be as ethnically diverse as possible—your whole lifestyle should reflect this diversity.

K: That is the one thing I am sorry about. I would have at least liked to have gone to a black church. We were hoping our church would become more integrated, but it didn't.

RR: What other advice can you offer to parents who are looking to adopt transracially or are in the process of raising their infant kids?

J: Prospective parents must know about black history. They need to be aware of the good things that black people have done. When I taught middle school, I really made a point of integrating many different cultures into my teaching, particularly emphasizing the significant contributions that black people in the Bible made—that just has to be known. For example, in my class we would study Africa or India and their respective cultures and history, and why these groups were in conflict with one another at times. (I brought that all out because of the whole colonization thing.) We delved into the literature and folktales of different people, and I instructed my students to then write folktales that coordinated with the folktales of the African people, to use the same images, I did that with India, et cetera. It was quite interesting. But certainly as a society we don't talk enough about the value of cultures other than our own.

RR: Do you have any other suggestions for families who have adopted?

J: I believe adoptive parents have to become knowledgeable, especially if we are going to teach our African American children how to build healthy self-esteem. Our black and biracial children need to know the positive attributes about their heritage and know how to build from that foundation. This is important, especially since our children are confronted with so many negative images about who they are.

K: That would be true for Hispanic or Chinese or Japanese — it's not enough to just say I'm going to be a good parent. Because in the real world people are judged on the basis of what they look like. If they look like Japanese, no one will assume they are being brought up by white people. If you are in a minority and you are put in a white home, the compensation has to be that you learn about your background and your parents have to be aware of that.

RR: This is not an easy path to travel.

K: The challenge is that on one hand these are kids, and we all know (for the most part) how to take care of kids, but on the other hand (and this is huge) there's a real world out there, and unfortunately it is a broken world, and it's a world that judges people on the basis of what you look like. Ned is an intelligent person, and often when he showed his intelligence, he was mocked by his peers. Who are you trying to impress, and that kind of thing. And that really came from the black community, the kids in the black community.

RR: Do you think that society has become more accepting of black people in America since 1968? Do you see a transition or change?

K: I think racism is a lot more subtle than it used to be.

J: I'm not sure it is any better.

K: I'm on a police chief advisory council because of problems we've had with the police department and so on, pertaining to the treatment of minorities. I am on that committee and the chief of police doesn't think there's any such thing as profiling by police. I know for a fact that there is. When Ned gets stopped by a policeman, it is a whole lot different than when I get stopped by a policeman.

J: Yes. Ned didn't put his blinker on one time — and he got stopped and frisked and laid over the car. He's been stopped more often than he has told us for these little infractions.

RR: So it is more subtle.

J: And they say that it happens in the stores —

K: And for other parents who adopt black children, specifically, I don't know if they are aware of how serious this problem is and that it could happen to their children. Maybe there should be classes on becoming aware of racial differences. I'm not sure parents go into this, transracial adoption, really knowing what they are doing.

J: There is so much ignorance and stereotyping out there. If you don't know what you are dealing with, it can be very overwhelming.

K: If you are going to adopt or even foster kids from different ethnic backgrounds, you need to learn about their ethnic community. It isn't enough to say we are all human beings, we're all the same. We are not all the same, we're not treated the same.

RR: How do you think black children and teenagers especially can overcome the "driving while black" phenomenon? How do they deal with the rage—what can they do?

K: The problem is that police don't even realize it is a problem.

J: And it is a problem.

K: They are offering this program now that teaches you how to act when you get pulled over. You have to be real polite and say, "I'm sorry, Officer; what do you want from me, Officer?" Certainly that makes sense, but there has to be more to it than that. There has to be attitudinal change on behalf of the police officers. Why do they stop more blacks than they stop whites?

RR: So what can parents who adopt transracially do if and when their child gets stopped by a police officer?

J: I think they have to report it. Ned didn't want to bother. In his mind it wouldn't do any good anyway. I'm more of an activist, and I feel that you have to do something.

RR: You have grandkids. What is your hope and expectation for them?

J: The first is, I hope they can develop their abilities to the best and that they will not be discriminated against based on the color of their skin. I want their self-esteem to blossom.

RR: Is there anything that I haven't asked you that you wanted to contribute?

K: I think I said something similar to this. I guess if I had to do it all over again, I'd be a little more sensitive about the race issue and try to have more images reflecting black culture. That's what Ned is doing with his kids. I wish we would have done more in that area.

J: Ned often asks me questions about black history that he wants to incorporate into his lesson plans at school.

RR: What is it that has helped your kids to feel comfortable to talk to you and to look to you as friends and parents and leaders?

J: Our integrity and honesty with them helps.

K: Also, I'm willing to say I'm sorry, to say I might have made a mistake, and I'm willing to learn from those mistakes.

J: It is important to be there all the time for any child, and I think they are dealing with more than what other children are because of transracial adoption.

K: Sometimes I wonder what it would be like if we had our own biological kids and what it would have looked like. I think it's been an interesting life, and I think we've learned a lot. I have a fundamental belief that all of us are more alike than we are different. Having gone through all these experiences has proven that. Looking back, I think it would be kind of boring if we just had kids who look like us.

J: As a result we have both been involved in outreach, and I am currently working with refugees. Actually, we've worked with refugees for twenty years through our church and helped initiate a program focusing on refugees. I think through it all we've kind of expanded ourselves into reaching out to people less fortunate than ourselves. I am not saying that Ned and Tonya were less fortunate, but it has really opened our eyes to what the needs are. I was just thinking of the tsunami disaster when they said how many hundreds of thousands of people died. I led a Bible study and my first question was, "We saw how the tsunami killed so many people, how about the 800,000 to a million that were killed in Rwanda? Was the whole world jumping to them—and that was in six months. Did anybody go over there and help them?" It kind of grinds me a little bit—where we put our efforts as a nation and as a people. Natural disasters are OK, but when people are killing each other with machetes, then we stay away, and is it because of Africa? I raise those questions with people all the time.

RR: Case scenario: If somebody said something untruthful or hurtful about the black community or a person specifically, would you speak up and say something to that situation because of your experience [with] adopting two biracial children?

K: Yes, I would do that real quickly. If kids in my class, not knowing that I was the father of black children, if they were to make derogatory remarks about any race, I'd tell them to stop. Or ask them, "Why do you think that way?" Or, "Do you understand the ramifications of that statement?" Those situations have come up. Ned went with me to one of my classes one time, and a student was complaining because people wanted *black* television networks. He said what if the whites wanted that? And Ned responded what about ABC, NBC, and CBS!?

J: In my working with refugees, I've seen discrimination. I took a Cuban man to the hospital because his foot was rotting off. The hospital staff was putting us off, and we couldn't get any response. The health care personnel just wanted to send him back home. It wasn't until I confronted the supervisors and practically stomped my feet on the floor and said, "Oh, yes, you are going to treat this man. There's no question about it. You have to. You are required to treat this man," did they do anything. A black minister was with me and he said to me, "Jean, I never would have gotten that response. You stood there, you're white, and you said, oh, yes, you're going to treat him and then he was treated." A year later his foot was healed.

RR: What would you attribute to the fact that your mind-set, when it comes to people from different ethnic backgrounds, is such where you put every-body on an equal platform? Especially since most of America, even black families, are struggling with similar race issues and putting value on it. How have you been able to look at your son and your daughter as equal human beings that deserve to be in this world?

J: I believe that every single person was created equally by God. There is no such thing as one that is better than another.

K: I don't know if you've ever heard of Eugene Debs, but he was a socialist many years ago. He was white, but he was jailed because he was involved in a lot of civil disobedience. At one point he said, "As long as there is one soul in prison, I am not free." That is my philosophy. I am not free if anybody is being mistreated.

RR: And that has gone from your mind to your heart. That's the transition that America hasn't yet arrived at. How do you make that transition?

K: Adopt kids from another culture.

WINNIE

FLORIDA

MARCH 2004

Winnie is 64 and divorced. She has three biological children, Stephen, Catherine, and Anne, and one adopted child, Peter. Peter was less than a year old when he was adopted. The children were raised near Ithaca, New York. Winnie, a Unitarian, has a Ph.D. in French literature and is a library assistant. She describes her economic status as working class.

I've gone through the struggles that every other black person has gone through in this society, just because of the color of my skin.

—PETE, 28, SEPTEMBER 1997

INTERVIEW

RR: Take me back thirty-some years ago [to] when you started your family. What was going on nationally as far as social issues dealing with race? And where did you live?

W: We lived in… New York [State], in the country. We weren't hearing very much about what was going on nationally, at least I wasn't. This is a question I probably can't answer very well. I was pretty unaware of such things except through exposure at church where, of course, it was very liberal, and we actually had a minister (I went to the Episcopal Church at Cornell at that time), and we had a minister who had spent a summer with Martin Luther King Jr., but it wasn't until a little bit later that there started to be some riots in Ithaca, New York, itself and some discussion of racial matters. But, really, we were just not exposed to any of those questions.

RR: Why did you and your husband Jim at the time choose to adopt trans-racially?

W: Let me tell you the story about why we did that. We both felt that we wanted four children. We thought that would be a good number of children for their sake, and we just thought that would be perfect for a family, and we also felt that we shouldn't add more than two children to the world's population.

So after we had two, we went to the adoption agency. We talked to them about adopting a third, and they were very discouraging. They said, "Are you sure you really want to do that?' and so forth and so on. And we weren't confident enough to say, "Yes, we do." So we went back and had another child. She's the one with Down syndrome. And then we were also going to have a fourth, but I had a miscarriage, and we wanted to have the four fairly close together.

By that time we had gained more confidence, because we were managing fine with the two little ones and the Down syndrome baby, and so we went back and this time they welcomed us with open arms. That was 1968. It was immediate. They said, "Oh would you be willing to adopt a hard-to-place child, because we have children of mixed race and they're not wanted by black families and they're not wanted by white families?" And we said, well, of course, we would be delighted. We certainly would want this child as much as a white child or any other child. So that's how it came about. And we probably would have got Peter even faster except that the social worker who was taking care of our case broke her wrist, and so it took us three months. And that is an amazingly short time to get a child. It took us three months, and during that time another adoption agency in Ithaca actually called us up and said, "We hear that you're looking for a hard-to-place child, are you interested?" And we said, "Well, we've already started the procedure with this other agency." But all of a sudden they just really wanted to give us children. And that was it. That's how we got Peter.

RR: As you were raising your children, what were the most important factors that you stressed in your home?

W: Tolerance, I would say, and love and accepting of each other. And we were, as far as Peter was concerned, we were totally color-blind. I mean, we felt that they were all our children and it just made no difference. What values we instilled? Well, we instilled the values that most parents would try to instill. We tried to set an example of loving and doing things together and respecting each other and we, really, I think, as I look back, we had a very happy time together. We also were nonconsumer people. And I remember in Peter's interview, he mentioned about wrapping things in brown paper bags at Christmas. He thought that was to save money. Actually, in some ways some of the things we did were because we didn't believe in going out and buying a lot of things. We could have just as much fun playing games and doing things of our own invention. That sort of attitude was in our family.

RR: Did race ever enter into the picture?

W: Race was not a focus at all. And we're talking about the first thirteen years of Peter's life when he was a child and an adolescent, and that was the first segment of our raising him. Peter and the rest of our family were totally accepted by the rural community where we lived. And when we spent the three years in Hawaii, there we were in a minority, because most of the people were Chinese and Japanese, but again everyone was very welcoming and accepting, and we were pretty color-blind, didn't really give it much thought. People would come up to me—someone came up to me when I was out with the four kids in Hawaii when Peter was tiny and in a stroller, and said, "Oh, how lovely, you've adopted a child." It took me a few minutes to realize why they knew that because I just totally forgot it most of the time. So, no, race was just definitely not an issue. But that had a lot to do, too, with Peter's personality in that his acceptance, wherever we were, had a lot to do with his wonderful, engaging personality.

I don't know whether this answer comes in here appropriately, but in my experience with adoption I feel that heredity is equally as important, if not more so, than upbringing in developing a child. In my experience a child is like a flower, and you give him sunshine and rain, but they are going to develop to be their own beautiful self. Peter was just extraordinary from the beginning in some of his ways, and he was socially just amazing. The other children were shy, as we are kind of shy, but Peter from the youngest age was outgoing and playing with other children. When we were in Hawaii, I remember when he was 2 years [old], he had a Korean best friend from the apartment next door, and they would sit in the box together going on and on about fishing the barracuda.

And another thing, as he grew a little older and I remember driving him places with his friends, there has been a lot of talk in the book from the kids about different language, different races. Peter would just amaze me because he spoke beautiful English at home. He would say things like "He and I don't have anything." He could talk like that. Yet he would get in the car with his friends and he would talk a totally different language. He could switch from one to the other—"Him and me ain't." And at home he could speak beautiful English, and he could do this from a very young age. He just had the gift. And he was always out playing with someone. If he wasn't at somebody's house playing, they were at our door wondering where he was so they could play with him at our house.

RR: So when he was being raised [in New York], did he ever bring up any issues while he was growing up about race or about feeling different?

W: No, he never did that I remember.

RR: What was his relationship like with his siblings?

W: His relationship with his siblings was good. He was a very active child. He never stopped. So he would play with whichever one of them was willing to be active with him. As he got into being 4 and 5 years old, he had neighbors who were exactly his age with whom he was very close. He got to spend more and more time playing with other kids too. There was often a huge crowd in our yard over the weekend. But his relationship with his siblings was great. It worked out well that one of them had Down syndrome, which left really only three to play together actively, because she didn't participate much. But they would pair up in different groups of two, and they never excluded him, and whichever two wanted to play the same thing. And also a unique thing that we did give him was the sibling who had Down syndrome. And I have only begun to realize that just very recently, that growing up and tending to a Down syndrome child, I learned and they learned all about what it is like to be retarded and to live with a retarded person. That has helped me just very recently, to help relationships between, for instance, people [who ride] the bus and a retarded person [on] the bus. I realized that we learned a lot by living with such a person, and I am sure that even though [Peter and his nondisabled siblings] may not realize it, it's just something that they know, because it happened to them.

RR: In his interview in *In Their Own Voices* he cites a time when he had the option of living at home or living with a friend of his who was African American.

W: No. That was much later. His friend that he went to live with—you see, my husband and I split up when Peter was about thirteen, and I went to live in the City of Ithaca. It's a very small town, but compared to where we lived, it was a city. Now Peter had two very best friends growing up. Both were only children. One of them was practically a next-door neighbor and the other one lived in the little town where his school was, which was twelve miles in the other direction. When I moved to Ithaca, had he moved with me, he would have had to change schools, or he could have lived with his father still out in the country ... but at that time Jim [Peter's father] was teaching most of the week at another college, so he wasn't home a lot. Then Peter had the option of living with this neighbor who was white, who was an only child—well, not an only child, but his brother had long grown up and gone away, so he was practically an only child. His father was a sports coach, and they just spent so much time together anyway, so he elected to do that for a year.

RR: And in that relationship, did he interact with people outside of his white friends?

W: No, that was later. Living with that family was just an experience in living with an only child in a family that was more sports oriented and probably had more stuff too—a wonderful family.

RR: And most kids like a lot of stuff.

W: Yes. He has so many mothers, it is incredible. She is like another mother to him too. But that was one year and, no, he did not interact with other black kids during that year. It was not until he moved to join me in Ithaca, which was when he was 14, I believe.

RR: And what was that experience like for him?

W: Well, that was very interesting because all of a sudden his life changed completely. My life changed completely because I was separated from my husband. It was just the most terrible time of my whole life. I was going through so much, and I felt even worse about it because we had adopted a child, and you're not supposed to adopt a child and then split up. What kind of stability is that? But we did, and there I was in Ithaca, and Peter was coming to live with me, which was very scary because I knew nothing about raising a teenager on my own. I had my Down syndrome daughter and my oldest son staying with me, too, in Ithaca. And my older daughter was in college then. So for me it was a traumatic time.

For Peter, I know it was a traumatic time too. He was suddenly in a whole new school district with more kids of color, being exposed to all kinds of things that he had never been exposed to before. As he said in *In Their Own Voices*, he had more freedom than the law allowed. Well, he was as mature as I was at that point, because I was going through so much. I just feel so much gratitude that he had the maturity, that we both got through it. And, again, his social skills helped and the fact that he was good at sports. Our little apartment was a changing room for the football team. They all came and practiced in the park across the way. They were always running in and out of our little apartment.

I had got the advice from a friend to let him help make decisions, not to get all upset if he did something, if he came in after curfew time or something, but to talk it over with him and to make rules with him. I tried to do that, and it seemed to work very well. I think I probably should have given him a lot more guidance, but on the other hand, I think if I had, I might have lost him because he was of an age where he could have rebelled. By giving him all that freedom, thank goodness, he had the maturity to accept it. He rose to the occasion, and he was a great support to me, too, for what I was going through. As he said in his interview, he found a really wonderful best friend who was a mixed-race girl, and they spent a lot of time talking. He had another best friend, the guy he said that he hung out with a lot, he called him a "wannabe," and the two of them actually ran away again one time. Peter left me a message, an alarm clock was set so that I would find his message, and he said don't worry, I'm running away with my friend because he's having a bad time. So I went over to his friend's house to let his mother know. And she was just panicked completely. Somehow I knew that Peter would be back. And in fact he was back the next day.

Peter just could have gotten into so many bad things then, but he managed to keep an even course and continue on and just feel more and more accepted by the new community that he was in. I am just so proud of him for what he did.

I've always been very proud of him, even when he was little. I just want to add this about his younger years. He might have felt that we spent more time—I think it came out that he thought that we were closer to the other children—but, as a matter of fact, Peter was so good at everything, he could teach himself everything that we had to spend a long time teaching the others, and he didn't need any help with socializing, so it may be that what he was feeling, and I am sorry if he did, was that we would give them a little bit of extra help with their connections with friends or just learning the sports skills and so forth, because he was always miles ahead.

RR: So the time that Peter was living with you in Ithaca, did you stretch and grow when it came to realizing the race factor?

W: I cannot say that I stretched and grew the way he did. I never understood how much a factor this was to him. I always accepted his black friends as being completely the same. I was color-blind the whole time. I was naive—I was much too naive. I needed someone to sit me down and tell me, "Look, this is a problem for your son, no matter what you think of the fact that all races are exactly the same. This is still going to be a problem for your son because there are some people who don't feel that way, and you need to learn more about this, and you need to face up to it." But I don't think that I ever really did. I felt completely at home with people of all colors, and there were people of all races and colors working with me at the library where I worked at Cornell. People from many different countries, so I think that was a big default in my growth. I apologize.

RR: Now that you have had a significant period of time to reflect on parenting children, one who is transracially adopted, is there anything that you think is paramount now in establishing and maintaining relationships with a child/adult who has been transracially adopted?

W: As far as what we should have done differently, you mean?

RR: Yes. Or even some of the things that you did do that you thought were effective.

W: I think that we completely accepted Peter and were color-blind was good in some ways. I believe formally bringing up racial differences and problems very early in his life would not have interested him. Peter was just so interested in what he was doing and in his friendships that discussing racial differences wouldn't have been pertinent to him at that point. But I also think that anyone who pursues transracial adoption should take courses, take some classes with the adoption agency, where they can be told about the importance of making some interracial ties with other families. Ironically, I have a very close friend right now who is black, whom I've worked with for the last twelve years, and we talk a lot about these things. Recently I have also been very active in raising money for a group in Haiti, and I have become very interested in that opportunity.

Now years later, yes, I think it would be very important for the agencies that place children to be sure that the [potential] parents are aware of aspects of transracial adoption. Those who are interested in interracially adopting a child should take a course in it and qualify. And, too, that there should be support groups that are required for adoptive parents, and maybe not only transracially adoptive parents but certainly transracially adoptive parents, that focus on maintaining ties with other parents in similar situations, long term, and with experts who know about the different stages [that] families who have interracially adopted may face. Because I think it would have been much better if there had been some preparation for Peter before the teen years. I think it is at those years that it is going to start making a difference as [transracially adopted kids] start to date and so forth.

Another thing that I think it is important to do is, and this would be for any adoptive parent, and this is something I would have done differently: I would have spent less time maintaining our rural lifestyle. We froze all of our vegetables, we had many animals, we spent a lot of time maintaining that kind of a life, for our kids too. Looking back on it, I would have bought more vegetables and given more time to the kids, especially if you are going to have a lot of kids, as we did. Four—that's pretty many. I would have spent less time on that stuff if I could have afforded to, but I would have spent more time at all the kids' functions. Even if Peter was at sports every other night, I would have tried to go more often. Unfortunately, it was physically impossible the way we lived, but I would have tried to make it possible.

RR: Can you tell me, in this whole process, what was your happiest memory with Peter, and what was your saddest memory?

W: Actually, my saddest memory was when he was about 9 or 10 years old, that would be one of the times when we had probably disciplined him or said no to something he wanted, and he said, "I was adopted by the wrong family!" That's not a very good example. But I remember that evening very clearly, because we are all so insecure anyway in our parenting and thinking, "Are we really doing this right?" And then his saying that, it's like a person whose parents have split up saying, "I wanted to be with the other parent, I don't love you."

One of the happiest things that has happened in the whole story of our adoption of Peter is his finding his birth parents. And I am just so happy, because it is just like a perfect closure, not closure because it is still going on, but it makes a perfect circle, because I have always been so grateful to have had a part in Peter's life. He brought so much to our family in the way of joy and an outgoing, friendly personality. He wore us out completely at many points but put a whole new dimension into the lives of everyone in our family, and I was so grateful to his birth parents for giving us this child. And I knew that they did it because they felt it was best for him. Then, when we found his birth mother, who it turns out was overjoyed to finally meet him, that was wonderful. After she had told her present husband, we arranged a reunion with our families. She and I became friends, and that was the most wonderful moment of the whole story. I felt as if, Wow! I can say thank you, and she was saying thank you to me, and there we both were and we're both Peter's mom, and I feel as if she's given me this wonderful privilege of sharing and I guess in a way she felt the same way that she was glad we had given him a good family. That was just so wonderful.

RR: What is Peter doing today?

W: That is another highlight of this story that I am so grateful for. He is a police officer and a volunteer fireman, and he is also the most wonderful father and husband. Sadly, I have not spent a lot of time with Peter and his family because I live in Florida, and they're in upstate New York. But, for instance, I spent a whole week with them Christmas before last. I am just floored by their parenting skills, the love in their household. I just don't know where they got it, because I think they do a lot better than we did. They are just incredible. Peter is just so good with those kids. I think it is just marvelous. And I am just so grateful to be a part of that.

RR: That's great.

W: Peter married a white woman who is the most wonderful girl and most wonderful mother. Yet at times I think it must be very hard for him as a black man that his kids appear to both be white. From my point of view, I just think that would be hard because then he has to go through this all again, that he went through all his life and his teenage years—that he goes out and society sees him as different. He even said one time that some people wonder if he is really their father. Other than that, my son has a wonderful family.

Peter does so much for people as a policeman and as a fireman. He's saved so many people's lives. He is so mature. I would go to him with problems or concerns of my own and trust his judgment. I am really grateful. I think we were just a very small part of it as his adoptive parents. I'm also very relieved that the mistakes that we made, mainly the fact that we split up, and the fact that I moved to Florida when he was going into his senior year of high school, did not debilitate him. If you recall, that was when he went to live with the black family. And, of course, I made sure before I moved to Florida that he did have a place where he would be loved and taken care of that year. Too, I made sure that he could graduate in the same school where he had finally found a niche after moving to Ithaca. (But that was really a very sad thing that I did move then, that I didn't postpone my own plans until he graduated.) Amazingly, that turned out to be the most important year of his life.

RR: Isn't that profound how it works out?

W: It must be I sensed that I couldn't do any more for him then. Whatever the reason, it was a gift that it worked out that way.

RR: What is your relationship with him now, and do you think that the divorce has impacted that relationship?

W: My relationship with Peter is amazing. He is very respectful and loving and keeps in touch. I think that the divorce, actually the only way that it impacted the relationship was that he rose to the occasion and became more mature to help me. It certainly has not made us further apart at all. I don't know how it has affected his relationship with his adoptive father, with Jim, but with me, if anything, [it] probably made us closer because he did live with me the years that I was going through the impact of that, and, as I said, he became more protective and more mature because of that.

RR: And basically you said it—the fact that you still feel committed to him.

W: I feel committed, but I don't feel at all possessive. I feel as if he belongs just as much to his birth mother, who sees more of him and of the grandchildren now than I do, and that's perfectly OK with me. I don't know how he can keep up with us all, but he does. I don't think we have to do any comparisons about who's closer. I think we are all close. I don't feel at all threatened by that. I also feel very grateful to his stepmother, because my ex was married in the meantime (he's now divorced from that person), but she was a wonderful stepmother to him all that time too. I feel very grateful for that. She was his mother, too, and then, too, John's mother, who took him in, and to the black family who took him in his senior year, whom I really don't know, but I know they are very close too. It's like these societies in Africa where everybody shares the raising of the child.

RR: That is such a beautiful gift.

W: It is not a very distant memory, but I guess those are probably the most wonderful aspects of the whole story for me, being able to evolve like that.

RR: Did the position by the National Association of Black Social Workers ever make a difference in how you thought of yourself as a mother, as the fact that both you and your former husband adopted a biracial child?

W: No, because we never knew about that position. And, as I said, the adoption agency that gave us Peter certainly led us to understand that we were adopting a child who very much needed adoption. They had only gratitude to us for doing it. The agency's attitude was that our adopting Peter was a wonderful act. So the belief that it might be a bad idea to adopt transracially was something that we never were aware of.

RR: Would you recommend [to] other families to adopt transracially?

W: We just had a message in church this morning about adoption. It was very interesting. And I understand that there are about 125,000 children in the United States in need of a home. Yes, I would certainly recommend transracial adoption, only with the provisions that I mentioned earlier, that the parents who are adopting be sure to be made aware of the issues and that they have an ongoing support group and some instruction. I think that the purpose of the ongoing support group should be to keep parents up to date on this issue and to help inform them of each stage of a transracially adopted child's life as to what they could expect to be talking over with their child. Retrospectively, we could have done a lot more of that. To our credit, we would answer any questions that came up from our kids, but I don't think we initiated topics. We weren't talkative and open enough as a family. We needed more guidance. Other than that, I think transracial adoption is a wonderful idea and certainly not to be discouraged.

RODNEY AND JOYCE PERRY

ROCHESTER, NEW YORK

AUGUST 2005

Rodney Perry is 60, and Joyce Perry is 61. They have three biological children, Seth, Amanda, and Nathan, and one adopted child, Britton. Britton was about 3 months old when he was adopted. The children were raised primarily in Rochester, New York. The Perrys are Quakers. Rodney Perry has an M.A. in library science, and Joyce Perry has a B.A. in English literature. They are both self-employed. They describe their economic status as middle class.

This is going to sound phony, like a cliché, but it's true. You have to recognize, find, and maintain your inner strength. No matter what it is, no matter where you get it from, because, when it comes down to it, you are all you have. You have to love yourself for who and what you are. From there you can go on to idolize, to have mentors, to find support. But most important is to have a firm belief in yourself and the strength that keeps you going from within.

—BRITTON PERRY, 27, DECEMBER 1996

INTERVIEW

RR: How old were you when you began your family?

JP: I was 27 and Rod was 26.

RR: What decision came [in]to play in choosing transracial adoption as an option for your family?

JP: Even before Rod and I married (we were very much products of the '60s and we were concerned about children out there without families), we said we wanted to have three or four kids, and we wanted to have some and adopt some. That was part of the plan before we married. The only thing that changed in the plan was that I had some infertility issues, and I was getting older without successfully becoming pregnant, so we decided that rather than adopt the kids on the end (we thought that we'd have a couple and then we'd adopt the last couple), we might as well get going, because we didn't know if we'd have any biological children. So it turned out that Brit was the first child—the adopted child came first. And that was the only thing that was a variation on what we had always said we would do.

RR: When you adopted Brit, where were you living at the time?

RP: We were in Boston.

JP: We started the process in Boston; when we actually got him, we had moved to the South Shore of Massachusetts. We were two years in the process—the paperwork and interviews—so we brought him home to the South Shore of Boston, where Rod was director of the public library there.

RR: Brit is biracial. Did that have any impact as to your decision of adopting a child or the process in which you ended up adopting Brit?

JP: Brit is actually triracial—African American, Caucasian, and Native American. We adopted Brit through Boston Children's Services, which is a very well-known, reputable, established agency in Boston—a hundred years old or whatever at the time. We had said from the beginning that we would take "a hard-to-place" child. We limited that; we were able to qualify the kind of child we would take. I did not feel emotionally prepared to deal with a severely physically handicapped child, but we were very open as to other situations.

RR: Had you known any African American people at the time?

RP: Yes, we had friends in college who were, and a friend of another friend.

JP: Yes. We had both known African Americans. I had a very close friend in college who was African American, who didn't actually finish school because she dropped out to stay in the civil rights movement, and we also had some good friends at the time who had two American biracial adopted children—as opposed to adopted Korean and South American children. I guess the way we felt about it was that we knew there were kids out there that, for lack of different resources, would sit in foster homes, and it didn't matter to us what the child's race or ethnicity was. It wasn't important to us.

RP: And I think that, at least from my point of view, when I kind of remember this for both of us, we were not that interested in "conventional adoption" in which, at least at that time, the agency even tries to match the look of the kid with the look of the parents. I mean, all kind of homogenizing or molding the whole thing as if it weren't an adoption; it was just a child with parents. And so we were interested in something different. Not for the sake of being different, but because we didn't really want to fit in with just a routine adoption, and also from a practical point of view, those adoptions took years and years.

JP: And I think, again, it didn't matter to us if we had a fair-haired blue-eyed child, and there were other people to whom that desperately mattered. It just didn't make any difference.

RR: What were your views about African Americans, generally?

RP: At the time integration was very high on the agenda in awareness. That was in 1970 and the civil rights movement, which we were both active in (Joyce more than I), had begun, say, in 1962–63, so within seven or eight years, the opportunity and also society's resistance against desegregation was there. And so, in a sense for me, having Britton is almost a statement of joining or sympathizing, if that is the right word, or getting as close to the oppressed as we could.

JP: You have to put this in the context of the times. We brought Britton home in 1970, but we started the process in 1968. We were two to two and a half full years going through the screening. Our social worker, who was not African American, had a poster on her wall that at the time was very popular and said, "Black Is Beautiful." As Rod said, I had friends who were freedom riders, who were jailed for the civil rights work. I felt very strongly that America had to learn to live together, and if taking one child out of foster care was the only thing I could do, then that would be something rather than nothing. So if this was the child that became available, then that was fine. That was wonderful. It was known from the beginning that we would be willing to take a mixed-racial child. Those kids were not being placed because they were not accepted in either camp. So they were languishing, and that to me seemed criminal.

RR: You had indicated that you essentially raised your kids primarily in Rochester, New York. After Brit you had three biological children. How did your family grow together and operate within your surroundings and also now as a blended family?

JP: Yes. But I would like to give you a little background on that. We had a fabulous social worker that we worked with through the adoption process. And one of the reasons that it took so long was that they had to feel very comfortable that we would be equipped emotionally and mentally for an interracial adoption, if that was what happened. So we were screened probably longer and in a different way than most cases. One of the things that I remember very clearly, as we were getting toward the end of the screening, was the statement, "If you should be given an interracial child, you will have to think about every life choice you make forever."

RR: Wow, you had a progressive social worker.

JP: Oh, yes. For example, she told us two stories and they just have stuck in my mind. One was of a couple who had finished the process. They were just about to be given the child, an interracial child that was going to be placed with them. They were in New England, had been in New England for years—he was professional military. And just at the point when they were actually going to get this child to take home, he was transferred to a southern military base. The agency would not place the child, because they said at that time, in that climate—again, we're talking about in the '60s—that for a Caucasian couple to bring an inter-racial child or an African American child into a southern military base would not be in the best interest of the child. So they wouldn't complete the adoption.

They told us another story, I remember, of a couple who had gone through the adoption process, and they had clearly requested or accepted an interracial child, and it turned out, this is a story our social worker told us, that the child was very fair skinned and probably her only real African American feature was her hair. And when the agency visited the family, as they do after they place the child in the first year, at least in Boston that was part of the routine that they make regular visits for the first year before they would finalize the adoption, they discovered the mother had dyed the child's hair blond. The agency was absolutely appalled because one of the things they talked to us about was, if we're going to take a child with African American background, then it will be our responsibility to nurture and guide the child in the child's cultural background and not to deny it and disguise it. They were just appalled. How could they have made such a mistake in interpreting this couple!

So we were told, "You are going to have to think about every street you ever live on, every house you ever buy, every school you ever send your kids to," and in fact and in truth, that has been the case for us. Our life has been carefully planned—what cities we lived in, what neighborhood we lived in, and what schools our children went to, so that all of our children, not just Brit, lived in a world where they were not unusual.

RP: We lived in Philadelphia from 1974, when Brit was 4 years old, to 1978, so there was a little bit of growing up in Massachusetts (1970–74) and then Brit from ages 4 to 8 lived in the suburbs of Philadelphia. So Brit was 8 when we moved to Rochester, New York, which is somewhat grownup, not a lot, but it may affect how you want to look at this.

JP: And in that area we had our first racial hurdle, I would say.

RR: In Massachusetts?

JP: No, in suburban Philadelphia. We lived in a working-class town—Rod worked on the Main Line—he worked in Bryn Mawr. That is fairly well-to-do—I don't know if you know that part of the world, but the Main Line would be in some ways like Westchester County, New York. The executives and the affluent commute into the city by train from there. But then there are some little working-class villages and more modest communities along the Main Line. When it came time to register Brit for kindergarten, we found out (after we bought our house) there was a neighborhood school not far down the road, and then there was another school about two miles away.

We found out that we were part of the neighborhood school that was closer since we lived on the one-hundred block of our street. When I went over to meet the principal of the school, he said most of the kids in that school were from working-class families, and he said to me, "You do not want your child in this school. He will be the only dark face in this building, and he will not be treated well." He told us to call the school district and ask to be transferred to the other neighborhood school, which was 30 to 40 percent integrated.

If we had lived on the two-hundred block of our street, we automatically would have gone to that other school, so we're talking maybe five houses different. The school district would not allow us to send Brit to the integrated school. We were in the one-hundred block, not the two-hundred block. And I fought the district and I called the American Civil Liberties Union. They asked us to file a lawsuit; they would represent us. The problem was it was going to take probably two years to get it through the courts, and by then he would have started school. So I threw up my hands.

And that was our first real test. What were we going to do? I refused to send my child to this school where he would be bullied. Around Philadelphia there are a lot of Quaker independent schools; they are expensive, and many of them are nationally known. In desperation I went in tears, sat down, and talked to the principal of one, and said here's my situation. She listened to me for five minutes and said "We will provide scholarships for your family. You don't have to go through that."

RR: What a blessing.

JP: We would have moved. No way was our child going to go to this neighborhood school when the principal said, "*You* don't want your child here.

It will not be pleasant." And if we hadn't gotten the response we did from the Quaker school, which was integrated, we would have filed the lawsuit, and we would have made a big stink regardless. We would have found a way. So that was the first time we had to really fight for what we knew was best for Brit and for the family.

RR: Did you have to fight in your other communities that you lived in?

JP: No, because the schools were all very well integrated and, in some cases, by the time the kids got to high school, our biological children were the racial minority. There were two high schools in Rochester—well, there are many, but four of our kids went to two different high schools. Brit and his youngest brother went to the School of the Arts because they had a strong arts bent, and our other two went to what in Rochester is known as the Comprehensive High School—regular traditional high school.

The high school where Brit's brother and sister went was 90 percent African American, and one of the things that I was always proudest about, Brit's brother, the one that is closest to him in age (they are ten months apart), was voted most popular in his high school class, in a class that was 90 percent African American—and Seth is white, biological from us—so what that means is that Brit's siblings have always been able to live in a mixed-race world because that's the way the family is. And Brit's sister has two best friends from growing up, her very closest friends from elementary school. One is white, one is black. Brit's youngest brother's two best friends from high school were both African American.

RR: As your children were growing up in this mixed-race community, what were your expectations that you had for your children?

RP: Behavioral or?

RR: Behavioral, what did you want them to strive toward? What were the values that you promoted in your family?

JP: We stressed academics—do the best you can because education in life is important. We expected our children to be decent, compassionate, kind, and thoughtful people.

RR: What was the relationship like between the sibling groups?

RP: We had three boys and one girl, and the two older boys, Brit and Seth, got along very well. Seth is very different, more introspective, quiet, and more cautious in his behavior. Brit was kind of—not wild but just kind of impetuous. They got along very well, I think.

JP: They were really inseparable until about the ages of 7 and 8 when they got into elementary school and began to build their own friends. They belonged to a neighborhood group of kids. Brit would gravitate more toward two or three of the kids in that group and Seth to another. They never fought, they always respected and liked each other. The older they got—Brit got into theater, and Seth was a very avid sports person—skier, tennis player, soccer player. Brit was in theater all the time, and they were in different high schools, so they lived different lives, but I don't think I ever—except once or twice in their whole lives—can remember them fighting. Because they were different enough, they didn't compete. They weren't so much alike that they wanted the same things.

RR: Was your family open to discuss internal issues that each one of your kids were going through, so, in other words, could Brit or could Seth or Amanda feel comfortable to talk to you about racial incidents or struggles with relationships that they might have had?

JP: We had one family rule as the kids were growing up. I went back to work when our youngest was in first grade. I had a three-quarter-time job, which meant that I was home at 3:30 in the afternoon, so I actually was home when the kids came home from school. I felt very strongly about being an on-the-scene parent, but I was at work while they were in school. The one rule we had, as the kids were growing up and as they got older, was that everyone was expected home for dinner. And if they had sports practice or other things on occasion, if there was a game and the game went over, it was understood that I was always told ahead of time.

But as a family rule, the children were expected to be at the dinner table. So that's the plan we had as they got older: everybody had a meal together, and we would laugh and talk, and the family could really be there as a unit. And then they would go off and do their homework. Sometimes one of them would be late, but it was not [like] you're out after school and you just don't show up. That didn't happen in our household. We had pretty strict expectations, and if any of the kids blew it, for example, if they had the car when they got older and they showed up at 1:30 in the morning and their curfew was midnight, they lost the car keys for three weeks. If they wanted to be able to drive, then they had to be home when they were supposed to be home. I remember Brit's once telling a friend, I don't remember the situation, but he was probably in high school or close to college and maybe he heard me talking to his younger brother, I don't remember the circumstance, but I said, "And if that doesn't happen, then this is the consequence," and Brit turns to his friend and says, "And she means it!"

RR: With all the thought and preparation that both you and your husband had gone through to decide on having a blended family, what do you think was the most dynamic part in this whole experience?

RP: I think for me personally, people from outside look at our family as a blended family, but from the inside I have no sense that it is anything but what it is. I don't label it as blended, I don't think of it that way, and it just made it clear to me, which I always had an intuition of, that it doesn't matter, race and whatever, at all. From an emotional point of view and from a connection point of view, I also saw with Britton a number of incidences, and prejudice, and stupidity, and that sort of thing that he faced. I recognize how much maturity, and goodwill, sense, and also realism Brit developed to deal with those prejudices against him that are basically socially based and sometimes individually based.

JP: I would add to that—we had an adopted child, [then] a very premature—a 7-month premature baby—and then a very unexpected third child, so we had three kids in twenty-two months. That's a pretty quick family; all different ages, all different schedules. Three in diapers, three in cribs but everybody on a totally different stage of development. Those three kids grew up in each other's pockets, and they are very close. Brit and his youngest brother, Nathan, are both extremely arts directed.

Nathan in some ways was a difficult child because he was extraordinarily bright and sensitive, and Brit, of all of our children, had the easiest, warmest nature. I mean, they're all great kids, but the other three have all had, at one phase or another, a stubborn streak—they were stubborn. Brit has remarkable characteristics—he is absolutely a people person, and he has always been in our family the mediator, the one that could smooth the waters among the other siblings. And I cannot imagine our family, as we grew from little ones to adults, having lived it the way we lived it, I cannot even imagine what it would have been like without him. Rod once said, "Brit's the glue that holds the family together." And it's true. And in this sense it was because he was adopted, not biracial, and he didn't inherit some of these family characteristics like the stubbornness—he had a whole different set of characteristics, genetic characteristics, that he brought into our family, and it made our family better.

RR: Do you think that Brit was able to feel comfortable sharing with you things that he was struggling with, or did he have a tendency of keeping it in so as not to bother you?

RP: I really don't know. I don't recall him coming to us with "Gee, I've got this problem or that problem." I think because Brit was so engaging and warm and adaptable and kind of a leader in his own way, I think that he didn't run into these things within his circle, with schoolmates, within the neighborhood, within the family. I'm sure he ran into it in the grocery story or out on the street and so forth, but he didn't really come to us and say this and that happened to me, it's so upsetting to me, and so forth. He was really very absorptive of those kinds of insults or situations, and he didn't turn them into minicrises.

JP: He did talk about things. I remember once, when we moved to a second house in Rochester, and we hadn't lived there very long, and he was pulled over by the police walking down our street on the way home from school, because obviously some neighbor on that block who hadn't recognized him, because we were new to the neighborhood, had seen this young African American man on our street and wanted to know what the heck that person was doing in our neighborhood.

RP: And that's when he was like 15 or 16 years old, which is when you begin to and he did begin to verbalize that. For many years he was not focused on those issues.

JP: And up until that time, I really don't think there were very many. Some very good friends of ours had five adopted children, all biracial. One son went to college in Rochester and had his first incidents in racism, he told his parents, when he was in the dormitory in college. Because the schools here are integrated, and the kids are so mixed, there doesn't tend to be much of that.

So it wasn't until Brit got to be toward high school that he talked to us about things. His best friend is adopted, and the two of them used to be called names by other African American kids. What was curious about that—I mean, when we first thought about it—was because they were both basically on an education track. They didn't talk street talk (they could if they wanted to and had to). Brit wanted to do that when he was in his high school. His high school was about 80 percent African American. He could switch his language; he was very good at that. But it became interesting; for example, my daughter's best friend who is African American and whose father was the assistant superintendent of schools, experienced the same thing because she was in classes preparing to go to college.

Rochester is a very, very poor city. Sixty-five percent of the kids in Rochester public schools are at the poverty level perpetuating this tremendous difference in socioeconomic backgrounds. So you have kids who have never even met their biological parents raised by grandmothers and aunts, and all the worst kinds of social situations you can imagine, going to school with a kid like Brit. Nobody in Brit's high school knew that he was adopted—his closest friends, yes, but as he was walking down the hall, how would they know? But they knew that he did different things, and his friend Steve, who was the best man at his wedding, both of these kids weren't hanging out on the street corner, and they weren't in gangs, which a lot of the kids in the school were. So they stood out as being different, and it wasn't because they were darker—they were different because they came from different kinds of families. And I know that was hard for the both of them, both Brit and his good friend, being in the Rochester city schools, because there were few middle-class African American kids. So it became, from that point of view, more of an economic distinction.

RR: What would you say is one of the paramount issues that you struggled with involving Brit? Or what is the saddest memory you have?

JP: The most difficult for me was that Brit had real learning disabilities. And the hardest thing for me in his early years was teachers saying to me, "He's a cute kid and he's so bright, but he's lazy." It was not until he was about 11 that we had him go through very sophisticated testing. We started having him tested before he was in first grade, because I originally thought he had a hearing problem, he had trouble following directions, and it's a long, long story.

But we knew that he had some difficulty. He was diagnosed [with] ADD [attention deficit disorder] when he was 2. He could not sit still. So it was always a struggle to keep him physically safe, because he climbed up on the roof, he jumped seventy feet from a tree, and he had no fear of heights; he loved to be moving, he loved to be high [up]. So keeping him physically safe was difficult, but I used to get very frustrated when he was young with teachers saying, "He's just not ready, he can't do this, and he can't do that. He's a sweet kid and everybody loves him. He's the most popular kid in the class, but he's just plain lazy." And I knew that he was not "just plain lazy," but I was not equipped to tell them—even though we had had the testing done. He was 10 or 11 before we had an extremely sophisticated battery of tests done where we were able to find out how to break down his learning disabilities. Because he struggled in school—

RP: And he wanted to do well, so I'm sure he was frustrated too. So he might not have known how to articulate that—that he was frustrated. I don't think that relates to race or adoption.

JP: But that was the hardest part. And the only way you can say the adoption entered into that is that our biological kids did not have these kinds of learning disabilities. So he had the distinction in the family of struggling more than his siblings did, and that was painful for me as a parent, because I never wanted him to feel that, because he had these problems, that we valued him less. So it was very hard as a parent to try to keep him on task, find a way to help him learn, which we did by tutoring.

Actually, I ended up going to court again with Brit, and I was the first person in New York State to get him into a nonspecial ed section. I brought in state advocates for him—I fought for this kid all my life. And we won the case. And then I was asked to be a parent advocate for other children in the same situation, because he wasn't retarded, he just had extraordinary issues in certain areas, and in other areas he was fine. When we finally got this information, the psychologist that did the testing said to us, "It's unfortunate that Brit is so good in these areas because he's in the ninety-third percentile in X and Y, he's extremely articulate and verbal, and therefore everybody thinks he's lazy, because he can talk his way in and out of anything he's not good at."

RP: He was always good at creating an impression—not lying, not any of that—but just creating the impression that everything was OK, or I can remember at times, when I was talking to him about something that he didn't want to talk about, and I realized that within two minutes he had changed the subject and without my knowledge. So—what happened? I laugh about it, now that I think back at what he was able to do to mask his difficulties because of his persuasive bent, and whether it was logic or reason, it is just the way he is.

RR: What would you say is the happiest memory you have with Brit or an exciting point in this journey?

RP: To me I haven't thought about this to make a long list, but he was a good actor. He liked acting and went to the School of the Arts, and they had a fabulous drama teacher in the early grades who really was great. There are several memories—one of them was in music theater, and the show for the seventh and eighth grade was *Joseph and the Amazing Technicolor Dreamcoat*, and Brit got the part of Levi, and his premier song is sort of this cowboy western song that Brit came up there and sang beautifully, but it just knocked me over to see him go from being a little boy to up on the stage doing this. It is the blossoming of that talent and that interest.

JP: Brit was at the School of the Arts, and School of the Arts was the place for him. He was one of the stars in the school; he was one of the popular people who got the lead or the sublead in every production. So we had six years [grades seven to twelve at his performing arts school] of seeing him shine on the stage. Every one of those moments—because he loved this, this was who he was. And just seeing his talent develop and seeing his person develop, he was so widely respected by the teachers and his peers.

I remember the moments that stand out for me as the happiest are because they meant a lot to Brit. One was, his senior year in high school

[when] the school district restructured, changed things, so that his school actually got separated. The point is, in his senior year he suddenly, instead of being in classes with thirty to thirty-five kids, was in a class of, I believe, twelve people, and this was in his English class. As his learning disabilities require him to have quiet concentration and be able to work at his own pace, he got his first A in English in high school. And the teacher said what a remarkable thing, it is amazing. You know, he might not be able to spell some of the words, but his thinking is so beyond what these other kids are doing. So he got an A. But she understood what was in his head and was able to give him the time and work with him as an individual. So I think that was the first time he made the honor roll. And of course the very fact that he graduated and then went to college, and now it looks like he is going to get his master's degree summa cum laude. He can't believe it. He is somebody who has struggled all of his life. He said he's never worked so hard in his life as he is right now in graduate school.

RR: What determination!

JP: So all of those big milestones—proud and happy for him, because he knew he'd done it, and everybody else could see he had done it too. Those were really big moments for him.

RR: Now tell me about what happened a few months ago.

RP: You mean getting married?

RR: Yes.

RP: Brit has always liked to have a lady around. He had various girlfriends, and some were working out well and some weren't. When he was in the Boston area, he was living there after graduating from Emerson, and he was teaching at an elementary school, and he had a girlfriend there whose name I forget, but it was at that point he decided he didn't always want to be a teacher, he wanted to become an actor. So he left his teaching job, gave that up, sold his car, and ended his relationship with this woman—when I talked with him about it, I thought it was more serious than maybe it was—but he left his girlfriend and took off to New York to become an actor. And the point is that he'd had girlfriends and so forth, and by the time he met Pam, he knew what he wanted, and it happened.

RR: Tell me about the type of person Pam is and how she has supported Brit from your perspective.

JP: She is a type-A personality, and we get along very well. She and I are a lot alike. Here's a situation again: she's African American and I'm not, but we're a lot alike, so I think Brit can deal with women like her because he's dealt with his mother. But she has been extraordinarily successful in her career. She's a lawyer. She has an undergraduate and law degree from Harvard University, so she is used to things being top of the line, high expectations. She has been very supportive of Brit's, for example, going to school, because she knows that education and degrees are how you get your meal ticket.

And so when he lost his job, he got laid off—he'd been working at a place for a couple of years, got laid off, couldn't find work—and so she said, "OK, this is time for you to go back to school because you're going to need that education." And he has worked very hard, partly to prove it to himself, but I also think because he wanted his wife to know that he would do it for her. She has been very supportive in helping him get through and proofreading his papers and things like that. And he wants to be the man he assumes Pam thinks he is. He is going to live up to the model—she's put him on a pedestal, and he's going to get himself on that pedestal too.

RR: Tell me about the wedding.

JP: The wedding was wonderful. There was a lot of the usual how many-people-can-we-invite, because both families are fairly large in terms of cousins and first cousins and second cousins, a lot of that—so numbers were an issue from the beginning. It was not an unfriendly issue, it was just how can we get the people we want the most to be here and afford this, because it was a New York City wedding? So there was a whole lot of "we have to invite this person, but maybe they won't come because they live so far away—" and it all got worked out on both sides.

Brit introduced us to Pam about April, and they got married the next March, so I think we first met her in April, and in July of that year he asked us if we could get together with him and Pam to meet her mother and stepfather, and so we all met for a weekend somewhere. And I remember thinking after two hours with Pam's mother (and they are a lot alike, so if you like Pam, you would like the mother—you can see where the daughter comes from—some of her qualities), I wish I had known her for ten years. We were so much on the same wavelength on things.

Brit had said to us, when he asked us to meet Pam for the first time, he said you won't believe it, but this relationship is going very quickly. (Maybe they had been into it four months.) He said it is getting pretty heavy. "Pam and I can't believe how much alike our families are. We are just raised exactly the same way." We laugh about it because every story she'd have, he had one that was the same, and that was real clear to both the families when they met. We were just so much alike, and our kids had been raised the same way. And, ironically, she came from Binghamton,

New York, which is not unlike Rochester in some ways, and they met in New York City, so that's the family.

The wedding was very personal, very simple, in a very lovely church, and it was all about, as several of our friends said, about the bride and the groom and the ceremony and the process of getting married rather than putting on a splashy wedding.

RR: And the guests were able to interact with one another?

JP: The reception was one of the nicest, I think for that reason. They worked very hard at seating people, and I would say about a third of the people at the wedding, roughly, were our relatives, about a third were Pam's relatives, and the other third were their friends. There were a lot of people, either cousins or friends, ranging from the ages of 25 to 40, the singles or the "young marrieds." And they worked very hard at how they seated people, and it was very much everybody mixing and enjoying each other.

RR: Now that you have raised your children, thirty-some years later, would you say that the position taken by the National Association of Black Social Workers affected your decision to adopt Brit?

RP: What is that position?

RR: The fact that in the early 1970s, actually when you were in the process of adopting Brit, the National Association of Black Social Workers was concerned that black children raised in white homes would not be able to grow up with a strong sense of who they were as black people and as individuals. And that they would not feel comfortable to be part of the black community. So did what they said ever impact—?

JP: My feeling is, if you have black families who can adopt black children, that is the best way to go. But I would rather see any child go to a family who will love that child than sit in a foster home forever. I do remember when we tried to adopt a second child, when we were in Pennsylvania, and we became aware of a young man who was sixteen, I believe, and he was in foster care or he was in some institution, I can't remember if it was Pennsylvania or New York—it might have been New York at the time. We were at that time very involved, when we were in Philadelphia, in the Council on Adoptable Children, and so somehow I heard about this young man. Of course, he was pretty much grownup, he was a teenager. We were very interested and we inquired about—we started the process, and we specifically inquired about this young man, and the response was—and it probably was because we were an interracial family, I can't remember if he was interracial or African American, but they didn't want to take him out of the environment where he was. That was the answer that we were given. So we never even had a chance to meet him and let him know that through an official situation, that we were interested in considering adopting him.

And I remember feeling at the time that I would like that young man to have had the opportunity to say, here's a family that wants me, even though I am 16, rather than keep me in this institution because they don't think he should switch high schools at this stage or something. So that's where I am on the issue. Sure, if there are families that are available, but I always think about the kids. I think any kid is better in a permanent and loving home than in a series of foster homes. And Brit is triracial, so where does he really fit?

RR: Would you recommend transracial adoption to other families like your own?

RP: Yes.

JP: Yes, if the children are available, why not? But with the caveat that if you are going to do it, then you owe the child that obligation of seeing that that child is in situations growing up where they are going to be in an environment with other children of all backgrounds and races. To take a child like that and be in a place where that child is going to be clearly the odd child out, I think that is unfortunate. Then you are not giving the child the best you can give the child.

RR: How were you able to come to that decision, where you recognized that it was a value for your child, your son, all of your children, to be exposed to people of different ethnic backgrounds?

JP: Partly, I was raised that way, thinking that that is important and that people are equal, and it is the real world we live in.

RR: That is a courageous move.

JP: Well, that's what I think. And, as I said before, our social worker was wonderful in the process of reminding us of the areas where we were going to have to be very conscious about what we did, and that was helpful, because if we knew it kind of intuitively before, it was absolutely clear that this would be expected of us. If we were going to do the best for this child, that part of the best might mean sometimes doing things that we might not have done otherwise. Where we bought a house—where we put the kids in school.

RR: Is there anything I haven't asked or anything that you haven't said that you want to say?

RP: My observation is that the richness of this experience comes from living it, not thinking about it or theorizing about it or any of that sort of thing. You have to plan, and you have to figure out what is best, but you also just kind of let it happen in as normal ways as you can, recognizing that you have an obligation to the child to remember that, even though he doesn't seem like a biracial or African American child or anything other than just one of your kids, he is biracial and he does face unique challenges in this life because of that.

I rarely see with Brit this kind of prejudice. I saw it two or three summers ago. We were at this place in Pennsylvania where we go sometimes, and Brit was there and it's a very — it takes people out of Philadelphia, and it's kind of upscale and stuff, and Brit and I went up to the boat window to rent a canoe, and the guy, kind of an old redneck-looking type — not to stereotype, but that's what he was — saw us and just kept standing there with his back to us. He wasn't going to come to the window. Brit and I stood there for a while, and he knew I was there, and I realized that this guy was not serving Brit because he was black. You couldn't see another black face in that entire place, unless it was a nanny. And there it was. It was just — and Brit at the time was 29, 30 years old. And it just drove it home to me — not in any dramatic way, but this is what it's like — people ignore you.

JP: And yet, here's a different example. Brit's youngest brother, whose two best friends in high school were African American, went to college in Boston, and a few years ago when he was there, he was riding the subway on his way home from college to his apartment, and he was jumped by a gang, which turned out — the police report said it was a black gang initiation, and they were trying to beat up, kill, white people. So our son happened to be the victim on the subway that night, just sitting there in a car, and suddenly there are all these people bloodying him.

Brit was living in Boston at the time, teaching, and he got the phone call from the emergency room saying we have a young man here who says he is your brother, and he's been beaten, and he's in the emergency room. And Brit got over there, and here's his baby brother who's been beaten by this gang. And Brit said his first instinct was to find these people and kill them. 'My brother is sitting there, minding his own business, and he's not a racist. Why did you do this to him? If you had to pick on somebody, pick on somebody that wouldn't support you.' He said he was enraged that the injustice, that it happened to his brother. And I thought that's interesting, because it happens both ways. He didn't use his race as an excuse to say, oh, gee, sorry this happened to you... .

We were concerned, and the police were concerned — they'd had a terrible rash of these incidents. He got on that train at a certain time of day, it was eleven at night, if they spotted him on the train again, they'd finish the job because they hadn't killed him. I lived in fear for days. He had no other way to get from the college, no other train, and no other bus that ran this time of night. I give Brit's brother credit. He doesn't think that way. He got on that train. He fell off the horse, but he got back on that train. But Brit was the one that was more outraged than his brother.

The only other comment I would like to make in general is that Brit's married. They hope to have family; we have this wonderful new set of extended family, and I am thrilled by the idea that our family is becoming more and more blended, because I truly believe that that is what America is going to be in the next twenty or thirty years—and I can't wait for the grandchildren. Our granddaughter was in Brit's wedding, and our family is very close—the siblings are very supportive of each other. Brit's flying up this coming weekend for his brother's 2-year-old child's birthday party. Pam has to be at a baptism, she can't come, but they felt it was important for at least one of them to be there. So they are really supportive of each other. I just love the fact that our family is going to be ahead of the curve in learning how to be and to live in this world.

PART 3

CONCLUSION

OF THE SIXTEEN PARENTS we interviewed—three mothers, two fathers, and eleven couples— all spoke warmly and lovingly of their adopted children. The Peltons are very grateful that Jessica and their other biracial daughter have found their way back to the black community, the mixed communities, and the white community. They are close to all their children, two of whom are living with them: the other biracial daughter and a birth son. Jessica lives thirty to forty miles away.

Alice Bandstra, Andrea's mother, talked especially warmly of her relationship with her daughter. While both parents are close to all their children (two sons and a daughter), Alice emphasized the intimate relationship she has with Andrea, who is the mother of three children. They talk about everything that is going on in their lives. The Bandstras recall that the saddest memory of their relationship with Andrea occurred when she told them she was going to be a single mother. They responded by assuring her that she could count on them for support and love.

Kim Stapert's parents state clearly that while they were aware of and to some extent participated in the upheavals of the '60s and '70s, and recognized the poor treatment that African Americans received in this country, those were not the reasons they opted to adopt. The Staperts adopted because they very much wanted children and they had not been successful in having children by birth. They adopted seven biracial children. Kim and her brothers and sisters always felt comfortable talking to their parents about any racial slurs slung at them by both white and black children. The Staperts report that Kim and her siblings were also harassed because they were adopted. On such occasions Kim would respond: "My parents want me! Yours don't want you." The Staperts felt strongly that as their children were growing up, they needed to have connections with a black world. Even before they adopted, the Staperts had black friends and lived in an integrated neighborhood. Kathy Stapert had been warned by white social workers that she would have a problem learning how to care for black children's hair. She and a close friend who is biracial enrolled in a class on learning how to fix black hair. And their children's pediatrician was black.

Ron and Dorothy, the adoptive parents of Shecara and the birth parents of ten other children, describe their current relationship with her as great. They communicate regularly and warmly. As Shecara related in *In Their Own Voices*, there were times when she and her parents did not get along, mostly during her adolescence. But she eventually moved back into their home, went back to school, and earned a degree in nursing.

Paul Goff's interview focused mostly on the extensive travels and cosmopolitan life that he, Ellen (Laurie's mother, who died before Laurie was interviewed for *In Their Own Voices*), and their children lived. They spent time in Sierra Leone and the Ivory Coast. In the United States they lived in New Orleans, Seattle, and Washington, D.C. He mentions, but chooses not to elaborate on, some difficult times he and Laurie have had since Ellen's death and his subsequent remarriage. At the time of the interview he felt that their relationship had improved, and he was proud of Laurie's accomplishments.

Barbara Tremitiere, a social worker, is the mother of three birth children and twelve black, Korean, and Vietnamese adopted children. Two of Barbara's twelve children appeared in *In Their Own Voices*: Chantel, a professional basketball player and the founder of Assist One, an adoption program based in Sacramento; and Nicolle, who at the time we interviewed her was the director of the York [Pennsylvania] YWCA's program for teenage mothers. Barbara talks very warmly about the close and loving relationship she has with all but one of her children. Much of her interview is devoted to her experiences in placing nonwhite children in white homes. Barbara is an ardent supporter of transracial adoption.

In *In Their Own Voices* Rachel had said that her mother, Nora Anker, held her back by always referring to Rachel's hip problem and worrying that Rachel was trying to do too much. Her father, Rachel said, kept telling her that "college isn't for everybody." Nora does not speak directly to those issues but did talk at length about Rachel's several surgeries and the amount of time she missed in high school, especially in her senior year. She did tell us that Rachel is completing her college degree and plans to go into teaching. Nora refers several times to Rachel's comments in *In Their Own Voices* about how little her parents did to expose her to black history or her racial background. Nora does not believe that Rachel's lack of exposure to the black community affected her daughter's identity, but Nora does talk at some length about Rachel's meeting with her birth mother and sister. Nora met them, too, and she urges Rachel to stay in contact with them.

The last parent of the daughters we interviewed is Marjorie Gray, the mother of the coauthor of this book, Rhonda M. Roorda. Marjorie describes her relationship with Rhonda as more of a sister relationship than a parent-child one. She and Rhonda were married (in Marjorie's case, remarried) within a year of each other, and that brought them closer together, as did Rhonda's decision to undertake the interviews for *In Their Own Voices*. Rhonda's career influenced Marjorie to become a published author as well. She writes poetry and has written a nonfiction book about the Bible that she is trying to get published. Marjorie is grateful to Rhonda for motivating her to write and publish.

We were able to interview both parents of six of the eight sons who appear in *In Their Own Voices*. Keith Bigelow, a minister who was adopted when he was 5 years old, had characterized his family as exceptionally wonderful. His parents, Ed and Judy Bigelow, also speak very positively about their family life. They are especially proud of Keith for what he has accomplished and wish they lived closer. Keith is in Michigan and his parents are in Vermont.

In 1998 Daniel Mennega told us that he was "entirely comfortable and happy" about his relationship with his family and about his social identity. Aaldert and Elisabeth Mennega came to the United States from the Netherlands after the Second World War and never had any contact with blacks until Aaldert was inducted into the army in 1951. The Mennegas hold strong Christian beliefs, and they feel they made the right decision when they sent their children (two transracially adopted and two birth) to Christian schools in Sioux Center, Iowa. As the children were growing up, their parents' highest priorities were to instill in them a love of God, raise them as good citizens, and have them become assets to the community and to their country. The overall tone of the Mennegas' interview suggests they believe they have accomplished those goals.

Tage's father, Rikk Larsen, is very proud of his son's accomplishments as a professional classical musician. He tells us that Tage is the first black musician that the Chicago Symphony ever hired full time. In his interview Tage credits his father for his initial interest in becoming a musician. Tage explained, "He [Rikk] was not a musician, but he loved classical music, he still does. Growing up, he would play Beethoven, Bach, and many other well-known classical musicians. And for some reason I latched onto this and connected to it with a passion." In his interview Rikk responds to Tage's attribution, saying, "I know that and I love it."

Rikk Larsen explains his desire to adopt a black child as a means of coming to grips with his own racism. Growing up in a very wealthy New York family, "the only black person I ever saw growing up was our cleaning lady." Through-out his elementary and high school years at upper-class private schools, Rikk had almost no contact with African Americans. In Rikk's words, "I was raised in a very, very white world and full of liberal Democrats. But I had virtually no exposure to minorities."

David Adams, like Daniel Mennega, grew up in a strong Dutch Reformed Christian environment in Sioux Center, Iowa. Like Daniel, David is proud of his family and proud of his Christianity. And his parents believe that "the most fundamental force that held our family together is the fact that all of us are committed Christians." They are also proud of David's parenting abilities.

Seth Himrod's parents report major changes in their son's life since we interviewed him for *In Their Own Voices*. In 1998 Seth worked as a stock-broker and was the single father of a 9-year-old boy. David and Lola Himrod report that Seth is employed as a sanitation worker for the City of Evanston, Illinois; he is married to DarLisa, an African American woman; and they have had five children, four girls and a boy. David and Lola believe they did a good job in making Seth comfortable in his relationships with black and white people. They report that when Seth was in the army, many black soldiers were angry at whites, and Seth would tell them that white people are not the monsters you think they are, that not all whites are the same. David and Lola see Seth and his family often.

Ned's parents, Ken and Jean, are the most radical of all the parents in this study. Not only are they ardent supporters of transracial adoption and strong Christians, but they advocate greater changes in our society that would ensure true equality among people of all races and ethnic groups. Jean works with refugees from eastern Europe and Cuba and stands up for them against government bureaucrats. Ned followed in his father's footsteps and became a high school teacher. It is clear from the interviews of both Ned and his par-ents that they are a close and loving family.

In her interview Winnie, the mother of Pete, talks a lot about the difficul-ties she faced after she and her husband split up and she moved to Ithaca, New York, with their daughter, who has Down syndrome. Pete moved in with her a year later, and she is very proud of how helpful Pete was and how much of a support he was to her. Indeed, her pride for Pete occupies much of her interview. She says that one of the happiest moments in her life with Pete came when he found his birth mother and the two families had a wonderful reunion. She is especially proud of Pete's career as a police officer and what a wonderful father he has proved to be.

Brit Perry told us in 1996 that one of his major goals was to find his birth parents, that he needed to know where he came from. Rodney and Joyce

Perry make no mention of Brit's search for his parents. They talk very positively about the adoptive experience and about Brit's close ties to his two stepsiblings, especially his older brother. They also speak enthusiastically about Brit's marriage to Pam, an African American woman who is a Harvard-trained lawyer, and of Brit's accomplishments as an actor and academic (he's working toward his master's). The Perrys also are delighted that they and Pam's family get along well and have much in common. The Perrys are enthusiastic advocates of transracial adoption but emphasize how important it is that the family live in a multicultural environment.

AFTERWORD

THE OTHER DAY I was waiting in the checkout line of a large supermarket in Brighton, Michigan. Behind me were a white couple and their gregarious 3-year-old African American son. As I stood there drawing in the images and the sounds of the little boy—his laughter, his words, and his tears, as his parents were instructing him not to pull things off the racks—thoughts about the many transracially adopted children I have met through the years flooded my mind, including thoughts about my own childhood as a black transracial adoptee. And ever-present in my consciousness were the voices of adoptive parents. These parents were sharing with me the hopes and dreams they had for their children and the challenges or triumphs they were experiencing in their own journeys as adoptive parents.

This story about transracial adoption is especially relevant today. According to the U.S. Department of Health and Human Services, more than 500,000 boys and girls are in our nation's foster care system, the majority children of color, all desperately in need of stable homes. Tens of thousands of those children are ready to be adopted.[1] Both legal and social changes since the early 1990s make it more likely that these children will find homes, probably with parents of a different racial/ethnic background, but the number of stable, permanent homes ready to receive the children is insufficient. Thanks to the Adoption and Safe Families Act, no one can block a transracial adoption simply because it is transracial. At the same time international adoptions have been booming, most notably involving thousands of Chinese children, to name but one ethnic group. Clearly, transracial adoption is a phenomenon that will affect increasing numbers of children and families, and it makes good sense for us to figure out how to do it right.

The interviewees in this book represent the first significant cohort of white parents who adopted transracially. Their decisions unfolded against the backdrop of the civil rights movement, amid the eruption of racial tensions across

America, and the outcry from organizations like the National Association of Black Social Workers, which opposed transracial adoption because of the perceived negative consequences. The NABSW's statement impelled researchers to begin looking into the effects of transracial adoption. After more than a dozen studies conducted over a twenty-year period, researchers concluded that transracial adoption was good public policy and in the best interests of the child, even if that child was not exposed to her or his racial or ethnic community. Researchers today are finding that while transracial adoption remains good policy, the formation of a solid racial identity, especially during late adolescent and adulthood years, is crucial to the development of transracial adoptees.[2] There is still much more that we need to learn about this phenomenon and its consequences. Researchers need the funding that will allow them to explore identity formation in these adoptees throughout their lives and the role played in that process by their adoptive families, their ethnic communities of origin, and how their white adoptive parents and members in the adoptees' ethnic communities of origin relate to one another. Crucial to the integrity of these studies is the collection of *universal and consistent* data on domestic adoptions, including transracial adoption, in this country. Demographic data on all domestic adoption, not just transracial adoption, are frightfully inadequate.

Now, more than thirty-five years later, we have come to a time when multiculturalism is more widely accepted in this country, and adoption is becoming a positive means of building a family, making what these parents and children have to say especially relevant. These veteran families have much to teach us in a powerful and genuine way about the necessity of moving ourselves beyond our comfort zone for the sake of our children. Winnie addresses this head-on when she says, "I needed someone to sit me down and tell me, 'Look, this is a problem for your son, no matter what you think of the fact that all races are exactly the same. This is still going to be a problem for your son because there are some people who don't feel that way, and you need to learn more about this, and you need to face up to it.' ... I also think that anyone who pursues transracial adoption should take courses, take some classes with the adoption agency, where they can be told about the importance of making some interracial ties with other families." Raising children transracially takes unequivocal commitment, humility, honesty, forgiveness, courage, perseverance, and love on the part of the adoptive parents. It also takes active involvement by extended family members so that this experience can be equally beneficial for everybody.

Transracial adoptive families today have more information available to them than these families did—from books to films to magazines to heritage camps to listening to adult adoptees as they reflect on their experiences—to assist them in this multifaceted experience. We—transracial adoptees and our families—must call on scholars and social work professionals to continue to provide useful curricula and training materials to help parents be as effective as possible. And we must at opportune times educate religious leaders, psychologists, teachers, physicians, and others about the needs and concerns intrinsic to transracial adoption.

Yes, I believe transracial adoption can and does work, but the operative word is *work*. It simply requires more of parents than opening their arms and hearts—they also must open their minds, learn to think in different ways, and have an actual plan in place for guiding their child through the particular thickets of being a transracial adoptee. As Joyce Perry relates, "One of the things that I remember very clearly, as we were getting toward the end of the [preadoption] screening, was the statement, 'If you should be given an interracial child, you will have to think about every life choice you make forever.' … And in fact and in truth, that has been the case for us. Our life has been carefully planned—what cities we lived in, what neighborhood we lived in, and what schools our children went to, so that all of our children, not just Brit, lived in a world where they were not unusual."

The parents in this book are not perfect, of course, but they have proved themselves sincere in their efforts to build a family through birth and adoption. Because of their openness in sharing both their triumphs and their mistakes, they have provided a blueprint for successful parenting, especially of transracial adoptees.

The clear message throughout the interviews is that these parents love their children and demonstrate that love in concrete ways. Jim and Alice Bandstra supported Andrea when she may have needed them the most: when she was confronted with being a single mother at a young age. They assured her that she could count on them, apparently instinctively aware that one of her deepest fears must have been that they would abandon her. "We told her that we were not going to leave her," Jim said. "And that we were always going to be her parents, and she could count on us." David and Lola Himrod had a similar experience with their son, Seth, who became a father in high school. "It took me about a day to react to the news," recalls David, who apparently did then react. "In those days, when we would have quarrels or were upset with each other, Seth usually went into a silent phase and didn't speak for a week, and then we would slowly come back together after that week. That is what happened in this situation." When I asked the Himrods what allowed them to maintain their commitment to Seth, Lola Himrod said, "We really love him.... Just as important is our understanding about adoption—that it's like a contract: it needs to be renewed over and over again." These are but two examples from the parents' stories that illustrate the power of love, but many more exist.

What fascinates me are the parents who courageously crossed the racial-cultural divide after their children married African Americans, and who did so in order to stay connected to their children and their families. But crossing racial boundaries, even for family, is not easy. Joyce and Rodney Perry found that they and the family of Pam, their daughter-in-law, have common interests and values, and the four parents have apparently established a meaningful and healthy relationship, something that could not have happened if both families had not been willing and able to cross the racial divide. Similarly, the Bandstras did not hesitate to extend their hearts to their son-in-law's family despite having to go outside their racial and cultural norm to do so. Other parents have demonstrated this same commitment. To me, that is love, and humility. Perhaps these parents can teach all of us to do that?

I also was struck by the priority these parents placed on raising children who would become self-possessed individuals. Whether it was Rikk Larsen and his former wife's efforts to help Tage harness his passion for classical music, or the efforts of Barbara Tremitiere, and Jim and Kathy Stapert to find the unique strengths in each of their children and then actively help them achieve their goals, these parents recognized that their role was to help their children find *their own* purpose in life, not to find theirs as parents.

In general the parents in this book were conspicuously thoughtful throughout key stages of the parenting process: they reflected on how they wanted to start their families and sought advice from friends and other family members; they had specific values they wanted to instill in their children, such as the importance of education, having a good work ethic, and treating others respectfully; they advocated for their kids in their schools and communities; they have remained committed throughout their children's lives, attending important events like graduations and weddings; and they have embraced their grandchildren with much joy and happiness. How did they do it? They pulled from the sources they had available, including support groups, friends, family members, and adoption agencies. Mostly they pulled from within themselves.

One of the few characteristics that the parents in this book have in common is that, at heart, they are nonconformists. That undoubtedly was a factor in their decision to adopt children of color, and that allowed them to model for their children, albeit somewhat obliquely, how to be comfortable with being different. Especially in light of the paucity of information available to the parents at the time, they did a remarkable job of raising their transracial adoptive children, who are an especially successful group. These parents truly are the pioneers of transracial adoption. They did not get a book of instruction on how to raise children of color (nor did the children get a manual describing how to grow up in a white family). Through their experiences we gain insights for making the experience of transracial adoption even better for all members of the family, particularly the transracial adoptee.

Not surprisingly, given the level of knowledge and lack of formal, ongoing support, the parents' stories tend to reflect a certain disconnect from the black experience and its diversity. The majority of these families chose, for their own reasons, to live in predominately white communities. This meant that the connections between the parents and members of their children's ethnic community were limited or nonexistent. Why is this of concern? As their interviews in *In Their Own Voices* attest, too many of the children were disillusioned when they went out into the world because they had little understanding about how to maneuver in life with dark skin. Having role models—in this case black and biracial role models or mentors—would have been hugely advantageous to the adoptees in guiding them proactively through experiences that result from the color of their skin and society's reactions to it. Indeed, many other parents in this book address the necessity of living in multiracial, multicultural communities, seeking out friends and professionals of color in an effort to make their adoptive children comfortable and to help them better understand not only their cultural and historical heritage but the societal obstacles they face as people of color and as people with feet in two or more cultures. Ken and Jean, the parents of twins Ned and Tonya, have put a lot of thought into this aspect of transracial adoption. Ken says flatly, "It isn't enough to say we are all human beings, we're all the same. We are not all the same, we're not treated the same."

These families badly need the assistance of a new breed of social worker who can help them learn how to expand their imaginations and embrace new people, foods, customs, ways of communicating, and traditions of worship and fellowship—not to mention how to negotiate prejudices they may never have encountered before—and thereby enrich the lives not only of their children but of themselves. Another important role for the social work profession is to establish a formal means of connecting these adoptive families and the African American community, an effort that also would benefit immensely from the proactive participation of black churches.

I would like to leave you with the list of suggestions that I have developed for transracially adoptive parents, suggestions reinforced by the parents' stories in this book. These suggestions are based on principles of love, respect, forgiveness, trustworthiness, kindness, and fostering a strong work ethic in children. And while they are designed for families of transracial adoptees, they are in fact guidelines for successful parenting:

- Examine your views about people from different ethnic and racial backgrounds; will your views have a positive or negative effect on your transracially adopted child?

- Develop an ongoing multiethnic personal support network of people who will help you in this adoption experience.

- Build a plan for your blended family that incorporates the voices and interests of all its members.

- Invest in literature about and by people from your child's ethnic community, as well as about child development.

- Talk with your child about adoption and race issues in an age-appropriate and timely manner; they affect your child in important ways.

- Participate as a family in activities in which people from your child's ethnic community of origin are likely to join in: sporting events, picnics, religious get-togethers, festivals, and fellowship meetings; this is a good step toward helping your child develop a healthy sense of self-worth, and to trust that you care about his or her ethnicity and community.

- Show your child how to find good role models and mentors from different racial and ethnic backgrounds. This is a process largely based on the personal relationships you build with people from racially and ethnically diverse backgrounds through work, your place of worship, and community activities.

- Support your child's unique interests. Identifying one's passion and gaining proficiency, even excellence, in that area helps a child to build strong character. Be your child's advocate.

- Be aware of the community you live in, the schools your child attends, your place of worship, and who you socialize with. These decisions directly affect the well-being and development of your child and should be well thought out. Do your decisions support your blended family's plan long term?

- Have fun! See where this journey can lead you and what bridges you can build. You are a gift.

RHONDA M. ROORDA

NOTES

1. Children's Bureau, U.S. Department of Health and Human Services, *The AFCARS Report: Preliminary FY 2005 Estimates as of 9/06*, October 12, 2006, www.acf.dhhs.gov/programs/cb/stats_research/afcars/tar/report13.htm.

2. A. L. Baden and R. J. Steward, "A Framework for Use with Racially and Culturally Integrated Families: The Cultural-Racial Identity Model as Applied to Transracial Adoption," *Journal of Social Distress & the Homeless* 9, no. 4 (2000): 309–37.

POSTSCRIPT

SO WHAT are the adult adoptees of *In Their Own Voices* whose parents did not appear in this book doing now?

Ronald Wilson, who used the pseudonym Taalib in the first volume, has decided to make his identity known. He is the presiding judge of a municipal court in southern Arizona—the youngest presiding judge in Arizona and the first African American to serve as chief justice in that state. He recently was named Man of the Year by the *Tucson Business Edge*, and he is the proud recipient of a 2006 Community Service Award from the Federal Bureau of Investigation. In 2006 he was also honored to receive the Rosa Parks Living History Makers Award from the NAACP.

He is an active volunteer and a member of, among other organizations, Omega Psi Phi Fraternity and the Sovereign Military Order of the Temple of Jerusalem. He also is taking classes to become a foster parent. Wilson works hard to decrease the recidivism rate among people who commit low-level misdemeanors and works with juveniles in the foster care system. He strongly believes that quality foster care and adoptive placements can reduce the number of young people who come to the attention of the criminal justice system.

Aaliyah (pseudonym) is still struggling to find her identity and a healthier sense of self-esteem. After living on her own for a short time she moved back home to live with her parents in western Michigan so she could save money and plan her future. With good counsel from her father, she is saving for a downpayment on a Habitat for Humanity house. Aaliyah now has two children, a 2-year-old son and a 6-year-old daughter, and is raising them as a single parent. Her life consists, she says, primarily of caring for her kids and transporting them to and from day care. She is employed at a rehabilitation hospital, where she does medical billing and is responsible for discharging patients.

When she was 24, she was reunited with her birth mother and not long after that was able to contact her birth father. Aaliyah visited with her birth parents many times until her birth father died in 2000. At his funeral she was able to meet many of her biological relatives. Aaliyah maintains a relationship with her adoptive parents and her adoptive siblings, who take an interest in her children. That, she says, is very helpful to her and makes her happy.

Asked to articulate how she is feeling today, Aaliyah said, "I am stressed, sad, angry, and lonely. I don't have any friends or a social life. I am now 35 years old and have children, but I am still answering to my parents." Aaliyah hopes that once she moves out on her own, she will gain more confidence and that it will help her to establish a more adult relationship with her parents.

We were unable to reach Donna Francis (pseudonym), Lester Smith Sr., and Chip. Also, Iris (pseudonym) declined to be interviewed because of pressing personal and professional obligations. We also were unable to reach Olympic decathlete Dan O'Brien, but we learned from the *New York Times* that in December 2006, he was inducted into the National Track and Field Hall of Fame.

ACKNOWLEDGMENTS

IN THEIR PARENTS' VOICES is a labor of love born out of the commitment to bring about greater understanding of U.S. domestic transracial adoptions. We hope that this book will be a useful resource.

In Their Parents' Voices was made possible because of the involvement of numerous people, especially the parents in this book, the editors of Columbia University Press, and people who saw the project's worth and were supportive from its inception. Rita Simon and I are very appreciative of that support. We are also thankful for the support of the adult adoptees from the first volume who also participated in this new book and remain committed to bringing about awareness of transracial adoption. Thank you.

I would be deeply remiss if I did not take this opportunity to thank my friend and coauthor, the eminent scholar Rita J. Simon: Your contribution to the field of transracial adoption has been absolutely remarkable. She has tirelessly dedicated more than thirty-five years to researching this issue and has been willing to put her research alongside the emerging voices of adult transracial adoptees and their adoptive parents'. For any nationally and internationally known scholar, that takes heart and courage, but most of all it speaks to her commitment to ensuring that the study of transracial adoption is a priority in academia and in the political and social arenas. Thank you, Rita.

I am grateful to my husband, Floyd Brumfield Jr., whose encouragement is constant. Thank you, Floyd, for helping me to stay committed to this project and still find the time to have fun. I love you. To my family, thank you for giving me the gift of adoption. To my godfather, W. Wilson Goode Sr., thank you for being in my life and believing in me. To my friends and mentors, you too are a godsend. Thank you. It is difficult to list everyone who made this project possible. For those whom I may have omitted, please do not charge it to my heart.

I especially want to thank Columbia University Press for its team behind this project: Lauren Dockett, Anne McCoy, Christine Mortlock, and Polly Kummel.

I want to thank the following people for sharing their expertise in foster care and adoption and for holding me accountable throughout this project; you are absolutely wonderful for doing that: Amanda Baden, Phil Bertelsen, Annie Fischer, Dick Fischer, Beth Hall, Kim Phagan Hansel, Michelle Johnson, Ron Nydam, John Raible, Mary Smit, Sook Wilkinson, Joyce Loninx-Wright, Frank Wu, and Kathy Yates. And finally, to my family and friends, thank you for being my "midnight oil" and for being available to talk things out and make me laugh. You are very dear to me: Hank Allen, Juliet Allen, Suzanne Barclay, Ida Bergsma, Reynard Blake, Flora Brumfield, Floyd Brumfield Sr., Anita Edwards, Earl Edwards, Amy Espuet, Kiffi Ford, Mendel Ford, Jim Henry, Nicole Henry, Dennis Hoover, Ruth Melkonian-Hoover, Dan Lodge, Lisa Lodge, Charissa Los, Anja Mast, Chuck Mast, Mugs Mast, Ramona Moore, Vernon Moore, George Nichols, Kelly Nichols, Cyril Pinder, Ethel Pippin, Howard Pippin Jr., Elaine Pinson, Leo Pinson, Laverne Rens, Anthony Robinson, Vivianne Robinson, Esther Solomon, Carol Triezenberg, Don Triezenberg, Michael VanderBrug, Cindy VanderKodde, Gordon Vander Till, Joni Vander Till, Gary Visscher, Siyroush Visscher, Lee Washington, Sharon Wrice, Tyrone Wrice, and Charla Yingling.

RHONDA M. ROORDA